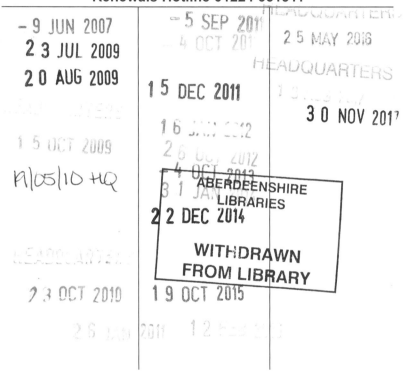
WOOLLEY, Monty

Cleanse their souls

# CLEANSE
# THEIR SOULS

# CLEANSE THEIR SOULS

*Peace-Keeping in Bosnia's Civil War
1992–1993*

by

## MONTY WOOLLEY

with a foreword by

## MARTIN BELL

Pen & Sword
**MILITARY**

First published in Great Britain in 2004 by
Pen & Sword Military
an imprint of
Pen & Sword Books Ltd
47 Church Street
Barnsley
South Yorkshire
S70 2AS

ISBN 1 84415 129 8

A CIP catalogue record for this book is
available from the British Library

Typeset in 11/13 Sabon by
Phoenix Typesetting, Auldgirth, Dumfriesshire

Printed and bound in England by
CPI UK

Pen & Sword Books Ltd incorporates the Imprints of Pen & Sword
Aviation, Pen & Sword Maritime, Pen & Sword Military, Wharncliffe
Local History, Pen & Sword Select, Pen & Sword Military Classics and
Leo Cooper.

For a complete list of Pen & Sword titles please contact
PEN & SWORD BOOKS LIMITED
47 Church Street, Barnsley, South Yorkshire, S70 2AS, England
E-mail: enquiries@pen-and-sword.co.uk
Website: www.pen-and-sword.co.uk

This book is dedicated to Mirjan and Svetlana

# CONTENTS

# FOREWORD

*by*

*Martin Bell*


The sword and the pen sometimes conflict and sometimes connect. There is a considerable history of both. The connection was seen at its most productive – and indeed immortal – in the work of the soldier poets of the Great War of 1914 to 1918. Siegfried Sassoon, Wilfred Owen, Robert Graves and Edmund Blunden were junior officers, captains and subalterns in relatively unfashionable regiments of the line exposed to the sacrificial strategies of the high command. "But still we were a good battalion," wrote Blunden of his 11th Royal Sussex in 1916, "and deserving of a battle, not a massacre".

The tradition went into abeyance and has recently seemed all but extinct. Monty Woolley of the 9th/12th Royal Lancers has revived it in the context of modern soldiering. As a young lieutenant on active service, he was attached to the battlegroup of the Cheshire Regiment in central Bosnia from November 1992 to May 1993. It was a baptism of fire for all of them, but the troop of light armoured vehicles which he commanded was closer than most to the front lines and to the dangers of trying to keep the peace in someone else's war. Nor was he thanked when, along "Bomb Alley" south of Tuzla, he robustly returned hostile fire against the Bosnian Serbs: "It is not open season," his commanding officer signalled. "Do not open fire unless cast iron case." He had expected praise for teaching the Serbs not to interfere with UN convoys. Instead the young officer received a dressing-down and a lesson of his own in the politics of UN peace-keeping, the most mysterious form of soldiering ever devised.

Monty Woolley kept a diary, in which he wrote clearly and vividly what he saw: the brutality of the three-sided war, the inadequacy of the United Nations mandate and the heroism of ordinary people in extraordinary times. He wouldn't claim to be a poet, but like the soldier poets of an earlier age his work draws its strength from his closeness to events and to the troops under his command. Generals and colonels are necessarily more remote from the blood and the mud and peculiar awfulness of the civil wars of our time.

This book also earns its place among the impartial narratives of the Bosnian war. The troop leader was the first blue-helmeted soldier at the scene of the infamous massacre in Ahmici in April 1993, when Croat paramilitaries surrounded a predominately Muslim village and murdered its inhabitants. This was an atrocity that shocked the world and led directly to the setting up of the International Criminal Tribunal at The Hague. Monty Woolley gave evidence there, and his written account is an important witness to history.

# PREFACE

*by*

*Charles Watts*

When one reflects upon the consequences of war in the Balkans in general and in the Former Republic of Yugoslavia in particular, one is immediately struck by the enormous loss of life caused there over the centuries; by the stark references to acts of exceptional brutality perpetrated by extremist groups during the Second World War (Croat Ustashe, Serb Chetniks and Nationalists) and, lastly, by the unspeakable suffering inflicted upon the hapless citizens of that much-troubled region of South-Eastern Europe.

During the Second World War it is estimated that the casualties in Yugoslavia alone numbered two million dead. These were Yugoslavs killed, not only by Germans or other Axis troops, but mainly by their own fellow countrymen. Even if this statistic is only partially accurate, its effects have left lingering, unquenched hatreds and unsettled scores among the survivors and succeeding generations, despite Marshal Tito's determined leadership to mould a new well-integrated Yugoslav society based upon Brotherhood and Unity (Bratstvo i Yedinstvo). These factors alone may explain, to some extent, the sheer scale of savagery unleashed after 1991 in that region of the Balkans. The post-1991 conflicts merely rekindled those former unresolved enmities and the killings continued, as before.

A further theme, among others, is the Serb nationalist fixation, evinced by leading figures (politicians, writers, poets and historians) of the constant reference to the date 28 June 1389, the date of the Battle of Kosovo Polje. This battle, which the Serbs lost, was fought near Pristina in Kosovo, between the Serbs led by Prince Lazar against the Ottoman Turkish invaders (although many other nationalities fought in the battle on both sides). Since that date, Serbian history and folklore is crammed with clarion call voices resolved to be avenged for that dreadful deed by action taken against the hated Musilmani, the Yugoslav name for the Turkish invaders. Indeed, many generations of Serb schoolchildren have been bombarded by anecdotal stories and historical tales to remind them of this, their prime national tragedy.

In the recent warring in Former Yugoslavia, after the death of Marshal Tito in 1980, 28 June 1389 and its consequences was effectively used as a rallying call to summon all Serbs to fight for their national prestige and their very survival.

It is therefore not without significance that the date 28 June 1989 was selected, by design or accident, by Slobodan Milosevic to visit Pristina and make his historic pronouncement that he would put an end to the violence unleashed against the Serb minority in Kosovo by the Kosovar (Albanian) majority. The visit was exactly 600 years after the date of the famous battle fought against the hated Turkish (Muslim) oppressors. The heroic deeds of this famous battle, much recounted and perhaps embroidered by elaborate tales, national folklore, poetry and songs (sung to the accompaniment of the Gusle, distinctive Serb musical instrument), recalling this single traumatic event, lie deep in the Serb psyche. These historic events were passionately exploited by prominent Bosnian Serbs and the Serb National Leadership in the period between the death of Marshal Tito in 1980 and the almost inevitable ensuing conflicts from June 1991 in Slovenia then Croatia, Bosnia and Kosovo in turn.

It is also significant that the tragic event in Sarajevo, in which the Bosnian Gavrilo Princip assassinated both the Austrian heir to the throne Franz Ferdinand and his wife, was carried out on the 28 June 1914, the anniversary of "The Field of the Blackbirds" (Battle of Kosovo Polje). This is considered to be the main *casus belli* which led directly to the outbreak of the First World War (1914 – 1918).

Following the defeat at Kosovo Polje 1389, large numbers of Serbs and their families fled north and settled along the northern bank of the Sava River on Croatian soil and also in a region of Croatia which became known as the Krajina, or frontier zone, immediately to the north-west of Bosnia. This territory of Croatia became the boundary or frontier between the Austro-Hungarian Empire and the Turkish Ottoman Empire. The history of these localities (East Slavonia; West Slavonia and the Krajina abutting Croatia/Bosnia) was established as a frontier protection zone, or 'The Military Frontier District'. From this territory Serbs fought for the Austro-Hungarians against the Turkish invaders. As a consequence of their lengthy stay on Croatian soil, (approximately 600 years) the Serbs established large communities, which, they claim, became, or were to become, part of present-day Serbia, in the modern era (i.e. Greater Serbia – Milosevich's dream).

The roots of conflict between Croats and Serbs in the recent fighting 1991 – 1994 stem partly from this outcome whereby the Croats felt compelled to fight for their nation to re-establish complete sovereignty over East Slavonia, West Slavonia and the Krajina and that these territories are indisputably part of Croatian national territory.

A further factor, which lies deep in Serbian memories, was that during the vicious fighting in the Second World War, Croats versus Serbs (i.e. Ustashe extremist actions against the Serb population as a whole), one prime Ustashe wartime slogan read "Remove a third, convert a third (to Catholicism), and finally eliminate a third" (an early form of ethnic cleansing). This wartime slogan speaks volumes about the atrocities committed by the Croat extremists against the Serbs and naturally these heinous acts featured strongly in the Serb national psyche and lasting memories of the Second World War. It is alleged, but hotly disputed by the Croats, that over 600,000 Serbs were massacred during the Second World War by the Croat Ustashe, led by Ante Pavelic. However, what equally and powerfully stirred Serbian blood in the post-1991 conflicts was that these atrocities were not the sole act and responsibility of the Croat Ustashe, but that Bosnian Muslims were also known to have actively participated in these acts of genocide. It is therefore relatively easy to establish how the present day Serbian focus of anti-Croat and anti-Bosnian Muslim feeling arose when one reflects on the dreadful events inflicted upon their nation in the early/mid twentieth century.

It has been said that Marshal Tito described Yugoslavia, the land he ruled with a very strong arm from after the Second World War until his death in 1980, as being a State consisting of:

| | |
|---|---|
| One Country | Six Republics |
| Two Alphabets | Seven Neighbouring States |
| Three Languages | Eight Ethnic Minorities |
| Four Religions | and |
| Five major nationalities | approximately 850,000 Gypsies |

From other well-documented research, it has been established that there are at least 15 other ethnic minorities in the population as a whole of Former Republic of Yugoslavia, many of whom were caught up in and deeply scarred by the tragic, recurring conflicts which characterize Yugoslavia's complex history.

The main purpose of Slobodan Milosevich's war in Yugoslavia was to create "Velika Srbija" – Greater Serbia, so that after the almost inevitable disintegration of the Former Federal Republic of Yugoslavia all Serb-dominated regions (within or without Serbia proper) would form the new enlarged Serb state. It is clear, from other notable researchers, that since virtually no Serbs lived in Slovenia, Milosevic was content to allow the Slovenes to gain independence, as it did not significantly affect his greater scheme for the Serbs as a people. However, he seriously miscalculated the subsequent reactions of Croatia and, in turn, Bosnia. Their bids for separate statehood propelled each in turn into serious outbreaks of violence, initially of localized fighting and then into wider conflicts. By the summer of 1991 the situation had rapidly deteriorated with major centres of fighting raging in East and West Slavonia and in the Krajina, and serious fighting had broken out in areas of Bosnia. The outbreak of fighting in Bosnia, by analogy, can be likened descriptively to the natural actions/reactions of hot mud/gas pools in the volcanic region of Rotorua in New Zealand. Gas accumulations from deep subterranean sources bubble to the surface and erupt violently, with the residue then seemingly subsiding, only to burst out again somewhere else with equal strength and ferocity. In Bosnia the multi-ethnic fighting which erupted between Croat/Serb/Muslim communities flared up in numerous widely dispersed localities, died down and were then re-ignited elsewhere with equal passion and uncontrolled fury. It was into this simmering, often explosive unpredictable cauldron that the 1st Battalion, the 22nd (Cheshire) Regiment, with its supporting elements, including B Squadron of 9th/12th Royal Lancers, was despatched to undertake their humanitarian peacekeeping rôle in late 1992.

# GLOSSARY

| | |
|---|---|
| AK-47 | Assault Rifle (calibre 7.62mm short) |
| APC | Armoured Personnel Carrier |
| ARBiH | Armija Bosnia i Hercegovina (abbreviated to BiH) (Bosnian Muslim Army) |
| ATO | Ammunition Technician Officer (Bomb Disposal) |
| Benz | Benzine (petrol) |
| BFPO | British Forces Post Office |
| BiH | Bosnia i Hercegovina (abbreviated form for ARBiH) |
| Bivi | Bivouac shelter |
| BSA | Bosnian Serb Army |
| BV | Boiling Vessel |
| C-130 | Military transport aircraft (Hercules) |
| Camel Trophy | Four-wheel-drive vehicle expedition |
| Click | Kilometre (slang) |
| CO | Commanding Officer |
| Coax | Machine gun mounted in the turret 'coaxially' (in parallel) with the main armament |
| COMBRITFOR | Commander British Forces |
| CSM | Company Sergeant-Major |
| CVR(T) | Combat Vehicle Reconnaissance (Tracked) |
| Diff-lock | Differential-lock (all 4 wheels driving) |
| Dhobi | Laundry – A term commonly used by soldiers, derived from India. |
| DM | Deutschmark |
| ECMM | European Community Monitoring Mission |
| FROG | Free-flight Rocket Over Ground (Soviet-built rocket launcher) |
| Gore-tex | Breathable waterproof fabric (jacket) |
| GPMG | General Purpose Machine Gun (Jimpy) |
| GPS | Global Positioning System |
| GV | Gornji Vakuf |

| | |
|---|---|
| HDZ | Hrvatska Demokratska Zajednica (Croat Democratic Union) |
| H.E. | High Explosive |
| HF | High Frequency (radio) |
| HOS | Hrvatske Oruzane Snaga (Croatian Armed Forces, estb 1944) |
| HQ BHC | Headquarters United Nations Forces in Bosnia Hercegovina |
| HV | Hrvatska Vojnik (Croatian Army) |
| HVO | Hrvatska Voisko Obrane ((Bosnian) Croat Defence Forces) |
| ICRC | International Commission for the Red Cross |
| ICTY | International Criminal Tribunal for Yugoslavia |
| JNA | Yugoslavian National Army |
| Kevlar | Composite armoured material (e.g. helmet) |
| LO | Liaison Officer |
| MST | Mobile Surgical Team |
| NAAFI | Navy Army Air Force Institute (shop) |
| NATO | North Atlantic Treaty Organization |
| NCO | Non-Commissioned Officer |
| ND | Negligent Discharge (of a firearm or weapon) |
| NGO | Non-Governmental Organisation |
| PIFWC | Person Indicted For War Crimes |
| P Info | Public Information (media) |
| RAF | Royal Air Force |
| RAMC | Royal Army Medical Corps |
| RE | Royal Engineers |
| Recce | Reconnaissance/Reconnoitre |
| REME | Royal Electrical Mechanical Engineers |
| RPG | Rocket Propelled Grenade (Soviet designed hand-held anti-armour weapon) |
| RQMS | Regimental Quartermaster Sergeant |
| R&R | Rest and Recuperation |
| RV | Rendezvous point |
| SA80 | British Army Individual Weapon (calibre 5.56mm) |
| Sappers | Royal Engineers |
| Scimitar | Armoured reconnaissance vehicle. Member of CVR(T) family |
| Scratchers | Beds |
| SFOR | Stabilisation Force |

| | |
|---|---|
| Shell | Name given to High Explosive ammunition in fire orders |
| SHQ | Squadron Headquarters |
| Sitrep | Situation Report |
| SQMS | Squadron Quartermaster Sergeant |
| TCP | Traffic Control Point |
| TSG | Tomislavgrad |
| UN | United Nations |
| UNHCR | United Nations Humanitarian Commission for Refugees |
| UNPROFOR | United Nations Protection Force |
| VHF | Very High Frequency (radio) |
| VRS | Voisko Republica Serbska |
| Warrior | British Army Armoured Infantry Fighting Vehicle |
| WEU | Western European Union |
| WOCS | War Office Controlled Stores |
| Zero | Radio call sign for a headquarters or controlling station |

## Serbo-Croat phrases

| | |
|---|---|
| Dobor dan | Good afternoon |
| Dobro | Good |
| Dobro jutro | Good morning |
| Dobro vece | Good evening |
| Dostar | Very |
| Dovidenja | Goodbye |
| Govorite | Speak |
| Hvala | Thanks |
| Ja sam | I am |
| Kapral | Corporal |
| Koliko | How many? |
| Nema | No |
| Pomoc | Humanitarian Aid |
| Pushka | Rifle |
| Razumijem | Understand |
| Slivovitz | Plum Brandy |
| Vojnik | Soldier |

AUSTRIA

• Ljubljana

SLOVENIA

• **Zagreb**

CROATIA

Banja Luka •

BOSNIA-
HERZEGOVINA

Vitez •

• Split

Mostar •

ITALY

*Adriatic Sea*

The Former Republics
of Yugoslavia

N

0        50        100 miles

0    50    100    150 km

HUNGARY

VOJVODINA

ROMANIA

Belgrade

Tuzla    Loznica

Sarajevo

SERBIA

MONTENEGRO

KOSOVO

BULGARIA

MACEDONIA

ALBANIA

GREECE

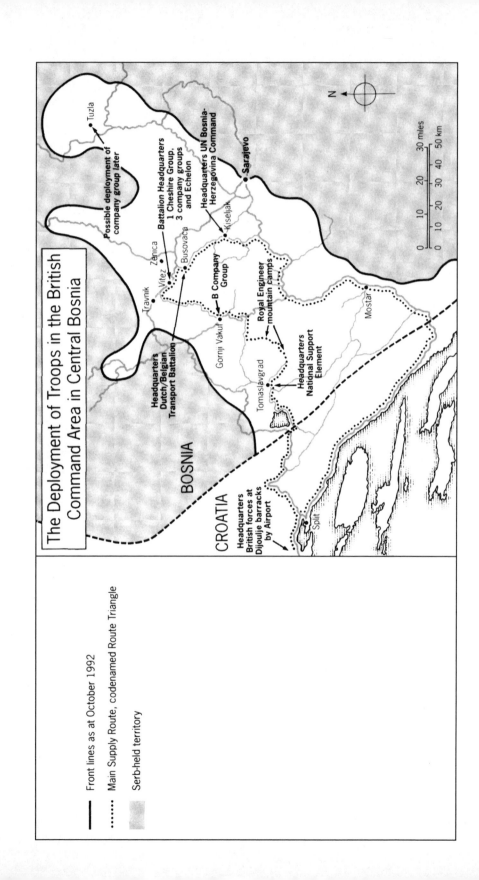

The Deployment of Troops in the British
Command Area in Central Bosnia

Front lines as at October 1992

Main Supply Route, codenamed Route Triangle

Serb-held territory

Tuzla

Possible deployment of
company group later

Battalion Headquarters
1 Cheshire Group,
3 company groups
and Echelon

Headquarters UN Bosnia-
Herzegovina Command

Sarajevo

Kiseljak

Zenica

Busovača

Vitez

B Company
Group

Travnik

Royal Engineer
mountain camps

Gornji Vakuf

Mostar

Headquarters
Dutch/Belgian
Transport Battalion

Tomaslavgrad

Headquarters
National Support
Element

BOSNIA

CROATIA

Headquarters
British forces at
Dijoulje barracks
by Airport

Split

N

30 miles

50 km

0    10    20    30    40

0    10    20    30

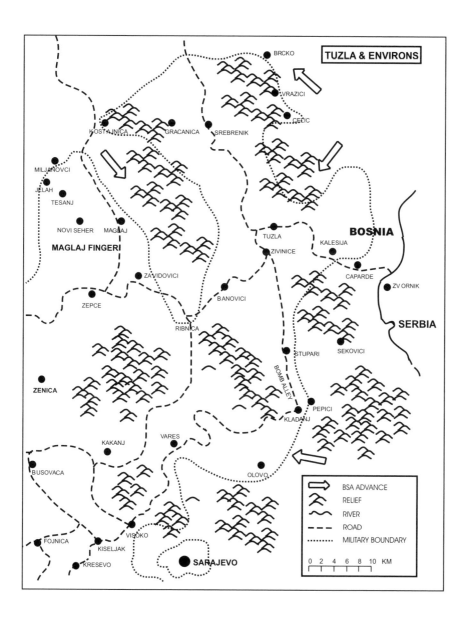

**TUZLA & ENVIRONS**

BRCKO

VRAZICI

CELIC

KOSTAJNICA  GRACANICA  SREBRENIK

MILJANOVCI

JELAH

TESANJ

NOVI SEHER  MAGLAJ

**MAGLAJ FINGERI**

ZAVIDOVICI

ZEPCE

RIBNICA

TUZLA  KALESIJA

**BOSNIA**

ZIVINICE

CAPARDE  ZVORNIK

**SERBIA**

BANOVICI

STUPARI  SEKOVICI

BOMB ALLEY

**ZENICA**

KAKANJ  VARES

PEPICI
KLADANJ

BUSOVACA

OLOVO

VISOKO

FOJNICA
KISELJAK

KRESEVO  **SARAJEVO**

| | BSA ADVANCE |
| | RELIEF |
| | RIVER |
| | ROAD |
| | MILITARY BOUNDARY |

0  2  4  6  8  10  KM

xxi

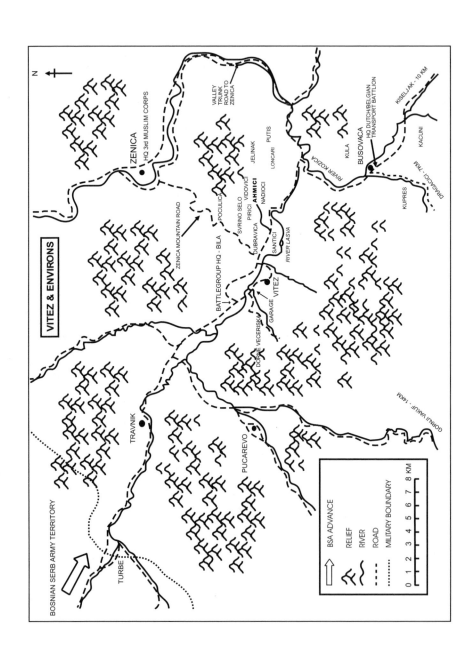

VITEZ & ENVIRONS

N

BOSNIAN SERB ARMY TERRITORY

TURBE

TRAVNIK

PUCAREVO

ZENICA

HQ 3rd MUSLIM CORPS

VALLEY
TRUNK
ROAD TO
ZENICA

ZENICA MOUNTAIN ROAD

BATTLEGROUP HQ - BILA

POCULICA

SVRINO SELO

PIRICI VIDOVICI

DUBRAVICA

AHMICI

NADIOCI

SANTICI

JELINAK

LONCARI

PUTIS

RIVER LASVA

DONJE VECERISKA

GARAGE

VITEZ

RIVER KOZICA

KULA

BUSOVACA

HQ DUTCH/BELGIAN
TRANSPORT BATTLION

KISELJAK - 10 KM

KACUNI

KUPRES

DRAGACICI - 7KM

GORNJI VAKUF - 14KM

BSA ADVANCE

RELIEF

RIVER

ROAD

MILITARY BOUNDARY

0 1 2 3 4 5 6 7 8 KM

# I

# LOVE THY NEIGHBOUR

The slender white column that had once elevated the minaret's siren towards the heavens had collapsed. Instead, rubble and debris were strewn across the surrounding homes beneath. Gutted by fire, structurally unsound and scarred by shell and bullet marks, these houses had been deserted long ago. The top section of the minaret had crashed through the Mosque's roof, breaking its fall. It now lay in the manner a tree might after a storm. Although beyond resurrection, its foundation undermined, the minaret was holding its head out of the dirt.

The scene is infamous on a global scale. Captured on film from every angle by every journalist in central Bosnia, it embodied the most striking and enduring symbol of ethnic cleansing in recent times. Ahmici's toppled minaret was so surreal, it looked like the creation of a sculptor whose interpretation of the Muslim massacre had been this abstract effigy: 'Allah slain by Christians' modelled in concrete.

Five years on, to the month this atrocity was committed, everything remained as it had fallen. This legacy of ethnic cleansing lay near the village entrance as a constant reminder to everyone who passed. How its condition was explained honestly to Croat children, too young to remember anything different, is difficult to comprehend. The wounds of this episode still gaped wide open; evidently time had healed very little.

The two Land Rovers were driven up Ahmici's only road, a simple dusty track. Near the top of the hill Mr Moskowitz, senior barrister for the prosecution, stopped near a row of breezeblock houses. As elsewhere in the village, these were all still empty, just roofless blackened shells. The cellar of one of these houses had been chosen as a refuge by a number of families on that fateful day, 16 April 1993. With the village surrounded, these victims of racial hatred had fled from their homes to the safest place they knew at a time of day when most of Europe was thinking about breakfast. While these old men and women, mothers and children had gone to ground to save their lives, Croat men of fighting age could be heard nearby ransacking

1

homes and executing any male old enough to pose a threat.

Unsurprisingly, most of the village's young men had been fighting on the front line for the collective good, but those with a reason to be at home were later found dead outside their front doors. Bodies discovered by patrol members were barely cold when laid side by side in a garden under the then towering minaret. With the instinct to escape death by burning, they had had no choice but to run from their blazing homes, only to be cut down by Croat squads firing automatic weapons, some of whom were their neighbours. A number of the families lucky or clever enough to evade certain death were still suffering the trauma of their experience when discovered hiding in the cellar early on that April afternoon.

Isolated, injured and at their lowest ebb, only hope was of comfort to this terrified group of civilians. Miraculously, their prayers seemed to be answered when an armoured United Nations patrol stopped after being flagged down by a brave female victim. The crammed cellar was guarded while first aid was given and rations distributed. The UN's fear of being accused of assisting ethnic cleansing had restricted the transportation of local people in UN vehicles. Fortunately common sense prevailed and these rules were ignored in order to evacuate the three worst injured to safety and professional treatment. For the people left behind hope vanished as the patrol departed. Once more they were plunged into uncertainty and danger, only worse; their hiding place had been compromised.

Half a decade before, I had failed to realize quite how significant the detail of our find would be. Neither did I expect to be called as a witness to give evidence at The Hague against People Indicted For War Crimes (PIFWCs). Returning to Ahmici with staff from the International Criminal Tribunal for Yugoslavia (ICTY), I was able to describe, with some accuracy, the scene as I had witnessed it at first hand. Initially I was unable to recall which of these breezeblock houses had given hope to those innocent people; the village was bigger than I remembered it. One might think that three hours among the groaning injured, crying children and screaming babies, accompanied by the tympani of rata-tat-tatting machine-gun fire and explosions outside should be indelible. A number of the houses were missing, however, and fences had since been removed for winter fuel. The stillness now was so out of context with the reality five springs ago.

JUDGE CASSESSE: Counsel Smith please continue with your questions.

Q. Major Woolley, can you tell the court about how many people you found in the cellar and what was the atmosphere like?

A. The cellar was very dark; there was no lighting. There was an awful smell generally of, I suppose, wounds, and there was also cigarette smoke. There were crying children, there was a woman breast-feeding, there were elderly people, children, and women. There were about 30 people probably in the cellar, five of whom had significant injuries.

Q. Did you do anything about those wounds?

A. Yes. Nearest the door was a small girl who I believe was about 12 or 13 years old. She had injuries on her left leg, on the lower limb of her left leg, and an injury on the inside of her thigh, on her right thigh, which again I — were consistent with some sort of, well, an entry wound that I thought was either from a low velocity bullet or maybe shrapnel. LCpl Priestly carried out some first aid on her left lower limb and the right thigh, the inner thigh.

Q. Did you record that injury in your diary?

A. Yes. I wrote about the injuries.

Q. You mentioned the injury of the young girl. Can you explain the injuries of the others?

A. Yes. The other one was in the far left-hand corner of the cellar, an elderly gentleman, and he, when we tried to move him — well, he was screaming because — of the pain. It was something like a pelvis or a hip injury, somewhere in his midriff that he was complaining about, injured either by shrapnel or more probably a gunshot wound.

Q. What about the other three?

A. The other — the third man — sorry, the third was an elderly man who had got a gunshot wound to the — if I recall correctly, the left shoulder, up in this sort of region here (indicating), and those three were the most significant, therefore we evacuated them in the back of a Warrior, in the space used for infantry personnel. There were two more, and I think they were both men, who had other sorts of smaller injuries. We didn't manage to evacuate them in the end.

3

Q. Major Woolley, did you record that in your diary as well?

A. Yes, I recorded five people being significantly injured hiding in this cellar.

Q. Can you explain to the Court the average age of these men and what they were wearing?

A. They were wearing civilian clothing, they were anywhere between maybe 45 and 65 years old. There were not many men anyway, but they were of that age. The rest were women and children and elderly women as well, and, you know, even children or, should I say, babies of breast-feeding age. All very scared, all very shocked in this dingy, dark cellar where they were taking cover.

Q. Did any of the men that you saw, these men that were injured, did any of them have weapons?

A. Not in the cellar, no, no.

Q. About how long did it take you to tend to all of these injuries?

A. Probably about a further hour.

Q. Was any drug given to any of these men?

A. Yes. The man in the — the second man I talked about who had the hip-type injury, we gave him morphine in his thigh because he was in such pain that when we tried to move him, he just yelped and screamed, and therefore, by administering some morphine, it enabled us to then move him using a sleeping bag, one of our own, as a stretcher.

Q. The most severe casualties went in the Warrior and the other two stayed at the house; is that correct?

A. That's correct, yes.

The people sheltering in the cellar were not the only huddle of Muslims who had been hiding in Ahmici that day and not the worst off. Several days after the assault, further investigations revealed more evidence of ethnic cleansing in its most disturbing form. Television cameras at the scene took millions of horrified spectators inside the cellar of one home where a family had been burnt alive. Twisted black limbs and

4

misshapen heads were barely recognizable as human among the melted remains of household objects covering the cellar's floor. Prominent above the detritus was a raised arm, the hand contracted by the intense heat like an evil black claw. These were the remains of a mother attempting to protect her children from a threat she stood no chance against. These grotesquely distorted bodies and contorted faces were seen fixed in a state that described an agonizing struggle at the point of death. This was not the Ottoman Empire of the eighteenth century but contemporary Europe nearing the end of the twentieth century and it was beyond imagination.

The next incident in the village would be easier for me to remember. There were only two bungalows at the top of the hill, I recalled; they were on the right-hand side. Nevertheless, the last time I had seen one of these pretty homes, a week after the assault on Ahmici, it had been burnt out. Everything wooden was destroyed, but the once-white walls and brick chimney had survived the blaze.

Strangely though, when the Land Rovers pulled up minutes later I was to find that the house had gone. Again, I spent a moment establishing where exactly it had been. Two concrete steps protruding from the foundations caught my eye. These were the same steps that a number of elderly men had stood on after the first wave of the massacre. Dazed by the events, they had peered through the front door to see their friend's wife dying on a makeshift stretcher. It was a miracle that the Croat-aimed bullet had not killed her instantly. While ordnance continued to be fired into the village from the safety of its peripheral slopes, she laid there, life ebbing away. The back of her skull had been blown away.

The base of the house was now heavily overgrown in newly surfaced weeds, made strong by the spring sunshine. Nothing of this former home stood higher. Quite what the point of completely levelling this house had been was beyond understanding. It was no more a disgraceful reminder to the few Croat families still living in the village than the minaret, and no one had dismantled the remnants of that.

Aware that untriggered mines or booby-traps might still be lurking to claim an unsuspecting victim, we moved with caution, keeping to the track. In bushes at the rear of the plot I could see the woman's cast-iron stove lying on its side. It was red with rust, the only thing that suggested anyone had ever lived here at all. Nothing else existed, not even one loose brick of rubble; it had all been conveniently swept away.

In the spring of 1993, before being tasked to confirm reports of burning houses in a place called Ahmici, this village had been just another random mixed community hardly known, just a place-name on the map. What was discovered unravelled one of the most emotive atrocities spanning the period of the civil war. As patrol leader, equipped with a camera and having kept a detailed diary, I became one of the ICTY's key witnesses. Photographs taken, despatched to The Hague for copying, were to be a valuable record of evidence during the case.

Regardless of being busy that day assisting members of the patrol carry out first aid, I had fortunately taken the opportunity to photograph the white bungalow, not realizing that it would soon be set alight. Ten days later, on the 26 April 1993, I was patrolling in the area and discovered the house burnt out as I have described it. ICTY staff explained the significance of these two pictures. The two dates in the photos' bottom corners were hard evidence that bracketed the chronology of events. It was to be invaluable in supporting the case for prosecuting six local Croat men, a number of them residents of Ahmici. Moreover, I had formerly been a member of the UN Protection Force (UNPROFOR) and as such was a credible and unbiased witness.

Mr Moskowitz and I went back down the hill to take in the scale of the carnage once more. It was fascinating as well as sickening to hear other horrifying stories of Muslim people caught in the Massacre of Ahmici, which was relevant as my evidence supported many of them. These events were taking place while my patrol had been tending to the few survivors lucky enough to have escaped alive. They described how Croats had used the most extreme methods to select who was to qualify as a neighbour. Many of the victims had known the killers all their lives; it was incomprehensible.

One family was duped by a local man known to them. Their young daughter opened the front door to answer a familiar and reassuring voice. The man exploited this toehold and the family was paraded outside at gunpoint. The mother and daughter watched as the father and two sons were murdered in cold blood in front of them. The mother was then raped. One of the sons shot in the head was to be lucky. The bullet went straight through one of his cheeks and out the other. Survival instincts and shock made him fall to the ground and play dead. The three bodies were dragged to a ditch where they were dumped among other corpses. Knowing it to be the only chance of survival, and frozen with fear, the teenager lay next to his dead father and brother for the rest of the day until night fell. Covered by darkness, he crawled away and, just when he thought his luck was changing, stumbled into a group of Croat soldiers. He was shot at once more and a hand grenade was lobbed at him, but the shrapnel missed and darkness concealed his escape and eventual safety.

This family's crime was being Muslim in the wrong village. Of the ten cantons designated to form the new Bosnia under the Vance-Owen Peace Plan, Ahmici fell into a canton earmarked to be Croat. The boundaries were about as sensitively or rationally thought out as the arbitrary straight lines drawn by colonialists to divide Africa over a century earlier.

In stark contrast to the majority of cleansed homes that we surveyed were a number of houses in very good condition. They looked just as if they had been homes anywhere else in southern Europe. While passing one very well kept house the downstairs curtains twitched. I was told that this was the home of the Kupreskic family. Two brothers and a cousin of this name were three of the six indicted for war crimes.

Having questioned me at length and taken abundant photographs, the ICTY staff departed in their white UN Land Rover for a hotel in Zenica where the laborious process of building the case would be continued.

Sergeant-Major Clarke and I drove home via Bila, near Vitez, where the Cheshire Battlegroup had been based at the time of the incident in question. The local school, previously the headquarters and home to four hundred British soldiers, was still standing, but now derelict. Coils of razor wire, once the only protection for soldiers going about their business in camp, remained as a perimeter that closed off the site. A house formerly used as the subalterns' accommodation had not changed and the family, who had let it to the UN at a significant profit, was living there once more. A legacy from more than three years of British military 'occupation' was a mural by the front door painted in black and yellow. Large letters spelt two famous British battle honours: TALAVERA and EGYPT. Another clue to the British past was issue pattern camouflaged trousers and green T-shirts hanging among other laundry from a washing line on the balcony. First appearances suggested that life for the local inhabitants had improved very little since the departure of British troops.

Continuing our journey freely through the former Serb/Muslim front line at Turbe was extraordinary. Five years before, this had been a village caught in the crossfire between two warring sides. It was also a dropping-off point for Muslims who, in order to secure their lives, had been forced to buy coach tickets to be ethnically cleansed. Innocent civilians in the wrong ethnic group had been kicked out of Serb coaches into the deep snow. Watching displaced Muslims fleeing down the hill at Turbe with all their possessions in suitcases, plastic carrier bags or, if lucky, in a wheelbarrow, was heart-wrenching. Only hundreds of metres short of the UN transport, and safety, the Bosnian Serbs had shot over their heads to hurry them on. The Cheshire Battlegroup's intervention was later criticized as condoning ethnic cleansing.

It was over two years later, in 1995, that the Dayton Peace Accord was signed and a multi-national force, under the stewardship of NATO, put in place to implement the Accord. While a commendable intent, the peace was in fact being artificially shored up. In 1998 deep rifts and scars were still apparent, but the international community was forcing the three major factions to comply with measures that were designed to establish lasting peace. Government buildings were forced to fly the new Bosnian flag. This blue and yellow symbol of 'unity', with stars and abstract shapes symbolizing new hope, was the design of Euro bureaucrats. It meant nothing to the majority of patriotic locals who had so recently and fiercely fought for their ethnic identity and who had a long-lasting memory. Similarly, drivers were obliged to register cars with a common Bosnian number plate. HVO (Bosnian Croat Army) and ARBiH (Muslim Army or BiH) armies were forced to co-operate in a united Bosnian Army or Federation, a façade of compliance which, to those who knew them better, failed to bond soldiers or erase old scores. It was all part of the international community's method of transforming Bosnia into a civilized country and it was proving a considerable challenge.

The NATO Stabilization Force (SFOR) monitored the cessation of fighting with continued patrols along the Zone of Separation, an overt presence designed to build confidence and trust on each side. Meanwhile, international money was poured into abundant projects, which the locals used to full effect. Targeting the most needy, teams of SFOR soldiers and NGOs would harness the skills of locals to rebuild their own communities. Homes, schools, dairies, bridges and much of the infrastructure were in a decrepit state; it was difficult to know where to start.

Probably the most challenging problem was the high volume of displaced people and refugees. Having been cleansed from their homes or forced to run away, five years later they laid claim to the house they had settled in, just like squatters. To return everyone to their original home, bearing in mind that many of the houses had been completely destroyed and remained beyond repair, created the biggest housing chain in Europe. Long after the fighting had stopped Bosnia's problems remained a nightmare, physical problems that would take years to rectify before even considering the emotional scars.

By 1998 there was a huge differential amongst the population, dependant on circumstance. Driving in the Land Rover down the hill from Mrkonjic Grad town to our SFOR camp, we overtook a farmer at the reins of a wooden horse-drawn cart, being pulled by a hardy and shaggy horse. A woman sat on the back wearing a white blouse, her long tangled hair blowing in the wind. Next to her was a small pig that had probably been bought from the market that day; the scene looked almost medieval, less the cart's rubber tyres and the tarmac road.

At the bottom of the hill, outside camp, children played in the street in the late afternoon and stray dogs roamed in packs of threes and fours. At the side of the road a number of shacks and shops were now being used to run thriving businesses selling pirate CDs and other attractive goods. The suppliers of these dirt-cheap products worked from eastern Europe, while soldiers with cash and time on their hands kept the demand alive. Relatively smart cars were parked outside the shops, many having mysteriously migrated from western Europe. Their owners were in business and enjoying the first taste of success. This was the other side to post-war Bosnia that had seen opportunity and struck.

The local situation was still fragile, but hopeful. The one incentive that promoted peace and fostered hope was economic, regardless of ethnic or class differences. Needless to say the entrepreneurs, perhaps people who had successfully played a leading role during the war, were getting richer and now had new reasons for flexing their muscles and ever more means to do so. The poor remained impoverished and struggled, supported by humanitarian handouts; t'was ever the case. This former communist state was indeed starting to understand the 'progress' of capitalism.

Thousands of international soldiers have served in Bosnia under the flags of the United Nations and NATO in the name of peace, many of them British. Some soldiers witnessed the bloodshed and chaos of a civil war, some the pathetic aftermath, a number both. All of them, however, have seen at first hand the devastation caused when peace becomes unachievable. Peace is the bedrock of a civilized democracy, a prerequisite for a nation's stability. Absence of such a key component undermines everything: the desire to make a family, build a home, the ability to work or plan for the future. For the majority who enjoy peace, such circumstances are incomprehensible, security rightly being taken for granted. Their only means to understand anything different, the horror and reality of war, is through the graphic scenes of television footage.

The vantage point that neutrality affords UN troops, on the other hand, is akin to being a 'fly on the wall'. For many it has provided a vicarious education in the consequences of politics failing and a civilized structure collapsing. One particular troop of Lancers, serving on the first British deployment to Bosnia, was put in a position to observe both sides of a civil war, men fighting men and whole communities fighting for survival and the right to exist. From the relative safety of the sidelines, this troop experienced a civil war that had the script of a bloodthirsty history book. Their experiences were written about in a diary. This forms a valuable record that tells the story of twelve soldiers who, engaged in the initially benign international humanitarian aid effort, later find themselves witnessing some of the most appalling war crimes in Europe since the Second World War. Hundreds of similar diaries exist, but their stories remain untold. All of them have their own opinions and conclusions, many doubtless reflecting the chapters within. This story is retold as it happened.

# 2

# NEW LIVERY

*The Balkans is not worth the life of one Pomeranian Grenadier*
*Chancellor Otto von Bismarck*

A random pattern of green blobs with off-white edging was cast against a rich cobalt blue canvas, illuminated brilliantly by natural light. Altitude had erased earthly imperfections to bless us with this magnificent image that belied reality. It was modern art indeed; abstract, living and created by the chance of a carefree hand. Its texture came slowly into focus as the aeroplane descended; terracotta-coloured squares, grey lines and agricultural terraces gradually emerged. Fishing boats came into view and eventually the white tips of small choppy waves could be seen. This was the Dalmatian coast, the same beautiful landscape that, through television, the world had witnessed being torn apart by senseless fighting for much of the year.

Pressing my face into the cold porthole I strained to see the mainland, but was beaten by an instruction to re-take my seat. Swivelling on the spot, I squeezed myself between camouflaged neighbours and secured the steel buckle. The noise and vibration of the undercarriage lowering, indicating the final approach to land, was obvious over the dull hum of four turbo-prop engines.

The aeroplane adopted an unusually sharp nose-down attitude. It was not nearly as severe as transporters seen on newsreel footage landing in Sarajevo, but a sufficient precaution against potential ground-to-air fire. Popping my ears and looking about, it was both amusing and reassuring to watch the concerned or exhilarated faces of other squadron members. Clearly many thought likewise. Had we been told to sit on our helmets for protection there would have been a legitimate cause for worry, but we had not.

Once the propellers had stopped turning the Loadmaster operated the hydraulic tail ramp controls and watched it lower safely. Activity outside was busy and organized. RAF ground crew wearing yellow high-visibility vests prepared for our disembarkation and a large forklift truck waited to unload our baggage. The flight was filled to capacity and so a mild scrummage ensued. Soldiers grabbed hand luggage and rifles from beneath the red webbing seats and formed single-file queues port and starboard of the cargo. Following the man in front, I stepped off the tail ramp and was forced to shield my eyes from the dazzling sunshine, made worse by the glare off the pale concrete pan.

Airport staff escorted us two hundred metres to the terminal where we were kept waiting in front of huge plate-glass doors. Above us was a concrete balcony emblazoned with large plastic letters, Split Kastela. One could imagine how holidaymakers had once stood on this vantage point and watched an aeroplane land on the single runway that would later take them home; that was the scale of this international airport! Peeling paintwork and long weeds rooted to unswept guttering was indicative of so much more than just under use of the balcony. Customers now were limited: humanitarian aid workers, UN soldiers and the media.

During the 1980s Yugoslavia's tourist trade exploded with success on account of being an alternative to Spain's cheap and sunny holidays. A significant proportion of its holidaymakers were from Great Britain, young and old. Consequently the local economies of quiet Croatian coastal villages had been buoyed, but at a price! Customers of Yugotour package deals included citizens who represented British fashion at its most impressive: A spectacle of pink arms and peeling bald heads, sandals with white socks, string vests and tattoos, white stiletto shoes and ankle chains, and lads parading football club jerseys and the Union Flag fashioned into shorts. For the small but conspicuous groups of holiday hooligans, alcohol and sunshine were the catalyst for frayed tempers, nightclub scuffles and obnoxious behaviour on the beach. Loutish booze culture was completely alien to the locals, who were indignant of the invasion, but happy to take the foreign currency. Yugoslavia's centuries-old culture was experiencing modern western interference, something that was to be proven as mild-mannered when set against a national demonstration of blood-letting in the following decade.

With not one passenger jet or tourist in sight now, it was puzzling that immigration control had managed to engineer such a bottleneck. "Why're we 'avin' our passports checked anyway, we're 'ere to 'elp these bludy spics . . . wod 're the' gonna do, send uz 'ome?" I overheard a tired and hot soldier exclaim. It too seemed odd to me, but then we had arrived in Croatia, which had become a state of respectability, not Bosnia the war-zone, our final destination. Dressed in combats for a cool German November morning, I broke from the queue and made for welcome shade offered by the balcony. This processing was going to take some time.

Behind us the trusty green C-130 transporter lay like an enormous lizard basking in the sunshine. Ground crew serviced the Hercules while the United States Air Force flight crew walked towards the terminal. Dressed in flying suits, adorned with colourful squadron badges and sporting aviator shades and blue side hats worn at jaunty angles, they were the essence of Hollywood's aviation heroes. The following day they would be back in Germany, smug faces clutching precious duty-free supplies, and able to tell economically truthful stories in their squadron bar about steep approaches and near misses. One could have been forgiven for thinking one had joined the wrong club!

The immigration officer was another stereotype, but instead a Mediterranean one. His chin could not have seen a razor for at least two days. He sported a bushy moustache, which drooped at the corners of his mouth matching his apathetic demeanour. His suspicious stare was hidden by the same aviator-style sunglasses, which to the discerning were undoubtedly imitations. Pinned to the left breast of his cheap blue bomber-jacket, with elasticated waistband, was an equally cheap chrome badge inscribed Hrvatska. Croatia's red and white chequerboard flag displayed beneath confirmed the nationality. This man had all the credentials to play the part of a dozy security guard in a 1970s movie. Looking up at my face and down at my passport photograph he thumbed through the pages with the speed of a bank clerk. His stern expression did not alter as he thumped the rubber stamp randomly at a skewed angle, spoiling a clean page: SPLIT 10.XI.92.

The bureaucracy got worse. Unquestioningly, the squadron formed an orderly queue for the metal detector archway. Each soldier passed his SA80 rifle over the adjacent desk before committing himself to the scrutiny of this nugatory procedure. Once past this test the squadron was subjected to a rigorous visual inspection from Croatian officers whose humourless stares must have been mastered during a special course. Another explanation might be the years spent suffering communist bureaucracy, cheap cigarettes and nagging wives with enormous backsides and no teeth. Whatever the reason the miserable buggers clearly had nothing to smile about.

On entering the arrivals hall the squadron fanned out in to a human delta and waited for further direction. It was no surprise to see a camera crew poised and ready to ambush a victim, perhaps a straggler who could be easily picked off from the herd. To have kept on shuffling along would have seen me go unnoticed, but, in an attempt to outflank this threat, my movement and the yellow pips on my shoulders caught their eye. Subalterns are easy prey, normally polite and sufficiently inventive to say something more original than the standard clichés, "We're just 'ere to do a job . . . Hi Mum."

"Excuse me, hello, I wonder if you would like to answer some questions," asked a short, blond-haired woman in her early thirties. Before being given a chance to reply, the cameraman had switched on a blinding light which had the effect of gluing me to the spot like a stunned rabbit in the beam of a car's headlights. It was the first time that a television camera had been pointed at me in anger.

"Right, look at me then tell us your name, regiment and where you're based," asked the reporter.

"Lieutenant Monty Woolley, 9th/12th Royal Lancers, Herford in Germany," I replied in a staccato manner, trying to suppress mild nerves.

"Lieutenant Woolley, what are your initial impressions now that you're here?" she asked.

"Well it's rather warmer and quieter than I had expected," came my weak answer.

"Have you got something you would like to tell the viewers at home, a message for your family and friends?" a verbatim line she delivered with a plastic grin and the sincerity of a trainee social worker. "Hope to see you in six months!" was my feeble reply and a wasted opportunity. A swipe at the enemy, the murderous Serbs, whose atrocious conduct was illustrated daily in newspapers and on television, might have been more fitting and worth risking a reprimand for.

As United Nations troops, however, there was no enemy in Bosnia-i-Herzegovina or anywhere, despite the media's war footage portraying Bosnian Serbs in such a light. The United Nations' task was not to enforce peace between the warring factions; it was not equipped for that. The UN posture was impartial, with a simple mandate to deliver emergency humanitarian aid to people in isolated Muslim and Croat regions. Our rules of engagement only permitted use of lethal force as a means of self-defence, and only as a last resort. Standing in the sunshine on the airport steps, I did not realize what a source of frustration our UN mandate would later become.

The package-tour theme continued when three 55-seater air-conditioned coaches pulled up in front of airport arrivals. These had seen better days, so too their drivers, who were more used to driving European tourists along the Dalmatian coast to the highly acclaimed and beautiful fishing ports and resorts. Dubrovnik, arguably the best known, was now heavily war-damaged from fighting, which had stopped in the summer since Croatia's declared independence, recognized only by Germany at this time.

The short excursion was no sightseeing tour; instead we were treated to the wisdom of a Royal Signals Staff Sergeant who delivered an amusing but cautionary brief of do's and don'ts during the three-minute drive to Divulje Barracks. The British Force (BRITFOR) now shared this former Yugoslavian National Army (JNA) camp over-looking the Adriatic Sea with the Croatian Army (HV).

The Squadron paraded next to the buses, each man with his bergen, webbing and grip at his feet. Meanwhile in true form the officers stood in a gaggle at the side of this formed body of men. Sergeant-Major Sterenberg explained the programme for the next twenty-four hours; timings, whose accommodation was where, tasks for the following day and more do's and don'ts. "Sir, would yer loike to address the squadrun?" the Sergeant-Major said, in his Brummy accent, handing over the parade with a salute to Major Abraham.

"Yes, thank you Sergeant-Major. Stand at ease; well we've arrived, finally, and since August it's been some journey, but thankfully we are all here in one piece. At nineteen hundred hours there will be an 'O' group (orders) in the cookhouse for Troop Leaders. If anybody needs me before then I'll be in the officers' accommodation. Take on board what the Sergeant-Major has said. I don't want any stupidity or disci-pline problems, and make sure you are prepared for an early start tomorrow. I've no more points, thank you Sergeant-Major, carry on."

"Roight, wun oy fal yer owt ged t'yer roomz and sort yerselves owt; troop sar'nts stay behoind, an' rememba whar-oi've sed, down't fuk ebowt with thouse Crow-ay-sh'n clownz nex' door, and down't leave yer fukin' kit loyin' ebowt for thievin' gypsoys; roight geraway."

Fooled by Mediterranean fashioned balconies and sunblinds, deflecting the afternoon's dying rays, our large white three-floor barrack block looked deceptively welcoming from outside. Dumping my heavy kit in a bare wooden-floored room was a pleasure. Although a brief siesta was tempting, my first responsibility lay with checking how the troop was settling in.

The Squadron junior ranks, about eighty soldiers in all, were squashed into a couple of large barrack rooms. A hubbub of normal banter and chatter emanated from within, the higher decibels of a familiar voice whingeing, ricocheted the length of the empty corridor as I approached. Inside green bergens sat on end half unpacked and kit lay everywhere. Camp beds were at different stages of assembly and some lucky enough to have secured a bunk bed were already spread-eagled to mark their new territory.

Sergeant Clarke had everything in hand, as one would expect from a soldier with fifteen years Service from the 'old school'. A drill instructor, he was not averse to raising his voice to achieve the necessary effect from young soldiers. Of course underneath he had a heart of gold. A Derby man, he had much in common with many of the squadron's soldiers who had joined the ranks from this prime regimental recruiting city.

A keen and competent NCO, Corporal Bremridge, would echo the troop sergeant, but was far less patient and more hands on, as troop corporals should be. He insisted on the utmost professionalism and if anything less occurred unleashed a quick temper. Another Derby soldier, he had said goodbye to his wife and young children in Germany that morning. Soldiers who are husbands and fathers can feel the separation worst and, having so much to lose, are generally more alert to unnecessary risks. Corporal Bremridge had promised to return home safely, reassurance that would be reflected in his prudent approach. This would be quite a contrast to most of the troop who, predominately young and single, had fewer responsibilities and sometimes the attitude of ten feet tall immortals.

The junior troop corporal, Chris Payne, was the clever one who could assimilate problems quickly. He was slick on the radio and a useful reconnaissance soldier. A wry wit and sarcastic nature was a front for a thinker who was adept in coaching younger soldiers and cared much about the welfare of the troop. A native of Leicester, the regiment's other key recruiting ground, he was fanatical about Leicester City Football Club and would be missing the chance to follow his team closely over the new season.

The troop seemed happy enough, despite being away from home and already missing their wives, families, girlfriends and comforts. The troopers were boisterous and light-hearted. I sensed an atmosphere of excitement, probably as a consequence of deploying on operations for the first time. Most of them were too young or too proud to dwell openly on the dangers that would soon threaten them, despite being constantly reminded by vivid television scenes. I was not aware of one soldier who did not want to be part of Operation GRAPPLE and, if there had been, we knew plenty of volunteers desperate to fill their boots. Three-quarters of the regiment had been left in Herford to continue with normal duties. B Squadron was lucky, for after a long Cold War that had required most British troops to remain at their station in Germany or UK, this small-scale expeditionary operation was something of a pioneering event.

The older soldiers, the NCOs, many with experience in the Gulf War and Northern Ireland, knew the form and were wiser. They understood that we might be kept waiting for political decisions, anticipated long periods of boredom, disappointment and frustration ahead, and moments of great uncertainty, possibly tragedy. In them I sensed impatience, but most of all relief. After three months of waiting and training, being stood down and stood to, we were finally getting somewhere.

The late afternoon sun had already dropped below the trees and the air cooled as fellow troop leaders strolled to the cookhouse for an early supper. This Yugoslavian camp had been well designed by someone, but not with anything particularly military in mind. Areas of sub-tropical vegetation were interspersed with pleasant gardens of a coarse grass bordered by white kerbstones. Red and white painted artillery shells stood as bollards and a neat assault course looked under-utilized, while birds and insects made the familiar sounds associated with more convivial circumstances. This all but perfected a sedate Mediterranean atmosphere, reassuringly absent of military bullshit and helpfully cathartic as we slowly adjusted to a new situation. One got the impression that before the war nothing too strenuous had occurred in this camp, which of course would soon change.

The first day had been unusually relaxed and unexpectedly warm for November, the harshness of Balkan winters being legendary. A more detailed study of the maps would later illustrate how the terrain climbs dramatically from sea level to mountain altitudes within a relatively short distance from the coast. We were not in Bosnia yet!

Five B Squadron troop leaders sat on wooden benches in the cookhouse in front of a large map of Croatia and southern Bosnia, pencils poised ready to receive orders. Behind us sat the second-in-command, Captain Tim Hercock, the Battle Captain, Stuart Ward, Squadron Sergeant-Major and other senior NCOs.

'Abes', our eccentric Old Etonian squadron leader, walked in just before 1900 hours. At six feet four inches tall he was an unmistakable figure, with prominent nose and eyebrows bushy enough to pull a shotgun through with. He craned over his notes in front of the map like a schoolmaster and picked up a radio antenna left there for him to use as a pointer.

"Gentlemen, good evening, these orders are for the Squadron's control of the Cheshire Battlegroup's regulated road move from the village of Lipa . . . here, along Route Triangle, and on to the release point south of Prozor . . . here," he said, following the black dotted line on the map trace with the tip of his pointer. "OK, Ground . . ." The Leader delivered his orders in great detail for more than an hour before we were allowed to ask questions.

The Bosnian Serb Army had thrust from the north-west to Bugojno, dissecting the metalled main road connecting Split and Vitez, the battlegroup's destination. The only other tarmac main road to Vitez went way to the south-east via Mostar, a town embroiled in heavy fighting. Triangle was the name given to the supply route stretching from Split to Vitez. The section of it that required traffic regulation was a forty-kilometre-long narrow logging track across mountains, 1500 metres above sea level. This was the only safe way to reach Vitez. The Squadron Leader's concept of operations was to deploy ten sections along this stretch of Route Triangle at points where the track was wide enough for local traffic to be held. With local traffic controlled by Squadron Headquarters, the Cheshires would then be able to send one packet of Warrior armoured infantry fighting vehicles and other assets along the route each day without interruption. Late into the evening my troop finally received a warning order for this first task inside Bosnia.

The sound of gunfire and the rumble of distant artillery were very real seconds before waking. But there were no guns; it was actually the window banging to and fro in its old paint-peeled wooden frame at just the right frequency to be annoying. Outside, the easily recognizable advance of a storm could be heard as its rolling barrage began battering the shoreline. Minutes later the first of many long forks of lightning bolted from clouds, followed by outrageous cracks, each resembling the sound of a tree being split in two. Milder, but not meek, was the clap of thunder that trailed behind it and let pour a torrent of rain of unbelievable proportions. Rain rattled on the glass and started coming in through the open and curtainless window as if someone had turned on a sprinkler. Luckily the majority was hitting Justin Freeland first. Looking like a green caterpillar on end, his sleeping bag around his shoulders, Justin had stood up to silence the banging window. He had checked the barrage from nature's guns, but sadly the peace and warmth of my generous sleeping bag were only to be enjoyed for a few moments longer. The luminous hands of my watch were not playing tricks; approaching 0530 hours, it was nearly time for reveille.

It was still yawningly dark and the rain almost horizontal when sodden soldiers with hunched shoulders boarded coaches after breakfast. The drive took us back past the airport on our way to Split North Port where the ferry, carrying our armoured vehicles, had docked the night before after a ten-day sail from the military port of Marchwood near Southampton.

The heavy clouds and downpour had inhibited the start of day, helping reduce motivation to a contrasting trickle. Fortunately the rain was abating and the driver slowed the enormous windscreen wipers to a speed in keeping with this reduction. He searched the radio channels to find some English music for us and when he did a favourite song gave me a false high for a few minutes.

This Croatian man was a chain-smoking lunatic who drove fast and recklessly with such ambivalence for road safety that the most counselled back-seat driver would have been scared. The lack of traffic was strangely conspicuous, as were vehicle registration plates. When a car did challenge the coach for primacy on the road it did so leaving dangerously little margin for error and made our driver look like an instructor.

Cliffs bear down on Split and much of the adjoining coastline. The town approaches had a large, relatively smart residential area sitting below these cliffs on the eastern side of the road. To the west was an obsolete run-down industrial complex, far from a holiday brochure sea view. Further on, a line of rusty and redundant derricks poked above scruffy buildings; between two of them was a battleship-grey funnel confirming the dock's location. Before turning in to the gatehouse a large red funnel could be seen, pinpointing the berth of the ferry and our vehicles.

Anyone who has served in Her Majesty's Armed Forces will be familiar with the expression 'hurry up and wait'. Having risen from our 'scratchers' at an ungodly hour, the Squadron now waited on the dockside for the ferry's crew and Army movers to assist our drivers with unloading. Five hours later, and almost midday, the first B Squadron vehicle was driven smartly down the ferry's wide steel ramp. Newly painted in gloss white, the United Nations livery, it gleamed in the dazzling sunlight that had since broken through the clouds to herald a fast-improving day. In large letters, U N had been stencilled in black paint on each side of every vehicle to advertise who we were, supposedly as much protection as the armoured cars' thin armour-plating itself.

Weeks before, the vehicles had been spray-painted, hiding the standard green and black British Army camouflage. The regiment's primary wartime role was medium reconnaissance for the British 4th Armoured Division. When I swore an Oath of Allegiance to Her Majesty Queen Elizabeth II, Her Heirs and Successors, in 1987, I had not expected to find myself in a white vehicle assisting with humanitarian relief in a multi-ethnic state in Europe, sucked in to a self-destructive internecine civil war. Then there had been an Iron Curtain dividing Europe. Such a scenario was unimaginable to the instructors at Sandhurst whose careers had always had the Cold War as a backdrop. Regardless of viewpoint or principle, this was now the job given us. It was not as if we were putting our lives on the line by fighting for someone else, we just had to deliver food and medical supplies; it was as simple as that.

Having disembarked, the vehicles were lined up for loading onto Scammel trucks for transportation up country to Tomislavgrad (TSG), a cheaper and more reliable method of moving armour. Wheeled vehicles were driven up country in convoy under their own steam. Wishing them luck and seeing them depart made an impact. Our first task inside Bosnia would start the next morning. It was an anxious time.

The next day's coach journey from Split to Tomislavgrad was another harrowing experience for the backseat driver. However, most of the lads managed to kip upright in the coach seats. Swaying, rocking and some dribbling, they were oblivious to their vulnerability and the beautiful countryside and relatively uninhabited villages we were passing. Once more the rain was relentless. Its effects could be measured by the disgruntled faces of the Croatian and Bosnian border guards who wore shower caps over their uniform peaked hats and rubberized capes around their shoulders.

Time went quickly and I too had nodded off. With eyes shut, I sensed the journey coming to an end by the reduced speed and increased number of turns being made. As the coach pulled up outside a disused school, which the grey weather made look even bleaker, I woke abruptly with a foul taste in my mouth. This was the National Support Element, a British logistic unit positioned halfway up country for the distribution of combat supplies.

Apparently tough soldiers were reluctant to leave the impermeable coach, the rain rattling on its roof so hard that its severity was amplified to an artificial level. Regardless, the Squadron mood was upbeat in anticipation of imminent reunion with our armoured vehicles and the prospect of soldiering.

Once the CVRTs* were unloaded we transferred personal kit into their stowage bins, mounted up and queued along a road waiting to pass through the ammunition collection point. Trooper 'Yozza' Hughes, my driver, pulled up next to a flatbed truck where a private soldier passed us ammunition. Brown steel boxes each containing a belt of two hundred 7.62mm ball machine gun rounds were passed across to Lance Corporal 'Elvis' Priestley, my gunner, who stowed these inside the turret. The private soldier also passed yellow-nosed clips of High Explosive (H.E.) 30mm rounds and Armour Piercing Discarding Sabot rounds, recognizable by their black plastic-covered noses or sabots (petals). Each clip of ammunition held three rounds, which Elvis stowed in the centre ready-rounds bin for easy access. Whether we would ever have to use this ammunition in self-defence was not in the forefront of my mind. All we cared about was getting inside the Scimitar and out of the rain as quickly as possible.

The Squadron moved out of Tomislavgrad as a single convoy, sometimes nose to tail because of regular checkpoints and the need to drive slowly through villages. This was not orthodox convoy discipline, but unavoidable and probably justifiable in the relatively benign circumstances. There were very few local people about. Those inquisitive enough to venture out of their houses, or who walked by, gave friendly but nonchalant waves. Excited children waved and clapped enthusiastically and, when progress was slow, ran alongside the convoy shouting, "bonbon, bonbon," a heart-warming picture that, in the weeks ahead, would lose its appeal to the extent of becoming highly irritating.

---

* The Squadron's armoured vehicles are British built by Alvis and belong to a family called Combat Vehicle Reconnaissance (Tracked) CVR(T), all weighing approximately eight tonnes. Sixteen Scimitars, each armed with a 30mm Rarden cannon and 7.62mm machine gun, made up the core of the squadron, split into four troops. Each troop's four Scimitars were usually operated as two 'sections'. The Troop Leader, either a 2nd lieutenant or lieutenant, led his section with the troop corporal. The troop sergeant led the other section with the junior troop corporal. The squadron's Support Troop, quasi infantry-assault engineers, was equipped with four Spartan Armoured Personnel Carriers. Other squadron CVR(T) included: one Samaritan armoured ambulance, two Sultan Command Vehicles, one Spartan APC fitted for radio relay and rebroadcast and two Spartans for the REME to support their Samson recovery vehicle.

The Sergeant-Major had gone forward to find a holding area. Just outside Lipa, fifteen kilometres east of TSG, he had discovered a large field, which the squadron vehicles were marshalled into as if parking up for an English county show. It was from here that we waited to start our journey along Route Triangle.

Before committing the whole squadron along the narrow pass, the Squadron Leader mounted another recce to ensure it was clear from obstruction and also to identify potential traffic control points. Unfortunately the Squadron Leader reported the movement of a large civilian truck convoy heading south, delaying our start further.

While standing in my turret clasping a brew under our huge green fishing umbrella, a reporter from a broadsheet newspaper asked to climb up onto the vehicle engine decks for a chat. He had been in Bosnia for a number of weeks and said that the threat to us around Lipa was negligible, which was reassuring, hence the non-tactical leaguer. Nevertheless, like many I'm sure, I was still experiencing mild anxiety, as I really had no idea what lay in store.

My impression of the Balkans had been coloured by the saturation of media coverage at home. Daily news emphasized the lethal effects that snipers, mines and mortars were having on Bosnian factions and innocent civilians. The situation had been portrayed so acutely that one could be forgiven for assuming that a sniper hid behind every tree and house and that tarmac surfaces were the only sanctuary from mines. As far as I was concerned, and until better informed, these stories were the worst-case scenario and thus would be treated with respect. Having already noticed a number of limbless men of fighting age relegated to the streets of their hometowns, I did not intend joining their ranks. Stray bullets, mines and mortars were infamous for having the right of way in this volatile land.

# 3

# TRIANGLE

A sense of foreboding struck me as the squadron penetrated the edge of a vast forest along a single dirt track. With vehicles literally nose-to-tail, it was akin to the tactics of a mule train, a situation not especially secure. The canopy of evergreen, combined with an overcast and dreary day, had the affect of accelerating twilight by at least an hour; it was a miserable moment, only made better by sharing it with my vehicle crew.

The Squadron had crossed the border into Bosnia-i-Herzegovina when south of Tomislavgrad, but I regarded this moment as the operational start line. With only an artificial sense of security from our numbers, we were keen to leave the enormous white 'caterpillar' and quickly establish our hide and checkpoint before the day's light completely failed. One at a time a section of Scimitars in front of us peeled away from the track to be allocated a traffic control point, each one several kilometres apart.

Around the next bend the track widened and the unmistakable figure of our lanky squadron leader could be seen pouring over a map on his Land Rover bonnet. "Monty," Abes shouted above the engine noise. "I think this widened stretch will serve as an ideal holding area for you; are you happy with what you need to do?"

"Absolutely," I shouted back.

"Good, well find yourself a clearing and I'll be back to visit you in a couple of days; good luck." An area of woodland where the trees were sparse was ideal, affording us only limited shelter from the elements, but communications were sound, access and space for our two Scimitars adequate, and there was level ground to pitch bivi shelters. For the first time in my career I established a checkpoint on a mountain and, not to do things by halves, one that was higher than Mt Snowdon.

Having quickly settled in, it was not long before Corporal Bremridge received a radio message regarding a broken-down bus south along Route Triangle and thus came our first order to halt traffic. Trooper Sparkes was on sentry by the track, thirty metres from our hide. He stepped forwards into the beam of an approaching vehicle's headlights and raised a hand confidently. The truck stopped and the driver switched off the old rattly engine before climbing down from the cab to talk. I made it my business to approach our first customer. "*Dobro vece; ja sam Britanski Oficir; govorite li Engleski?*" I said, plucking from memory one of the set-piece phrases I had learnt during my short Serbo-Croat language course.

"*Dobro vece, ne govorim Engleski,*" he replied, then garbled something else which I failed to understand.

"*Dobre, ne razumijem; Sprechen sie Deutsch?*" I said, not understanding him.

"*Ya. Ich Spreche Deutsch,*" this time followed by a German sentence, which I also failed to understand. That's the problem if you ask a practised one-liner; you often get a fluent reply you can't translate.

"Oh, well I don't; *nicht verstehen . . . nicht verstehen,*" I repeated loudly to make him stop jabbering in German.

"Why did you ask 'im then Sir?" piped Sparky with his trademark cheeky grin.

"Because if he'd said no, he would have presumed I wasn't just another linguistically ignorant Brit," I replied defensively, while unintentionally pointing my torch beam in Sparky's face. Unable to communicate, I returned to the hide to find Yozza, who soon engaged the middle-aged man in passable German. Yozza had been brought up in Germany, his father formerly a sergeant in the regiment. The Croat man was amenable, so I used the opportunity to practice a few Serbo-Croat phrases from my aide-memoire. The man stood chuckling at my random questions and statements, such as "*Polozite oruzje, nosimo samo hran*": Lay down your weapons, we are only carrying food.

The driver reached into his cab and from the dashboard removed a scabby brown paper bag. From it he extracted something that I could make out as a large chunk of black meat. Offering me a piece, he also tore a chunk of bread from what looked like a freshly baked loaf. "Oh Lord, how nice," I said sarcastically for a cheap laugh, while forcing a grin like a ventriloquist, knowing he would not understand me. It is difficult to make a tapeworm assessment by eye, but I had a go. Refusing this kind gesture would be to risk offending him; however to my delight the meat was delicious. This cultural intercourse was rather enjoyable and I surprised myself by hoping to be offered more. I was in luck, but before I could say "I'll do tha . . . t," he proudly ripped the meat with his enormous filthy hands "*Hvala,*" I thanked him.

In this short time about eight trucks had pulled into our holding area behind him. Yozza walked along the line of aged eastern-European-built wagons and explained the delay to as many of the drivers as he could. They were surprisingly co-operative while sitting in the queue, none of them troubling us at all. Thank goodness for Yozza. I was grateful and impressed.

The familiar sound of the bivi zip opening was not what I wanted to hear. "Sir, you're on stag; are you awake?" whispered Elvis shaking my shoulder.

"Yes, what's the time?" I inquired automatically, although knowing the approximate answer.

"Its ten to four sir; are you awake?" Elvis repeated, not completely trusting me.

"Yes, yes, Elvis, I'm getting up, I'm getting up," I whispered in an impatient voice. The off-going stag is always keen to wake up his relief in sufficient time to avoid doing even one minute longer on duty than necessary. Mumbled words from a prostrate soldier in a zipped-up sleeping bag are not as convincing as seeing the man sit up. To find your relief selfishly curled up at five minutes past the hour can be irritating when you are tired.

With the sleeping bag around my head and shoulders I sat upright with my face against the canvas. It was icy-wet with condensation and the temperature in the bivi was two profanities worse than "bloody cold". The huge volume of my breath vapour, made visible by Elvis's torchlight, which he kept switched on while I rummaged for my top layers, was a good indication of how cold. Fighting with my jersey, I put it on as quickly as possible and cursed under my breath. Inexplicably this habit helps alleviate the sensation of cold, as does remembering the saying, "it's only a sensation!" All the while I was trying not to wake the three green amorphous lumps next to me, but none of these would be making voluntary appearances from their warm cocoons. Of that I was certain.

A modest sprinkling of snow partially covered the ground, which, with half a moon exposed through broken cloud, reflected ambient light well in the otherwise dark woods. Elvis was only just recognizable with the flaps of his camouflaged deerstalker pulled down over his ears, a gift for anyone wishing to creep up unnoticed behind him. He stood at the front of our Scimitar on sentry, cradling his rifle in his arms, so when I tapped him on the shoulder to make this point, he replied loudly, "Why do they issue them then, Sir?" Honest logic from

25

a typical British soldier. He then whispered that there was nothing to report and, almost before he had finished his sentence, was heading for the bivi. "Yep, something to discuss tomorrow. Cheers Elvis; see you in the morning."

Trooper Kusbish was standing up, waist-high out of the turret underneath the fishing umbrella. He was wearing a black woollen hat pulled down over his forehead and a radio headset over his ears. Removing the headset, he climbed down onto the vehicle's engine decks to take up Elvis's position. The stag was one hour in the turret monitoring the radio, followed by one hour on sentry watching for traffic, a simple and fair system when there are only six of you in a team.

Having clambered into the cold and damp turret, I made sure the hatch was closed properly before turning on an internal light. I took advantage of the time to update my diary and write a 'bluey' aerogramme to my parents. They would be tucked up and fast asleep, secure in the warmth at home. Gibbering with cold in the turret, it was tempting to think of my soft bed in the Officers' Mess, but, given the choice, I was certain that Bosnia was where I preferred to be.

Standing in the woods an hour later was wonderfully peaceful. Not even the rustle of small animals or birds in the undergrowth disturbed the night, they too being sensibly asleep. Within the hour it had started snowing and by the end of my duty the snow had fallen so heavily that the weight of a thick white blanket covering the bivis was making them sag. The white Scimitars no longer looked incongruous in the Bosnian woods, their new livery being ideal but unnecessary camouflage against the snow-covered surrounds.

Operating alone at last on our first proper job in Bosnia was a pleasure. The three months of intensive pre-deployment training in Germany felt strangely distant. It had been far more demanding than this real task. Training tends to be harder than operations, being designed to instil the discipline and confidence to prepare troops for the worst eventuality. Strict procedures, such as minimizing noise and radio transmissions and restricting the use of white light, become second nature and foster professionalism. During UN operations, however, where transparency and overtness are the *modus operandi,* these practices are less relevant, while professionalism remains paramount. Consequently, discipline can be easily eroded and core skills do fade. Furthermore, most young troopers want an easy life and will usually try to short-cut procedures they regard as nugatory constraints. Nevertheless, continuing to observe essential basic procedures, while unpopular, is the easiest way to uphold discipline. How do you explain that it is acceptable to stop a truck using white light so not to be run down, while also refusing soldiers the luxury of ambling around the hide with white light as this is unprofessional? All Standard Operating Procedures for war fighting were maintained, where practicable, at least until more was known about the actual threat in our new environment.

*Friday 13 November: Traffic relatively heavy in the morning; cars, taxis, trucks and coaches mainly moving south into Croatia, which despite Triangle being a muddy logging track, is proving a real alternative. There are a number of Germans coming along Triangle, from where in Bosnia we do not know. Today this included a coach-load of jovial sausage-eating pensioners who were returning to Munich. Perhaps they had been visiting some Croat 'relatives' or friends from WWII!*

*I stood on the track viewing the spectacle of assorted traffic arriving at our checkpoint for some time. I have enjoyed making use of my limited Serbo-Croat, explaining to transitees the reason for their delay, in today's case B Company 1 Cheshire, the first packet. Four Bosnian Croat Army (HVO) soldiers (Vojnik) in two trucks stopped in the queue. The soldiers were very engaging. All in their late twenties and early thirties, they had ruddy looks, were unshaven and wore a mix of military and civilian clothes. They were in high spirits, laughing and passing a bottle of slivovitz (plum brandy) around. Despite the time of day I accepted a slurp; I felt I should. I made sure to wipe their saliva away first! It is one of the most unpleasant and caustic tipples I have had the misfortune to sample, but I swigged it with feigned alacrity to keep up appearances. Bosnia is a man's world and I think drinking is a respected pastime. Were they conscripts? Do they believe in the war? How long have they been fighting? How many soldiers have committed war atrocities by simply following orders? Surely not these normal looking men; not that I dared ask. My meagre vocabulary has prevented me from holding a meaningful conversation, instead I am limited to short comments about who we are and what we are doing, but the soldiers were only interested in my rifle and ammunition, and their translucent brandy. I wished I could have had a proper chat.*

"*Moi pushka dostar dobro, pet, pet, shest* (5.56mm), *dostar malo* (very small)." They laughed at the size of the standard NATO calibre rounds in my magazine. The soldiers shook their heads in disapproval and compared their larger calibre ammunition. "*Dobro, sedam shest dva* (7.62mm), *velk* (big)," I said before they did. Their ammo was larger, the Soviet 7.62mm short round, tried and tested in every corner of the globe. These men seemed proud, happy and confidently at ease, very much men's men. Their respect for size and strength was clearly part of their culture. One of the soldiers was enviously eyeing up my new gore-tex lined boots. He placed his foot alongside mine. "*Dobro*" means good, but seems to be used for just about anything. Pointing to his worn-out boots and pulling out his bayonet, he offered them in exchange. Perhaps in less favourable circumstances I would have been forced to oblige, but this time I politely declined the offer with a nervous laugh.

At the same time, but further down the queue, Sparky had been accepting brandy from a man in a Lada car whose wife and children had been grateful for some compo ration boiled sweets. For years I had wondered why ration packs contained so many boiled sweets and who actually ate them. In the months ahead they would prove to be very useful, although a 'double-edged sword' if you don't like attracting annoying children who will nick anything that is not welded down.

Later that morning a radio message was received that two of B Company's Warriors had slid off Route Triangle as conditions along the track were treacherously icy. Consequently B Company had stopped and was made to leaguer up at Traffic Control Point 2 with Sergeant Finlay's section for six hours, while the Royal Engineers gritted the route. Once complete, we were cleared to release civilian traffic from our layby, travellers who were becoming increasingly anxious and difficult to detain. Truck drivers with deliveries to make and coaches loaded with impatient passengers were understandably unimpressed by any delay in the mountains, especially in the late afternoon when temperatures routinely fell well below zero. We were not particularly happy either, but it was our job.

Once the travellers had disappeared south, leaving the mountain quiet, a woman in her early forties, dressed for an afternoon at the shops, walked along the snowy mountain track towards our checkpoint. Yozza spoke to her in German. It transpired that while waiting in the layby she had got off the coach for a call of nature, but, not realizing, the coach driver had then driven off without her. She was in an extraordinarily good mood under the circumstances, much helped by drink, which was evident from her slurred speech and long-range breath. After chatting for a while and refusing any assistance, she continued walking south. With the evening approaching and at nearly 4000 feet above sea level, it would have been interesting to compare the attitude and behaviour of a British woman, or man, in the same circumstances, regardless of intoxication. These people were tough, or mad.

B Company re-attempted Route Triangle in two small packets in the early evening. Their thirty-tonne Warrior beasts drove past our position gingerly, but, regardless, churned up the track. Most crews made an effort to greet us by nodding their heads or lifting a hand in recognition of our patient marshalling. The first company packet was successfully through.

When not on duty manning the checkpoint the section would rest, listen to the radio net or fulfil the seemingly never-ending demands of daily administration. Naturally in the morning everyone would wash and shave, powder feet, polish wet boots and strip, de-gunge and oil personal weapons. The Scimitars would be 'first paraded' by their drivers; coolant and oil levels checked and tracks and wheels inspected, while the two gunners would each clean their GPMG. The hot engine decks were a favourite place to sit and, if vacant, would be used to dry out wet kit. When all the chores were complete, the equipment would be stowed away to prevent damage, loss and maintain readiness.

The section carried out these chores in the field every day. They were the accepted norm, discipline inculcated during basic military training. A recruit undergoing basic training who cannot understand the reason behind the seemingly ridiculous levels of cleanliness and unnecessary bullshit demanded of him is likely to be in the wrong profession, probably having a limited sense of humour. To the instructor, and hopefully the recruit, it is in fact just a game. But there is a serious side; for exactly the same reasons as insisting on rigorous standards of fieldcraft, it is only by aiming unrealistically high during training that habits are drilled home and in the final analysis, when under pressure during operations, an appropriate or satisfactory standard is achieved. As long as a soldier is allowed to get on with his job without interference and is not needlessly messed around, he enjoys knowing where he stands and will take pride in conducting himself in a thoroughly professional manner. On the other hand, the soldier who is badly led and allowed to get away with being idle, will lose respect for himself and consequently have lower morale, reducing his effectiveness in barracks and in combat. That is why it is said, "There are no bad soldiers, only bad officers."

Having established a routine, life was being made as comfortable as possible. The constant need to keep vehicles batteries charged and the convenience of using the vehicle boiling vessels (BVs) to make hot beverages was consuming petrol at an alarming rate. Not yet due replenishment, I registered my concern with Squadron HQ during a situation report (sitrep). It was comforting to learn that most sections were in the same predicament. Nevertheless, fuel had to be conserved by limiting engine running, which also precluded the drying of kit on the decks under the excuse of charging turret batteries! When I found Trooper Kusbish ignoring this advice I did not need to rebuke him as the discovery of his gloves melted on to the Scimitar exhaust-pipe was enough for him to realize his error. He was inconsolable, understandable on a snowy Bosnian mountain with three more days ahead, but cheap morale for the five of us who still had serviceable gloves.

Of all the activities on the mountain eating was the most popular after sleeping. Cooking was normally a vehicle crew affair, prepared from four-man ration boxes, but on a Scimitar shared between three. Elvis usually cooked our meals, a task he did with much pride. He would add various non-issue seasonings to create some variety from the eight compo ration menus. Avoiding cooking as a rule, I felt compelled to wash the crew's three mess tins instead, which to save water I normally did with snow or leaves. It would be fair to say that our time on the mountain was in fact more like a camping trip than a military operation.

After supper on 14 December I lay in the bivi attempting to sleep while awaiting my next duty, something never more than four hours away. The temperature on the mountain had noticeably risen, although the boys refused to believe it, but was manifest by the snow vanishing in short order. This mild weather stayed with us for the next three days, but so did the rain, which fell hard when it came and pattered noisily on the canvas and metal, almost as depressing as its wetness. A few degrees lower and we would have been snowed in until spring.

Having just nodded off, an excited Elvis shook my shoulder. "Sir, the SQMS is here with mail, gore-tex and benz." Sure enough Staff Sergeant Pearce had arrived in a truck that carried waterproof suits, arctic smocks and trousers, promised by the system days before. As important, in these boring circumstances, was a small bundle of mail and jerrycans of fuel to supplement us until the fuel bowser arrived from Split. There was only one letter for me, but heavily scented. I pocketed it for something to read during my imminent radio stag.

With the SQMS departed and the excitement over, the only sound that could be heard in those dark woods was the rain, which that night was particularly wet, and occasionally a sustained gust of wind. On duty again, I sat in Corporal Bremridge's vehicle monitoring the radios with the hatches shut and rainwater leaking from what I convinced myself was every orifice of the turret. Boredom later led me to record more than twenty drips in the minute from the incorrectly sealed commander's sight. My plastic map case doubled very nicely as a water-resistant apron, easier than fighting with my new gore-tex trousers in the confined turret.

The anticipation of reading mail was exciting and almost as enjoyable as actually doing so and thus I first tended to all turret matters, including despatching a new sitrep by radio, before making myself comfortable for the day's highlight. Opening the 'bluey' released the sweet smell of a girl's scent in the confined space, inconsistent amongst the oil, sweat and other turret odours. "*Dearest Monty . . . .*"

In the following days it was a relief to see 'A' and 'C' Companies and finally HQ Company steam past our position unobstructed by ice or civilians. As one company passed us each day the monotonous stag of two hours on four hours off continued. Traffic control became slicker as new problems became fewer. The daily business of cleaning, cooking and sleeping became a blur, even in this short time, outside influences capable of changing the pattern of a given day being limited in the forest.

At the end of another duty I jumped down from the engine decks of my Scimitar aware that it was likely to be one of my last on the mountain. Our task was complete, except for the possibility of a few Cheshire stragglers. It was 17 November, a day of relentless precipitation which made the forest dank and gloomy, dampening our spirits, literally. The noise of raindrops hitting the forest's floor of decomposing leaves and soggy pine needles, and the 'plink' of raindrops landing on Scimitar stowage bins was becoming tedious. If not on duty the boys had been in their bivis sleeping; bored after five days of traffic control, they just wanted to get on to the next stage. The vehicles needed a good run, as did my legs, having not moved further than 200 metres either way along the track all week.

The prospect of curling up and sleeping for four hours was all that I cared about at the end of this duty. To my annoyance, however, I was delayed when I discovered the bottom half of my sleeping bag had been acting as a sponge for the re-directed River Bosna. The ground inside the tent was so wet that my gore-tex bivi-bag had failed to protect it. Elvis lay fast asleep in his green maggot oblivious to my plight, or in fact his own, providing me with much needed *schadenfreude*. There are few misfortunes more depressing for a soldier than discovering his sleeping bag soaked; it is a lifeline. Fortunately I was distracted from self-pity when the SQMS arrived in his Land Rover to inform us of the Squadron's immediate move to Vitez. A warning order over the radio would have been desirable and would have prevented the consequent rush, but there was no time to grumble.

The three crewmen who had been sleeping took a while to wind into action. Although glad to be leaving the godforsaken mountain, remaining in their sleeping bags was all they seemed to care about when woken; who could blame them? Dropping the bivis was the only substantial task, the canvas being wet, heavy and very difficult to re-pack. Sparky and Yozza courteously filled in the sentry's trench, which in five days had only reached a depth of eighteen inches after meeting rock, some of which we had used to build up around the pathetic hole, like a sangar.

Other B Squadron troops, having received the message earlier, were now whizzing past our position from the south. They were racing to the squadron *rendezvous* point, their enthusiastic speeds suggesting that 3 Troop were not the only ones relieved to be on the move. The majority of troops either waved or gestured with two fingers in fraternal banter, determined not to be last to the RV. Sergeant Clarke's section pulled up on the track and waited impatiently for us to join them. A quick count of weapons and WOCS (War Office Controlled Stores) e.g. binoculars, and a check in the woods for anything left behind, and the troop was soon spluttering down the track steering around potholes on a northerly course.

Once clear of the forest the countryside opened up into green rolling pastures, interspersed with small shack-like farmsteads and, very occasionally, goatherds by the roadside. This was not the ethnically cleansed Bosnian countryside depicted by vivid television images, but more like a chocolate box scene of Austria. The troop descended the mountain towards a lake named Ramsko Jezero. Our drivers had done well to catch up with 4 Troop in front, before arriving at the squadron column parked along a pink shingle track on the western edge of the lake.

At Rombici, on the northern edge of the lake, excited local boys ran out to greet us and tried to keep up with the vehicles. An occasional boiled sweet lofted overboard would cause a furious scramble of bodies desperate for a treat. Two girls looked on from the security of their mother's side while standing in their garden feeding free running chickens; a subsistence life indeed.

By the time we reached Prozor, one quarter of the journey completed, it was dark. The mixed Muslim and Croat town had been the scene of heavy fighting ten days before. The streets were all but deserted. The few people we saw ignored us, their heads down to avoid the rain, instead of the smiling faces and cheerful waves that had greeted us hitherto. Had it still been light I doubt whether the children would have been allowed to greet us anyway. They would be safe at home, away from the ghastly remnants of fighting, an unwelcome reality that had brought privation and must surely have robbed them of their childhood and innocence.

Between the shadows of intermittent orange street lighting the physical scars of combat were difficult to miss. A number of houses were burnt out and roofless, with only charred timbers remaining and window surrounds blackened from fire. Bullet holes and the splash marks of mortar and artillery fire were evident on brickwork and only the unbroken windows were noticed. The squadron drove past an eastern European car that had been torched to a rusty brown shell with a few lucky patches of white paintwork having survived.

These symptoms of fighting were a pointed reminder of exactly why we had deployed to Bosnia. Who had done this was, at first, difficult to discern. Further along the road, however, I was left in little doubt from proud displays of graffiti on the shells of former homes. Letters two feet high daubed in white paint announced who the responsible factions were: HVO, HDZ, HOS.*

Two Croat policemen dressed in blue-camouflaged patterned para-military uniforms, Kalashnikov rifles slung from their shoulders, stood by a patrol car at the next junction. What part had they played in this fighting? Had they turned a blind eye or assisted the army? Were they in denial or proud of what had been done? They stared at the long convoy looking resentful of the intrusion, but aloof and disinterested in the same way I believe I would look if a UN contingent rumbled through my home town in England. What would foreign UN soldiers

---

* The HOS was established in late 1944 to try and stem the rapid decline in morale in Croatia's regular armed forces by mixing the men there with more fanatical and loyal Ustase.

understand of our people, culture, politics, religion and centuries of conflict that has divided parts of our nation? Nothing, as we barely understood the affairs dividing Bosnia.

The atmosphere and state of the town embodied my perception of Bosnia: destruction, carnage and misery, not helped by the drizzling rain, a distraction that needed constant wiping from my goggles. The convoy continued north through Gornji Vakuf, where the Battlegroup had staged to refuel both vehicles and men the previous night. A half-hour stop was sufficient before continuing north through Pucarevo and finally arriving at the British camp in a small village called Bila, just outside Vitez. There had been no fighting here; everything looked quite normal.

# 4

## NO CAMELS – NO TROPHIES

The last lesson had not been wiped from the blackboard and broken pieces of chalk lay on the window ledge. Colourful pictures and montages adorned the classroom's yellow walls, the names and ages of the children written in the teacher's handwriting at the bottom of each: Mirjan 6, Svetlana 7, and so on. The chairs and desks had been removed to make space for camp beds, squeezed so close together the wooden floor was barely visible. Despite the cultural differences, this was all very familiar, even that cheesy classroom smell.

Combat jackets hung from pegs where children's coats would have been only weeks before. Corridors bustled with uniformed bodies, but not on their way to lessons. Instead, soldiers busied themselves humping equipment and boxes into classrooms under NCO supervision; signallers ducted cables and wires along walls and subalterns enthusiastically stuck Bosnian maps up in the operations room, marking them with military symbols and boundaries. The battlegroup staff officers discussed and directed the conversion of school to headquarters and the implementation of humanitarian operations in a new theatre.

The Commanding Officer, Lieutenant Colonel Bob Stewart, resided in the Headmaster's study. As Commanding Officers go, he was very in touch with his soldiers and always led from the front. He was not the most senior British officer in Bosnia, but a combination of his down-to-earth nature and habit of being where the trouble was made him the ideal spokesman. Colonel Bob was natural in front of the camera, which the media latched on to straight away, very quickly elevating him to national status. He was the man who was not scared to grapple with Bosnia's problems head on, making him loved by the public and jealously derided by many senior to him. He certainly put the British Army on the Bosnian map.

Soccer would not be on the school timetable for some time to come. A football pitch on the northern side of the school was now home for nearly two hundred men. They were not roughing it in trenches or under ponchos, but had been afforded the luxury of green 18 x 24 feet tents that formed a small village. Duckboards covering the ground and hot air space heaters made life bearable for the inhabitants. These tents were only a temporary measure, but enough to keep out the imminent Bosnian winter until portakabins could be erected.

In front of the school, on another grass playing field, the Royal Engineers (Sappers) were laying hundreds of tons of hardcore. This was in preparation for the portakabin accommodation, large electricity generators and parking space for some forty armoured vehicles. A number of these vehicles were already being employed on familiarization patrols of routes and villages around Vitez to establish the UN presence. As yet no aid convoys had been escorted.

The officers were billeted in four civilian houses adjacent to the school: Field Officers, logisticians and engineers, subalterns and captains. The UN had rented the houses from locals for 600 Deutschmarks per month. This was a fortune when the average monthly wage in Vitez, if you had a job, was no more than 100DM. It was not surprising, therefore, to find the owners of the captains' house living in their former cowshed, which the owner had decorated to a habitable standard. The cow was never seen again!

Compared with western standards, the subalterns' house was merely a shell, built from breezeblocks within a concrete frame. The adjoining garage was piled high with the owner's furniture and property, leaving us plenty of space. The house was not a professional build, perhaps slapped together in quintessential Mediterranean fashion by a team of brothers and cousins during a holiday. The house had no insulation whatsoever, the electricity was intermittent and when it did work the fuses blew if a kettle was switched on. The only heater was a wood burner in the sitting room and the bathroom hot water tank only had the capacity to provide a few inches of hot bath water per day. There were no carpets, only concrete downstairs and draughty floorboards upstairs; there were no curtains, nor putty in the window frames. The lavatory cistern had to be manually filled with water, which we did with a catering-size baked beans tin before every flush; and the ball-cock had to be fiddled with, an art that would be mastered several weeks later after much practice. For those not getting enough fresh air, the balcony was an added bonus, but recommended as safe for one man at a time, and then only if belayed from two secure points. War or no war, the house was a health and safety nightmare.

Eleven subalterns, two local interpreters and a number of Bosnian rodents shared this billet. As senior subaltern I allocated myself the luxury of a small private alcove annexed from the largest bedroom, where Lieutenants Billy Fooks, Justin Freeland and Ben Beddard slept. While I am sure that more than one soldier must have said "lucky bastards," we all felt rather guilty about living in a house when our troops were under canvas. But the soldiers would be having the last laugh when the winter set in and its effect on our breezeblock 'fridge' was fully realized.

Behind the school's bike sheds stood the tented cookhouse and field kitchen equipped with unsophisticated cook trailers, the very best in outside catering. In order to keep everyone fed the Army Catering Corps chefs cooked around the clock, and after our first supper where there were six main course choices of good old English stodge, they had already won their spurs.

As if we were not spoiled enough, a Mobile Bath and Laundry Unit had deployed to Vitez. This unit's men and women would be washing and drying *dhobi* all day, and sometimes all night, for the next six months. As the unit's title suggests, they also operated a shower tent, but with a limited capacity, only guaranteeing a soldier one shower a week. The school's changing rooms, which had seen many a child's dirty knee, were inadequate for four hundred men a day, so wash tents furnished with trestle tables and steel bowls were made available for everyday ablutions in the tented camp. As temperatures dropped the enthusiasm for this *al fresco* hygiene was lost.

Before supper on our second evening a squadron 'O' group was convened for the troop leaders. The first humanitarian aid (Pomoc) convoy was to be escorted to Tuzla the following day, a task awarded to Lieutenant Mark Jones and his troop. My troop would be disappointed, but at the same time glad to be able to settle in, while I was given a personal task for the morrow.

Intelligence reports indicated the Bosnian Serb Army's continued south-easterly advance from Jajce into central Bosnia. Their short-term target was Turbe, a village twenty kilometres from Vitez. Holding the ground between were the Croat HVO and Muslim BiH armies. In this area they were loosely co-operating in an alliance against their common enemy. If the BSA's rate of advance were to continue, the battlegroup would soon be dangerously within range of the BSA's largest artillery piece, an enormous 175mm howitzer nicknamed 'Big Bertha'. Colonel Bob could not afford to let this situation threaten battlegroup security or operations, so tasked Major Jamie Sage and 42 Field Squadron, Royal Engineers, to build personnel shelters in case of a bombardment. The battlegroup was suitably trained but not equipped for a fighting withdrawal, so it was critical that a contingency to identify secure alternative routes south out of Vitez towards Fojnica and Gornji Vakuf was made. It was these routes that I was to reconnoitre for the Commanding Officer.

My recce team was an *ad hoc* grouping from the Squadron mounted in two Land Rovers, which were by far the best means for mobility within the then low-threat environment. Lieutenant Simon George and his driver, both Sappers, came with us to offer professional advice about route and bridge classifications. Ben and Justin came for the ride and the Sergeant-Major accompanied the team to keep us on the straight and narrow.

As reconnaissance soldiers we were not only trying to identify routes but also establish the presence of choke points, obstacles, military faction dispositions and holding areas similar to those on Route Triangle. Any opportune intelligence, or military information as we were encouraged to call it while working under the UN's neutral flag, would be a bonus.

Vitez was one of many habitations that sat along the Lasva Valley and, although only the size of a typical English village, in Bosnia it qualified as a small town. Vitez is surrounded by hills, most about 2500 feet above sea level, but to the north a few rising to altitudes as high as 4500 feet. Our first journey from the School took us east along the valley on a by-pass around Vitez and through an HVO checkpoint at Dubravica, which we would come to know and love. Further east were a series of small dwellings, more like hamlets, separated from one another by pastureland: Sivrino Selo, Santici, Pirici, Vidovici, Ahmici and Nadioci, to name just a few. Generally these had mixed ethnicities, but some predominated in Muslims or Croats.

My map had black square dots on it depicting the approximate location of houses. Although most of the house planning conformed to a linear pattern following the roads and tracks, planning permission was clearly such that locals had been allowed to build a house pretty much where they liked. Consequently the map looked like a nest of ants that had lost their leader. Until 1969 Muslim houses were built with pyramidical-shaped roofs, whereas Croat houses were built with two-sided roofs, similar to alpine chalets. This was later to become a useful guideline when assessing the principal religion of a village. Passing Ahmici it was not difficult to tell what religion predominated there. Houses on the lower slopes of the village surrounded a prominent white minaret, with castellated turret, which stood like a rocket ready to be launched.

East of Vitez, near a village called Busovaca, we arrived at the first bridge for Simon to survey. Two scruffy HVO soldiers, one slumped on a chair, were manning a checkpoint in the middle of the span. When they saw us approaching their postures improved, both focusing on us with swarthy stares and the nearest soldier taking a proper hold of his AK-47. Anticipating the need to prove my identity, I slid the window open, but realizing they were not going to stop us, called out, "*Dobro jutro*" and carried on driving. As we crossed the bridge I scanned its sturdy concrete structure and Simon looked out of the back window for the same purpose. Stopping to examine the bridge properly and use engineer paraphernalia would have been an invitation for questions and a delay I predicted we could not afford. Even to a layman this European-quality bridge on an arterial route looked good for a seventy-tonne vehicle.

The next bridge, which this time I was keen for us to survey accurately, was a kilometre up the road in Busovaca near the base of the Dutch/Belgian UN transport battalion. It stood to reason that it would be the same classification as the previous bridge, but this was Bosnia. I stepped out of the Rover to confirm our position by taking a reading from the Global Positioning System (GPS), but found the grid reference several hundred metres different from the Yugoslavian maps. Simon paced the bridge's length and width and, bending at the waist with Ben holding on to his ankles, hung over the parapet while using a tape measure to estimate the weight-bearing capacity. The fully laden Warrior weighs over thirty tonnes and is 3.7 metres wide. Simon's calculations estimated the bridge as Class 60, strong enough to bear the load of any known armoured vehicle in Bosnia, whether UN or former JNA. With no time to waste, I climbed back into the Rover and drove off.

Half-turning my head while driving I said, "Justin do you want to plot the next bridge? . . . Freeland you deaf bastard . . . Justin?" I stopped the Rover and looked at the Sergeant-Major, who looked at me "Bollocks," we said in unison. Justin had been talking to a number of Dutch soldiers nearby when we had left. Seconds later Simon and Ben pulled up behind us in their Rover. They jumped out and with a poorly acted look of panic asked, "Where's Justin," before we had even told them he was missing, a dismal attempt at winding us up. We were glad to see him emerge from the back of their Rover, despite a sarcastic, "Cheers mate!" directed at me.

The Kozica Valley provides a main artery from Busovaca to Kiseljak and, further along, Jablanica, which, in the event of withdrawal from hostile local factions, would be an obvious route to deny the UN contingents. The thick orange line on the map indicated the road to be suitable for heavy vehicles, so we trusted our judgement and disregarded it in favour of identifying a less obvious alternative. This in mind, we headed south out of the valley and journeyed up a minor road following a Kozica river tributary for Fojnica. There were very few signposts.

A metalled road took us into the foothills of the Zivcicka Planina (mountains) and past a tiny village called Kupres; so far so good. But after four kilometres and at 2500 feet the tarmac ended, a gravel track started and we came across a switchback, which I assessed a Warrior would be incapable of negotiating. It was still worthwhile continuing the recce, but only with the use of Scimitars in mind. This route might provide a flank protection option for the battlegroup withdrawing along the Kozica Valley.

With the track becoming narrower and steeper it looked increasingly unconvincing as a viable route for anything. We met the snow line at about 3000 feet, which, combined with the other factors, confirmed my doubts. It was pointless to continue, but I was enjoying the remoteness and, with no time to start exploring another axis, was keen to see where this track led. If we could reach Fojnica it would at least be an achievement and prove an escape route was possible, even if only in a Land Rover.

The highest inhabited point that we came to was a group of houses called Dragacici. As we neared this hamlet the track stopped abruptly at the foot of a narrow snow-covered streambed with a steep bank to our left hand side. "Bugger, we seem to have run out of road Sar'nt-Major," I said cautiously, not wishing to suggest that his map-reading was in any way at fault, which I'm sure it wasn't. The Sergeant-Major leant over and rested the map on the steering wheel to point out a fine black line representing a path from the end of the track up to the hamlet. "This is the bludy track sir, I'm tellin' ya, an' Draga-fukin'-cici is just at the top of this slope," the Sergeant-Major replied, leaving me in no doubt of his conviction.

The two of us got out and walked the first twenty metres of the track-cum-stream until we could see the top. More than a foot of snow covered it, except for a meandering slit down the centre of the snow, melted away by a trickle of water. The ground seemed firm under foot. "Looks okay to me Simon," I said, chucking a stone from the riverbed over the precipice. Justin and Ben moved a couple of small logs blocking our progress. "Monty, we're watching you all the way mate," Simon said in a reassuringly sarcastic manner.

"Well if I make it you have no choice but to follow, because I ain't coming down; ready Sar'nt-Major?" I said, climbing into the Rover. Donning kevlar helmets as crash hats is not normal but was insurance worth taking with a lethal drop to our left. Not caring a fig for the welfare of this diesel Land Rover, other than its ability to get us home, I accelerated up the streambed in true Camel Trophy style. The diff-lock was engaged to help us through the snow, the engine revs were higher than sounded comfortable, and all without the aid of snow chains. It was critical not to hesitate, but to keep my foot hard on the accelerator as the vehicle hit small boulders and bounced us around like crash-test dummies. To slow down would have ended with us stalling, leaving us no alternative but to descend the dangerous stream backwards with far less control.

Near the top of the stream the Land Rover revs reached a crescendo, making me wonder whether it had the guts to complete the climb, but somehow the tyres kept on gripping the snow-covered rocks. The streambed petered out and the tyres were reunited with a firmer surface. I felt mildly exulted with our not inconsiderable ascent. The Sergeant-Major summed up my feelings with some of his own well chosen words of relief, "Thank fukin' goodness for that; good on ya sir." Having proved the route, it was now Simon's turn. The Sergeant-Major stood at the top of the slope and shouted down some advice and encouragement, "Give it plenty of fukin' welly sir." He did, and two minutes later we came across a farm and a series of tracks we assumed to be Dragacici.

The Sergeant-Major was cursing under his breath because there were so many tracks not marked on the map. Map-reading in these hills on small-scale maps (1:100,000) is easier said than done. Ahead of us stood an old man on the track's verge holding a rope attached around the hind leg of a small pig. "I wonder if he knows there's a war on, Sar'nt-Major?" I said, slowing the Rover down as we closed on him. "He might not even know that Tito is dead," I joked.

"I doubt he ever heard of fukin' Tito up here," the Sergeant-Major muttered drolly, as we pulled up to confirm our exact location. The man was stocky and looked hardier than an ox. He wore an ancient tweed coat and army boots, probably issued him during the Second World War. "*Dobar dan*," I greeted him, not that we thought it a good afternoon under the circumstances.

"*Dobar dan, dobar dan*," he replied in a happy but croaky voice. A motor vehicle at 3000 feet in such a rural backwater must have been a rare sight. He was then joined by a boy, possibly a grandson, whom the Sergeant-Major gave his left-over rations to, which guessing by the size of the boy's eyes, were gladly received.

"*Dragacici?*" I said pointing to the ground, "*Dragacici? . . . koliko* kilometres *Fojnica? . . . Fojnica,*" I said, pointing straight ahead.

"*Dobro, Fojnica!*" the old man said as if he suddenly understood me and pointed down the same track.

"*Dobro, hvala,*" I thanked him. "Right Sar'nt-Major, Fojnica's straight ahead, never mind which track we're on, they all go to the bottom of this bloody mountain . . . *Dovidenja, hvala,*" I called out to the farmer, as we drove away towards the extremely steep track he had pointed to. "Stop sir, it's a dead end; it's the stupid basta'd's farm," exclaimed the Sergeant-Major, swinging around in his seat to look back up the track. We had only just committed ourselves, but slid on ice for several metres because of my reflex to dab the brakes. "I think we're going to be better off reversing Sar'nt-Major." Within moments half a dozen old men and women emerged from a nearby house to witness the spectacle of the year. Stupidly we did not have a tow rope and so the locals enjoyed watching five crazy soldiers pushing a white Land Rover backwards with wheels spinning. Evidently they were mesmerized by this extraordinary event as not one of them bothered to help.

Everything I had seen so far indicated that the way of life for farmers in the hills and plains of Bosnia had remained unchanged for hundreds of years. One exception was the breezeblock farmhouses that the majority of farmers lived in, most old stone buildings clearly having been levelled by successive Balkan wars. The principal fuel for heating these houses was wood, which was abundant in the hills. It was mainly in the besieged capital of Sarajevo that stories were reported of families keeping warm by burning their furniture and derelict houses' roof rafters.

Fields were, in the main, still ploughed and cultivated by horse-drawn machinery, antiquated and rusty but effective. It was essential equipment handed down through generations. Horse-drawn carts were more common than cars in the rural villages, for many the only means of transport. Hay was most commonly stored on long wooden spikes stuck in the ground, peculiar features that were plentiful on the landscape. Weathering made the outer layers of hay turn grey, but protected beneath was clean hay, the yellowness of which would often be revealed by farmers who had cut away their livestock's daily feed. The shape and utility of these haystacks reminded me of vertical spits of doner kebab meat, strangely enough both with their practicalities and both popular in this corner of Europe.

Pigs, goats and chickens roamed the hamlet rooting along the hedges and verges, but where had the locals been? In two days I had formed the opinion that hibernation was the only sensible thing to do during a Bosnian winter. It was easy to imagine a grandmother in front of the fire making socks, a mother and her daughters scrubbing clothes in a tub, or cooking on a wood-burning stove, sons chopping logs and the father idly drinking home-brewed slivovitz and smoking strong cigarettes in front of the fire. This was the kind of place where women are sought for their child-bearing ability and cooking prowess, because beauty, which we certainly witnessed, did not appear to last any longer than thirty years owing to the harsh agrarian environment and diet. Judging by the competition it was definitely a low priority in a farmer's eye.

Knowing the speed, stress and avarice that western European lifestyles can bring, I imagined that these rural folk lived a pleasantly simple, healthy and rewarding existence, albeit hard graft. In Dragacici there was no traffic, crime or litter, no computers or loud music, in fact there wasn't much at all. While this might seem blissful to many I had heard that it did not inspire the young. Quite often they drifted to the towns and cities attracted by word of work and, before the war started, the lure of 'bright lights'. The future of this centuries-old subsistence lifestyle remained and remains with the return of those young people. The farmer's life is a tough one, but the Bosnian soil is rich and the country folk are expert in subsisting from it; generations have done so against the steepest odds. I hoped that those who did not care for wars but cared for their families and livelihoods would be able to do the same again.

After choosing the correct track we descended very quickly into the Fojnica Valley and headed for the nearest restaurant. Six orders of Wiener schnitzel, a round of drinks and a tip made us 35DM (£14) worse off and not being locals we were sure to have been ripped off. Replete, the team was back on the trail for Gornji Vakuf in an attempt to make a circle back to Vitez. The Matorac Mountains, at over 5000 feet, stood between the two towns and on them was our next obstacle, a small coach in the middle of a wood.

The Land Rovers were literally squeezed past the coach, which belonged to a group of fairly elderly hunting gentlemen. They were stylishly dressed in greens and browns, with feathers stuck in

Tyrolean-type hats and were equipped with shotguns and hunting rifles. I parked the Rover in front of their coach and strolled over to them for a chat, which, except for exchanging pleasantries, bore no fruit.

The hunters were in extremely good cheer and appeared too well groomed to be from these parts. Something they did understand was my sign language for a photograph, an offer that enthused them greatly, all proudly displaying their cherished weapons for the camera. Sadly there were no trophies to boast of, their bag being quite empty. A bear or wolf carcass would have fulfilled my preconception of eastern European hunters, or in these times a Serb corpse. Perhaps they weren't hunters at all, but the local militia patrolling. If so they were wasting their time as no one would be foolish enough to attempt crossing over these mountains into their territory, at least not without elephants!

Further up the track we came across another small group of 'hunters' at a roadblock. They looked fairly rag-bag, although one was equipped with a well-oiled German Second World War MG-42, a reliable machine gun with a feared reputation that rattled our grandfathers. Given its condition, it would still have been very effective. Its custodian was either an elderly soldier or a particularly unsporting hunter. He insisted we sign a form before continuing, very typical communist mentality, something I would soon discover to be the norm. Not understanding a word of the text, nor caring, I signed happily and continued on up the track for several hundred metres only to find our favoured mountain route dissected by a deep drainage ditch. With the only mapped route over the Matorac denied us, our Land Rover exploration had come to an end.

My family had not forgotten 21 November, my quarter-century. General Wilkes, Commander-in-Chief United Kingdom Land Forces, was visiting Vitez that day and addressed the officers to congratulate everyone on a splendid job so far. He also reassured us of the contingencies in train with the US Air Force and Navy to provide air cover during any Serb advance, a threat that looked increasingly real.

My birthday cake, iced fruitcake, skilfully baked by my grandmother, had survived the journey from England. This treacherous path included some close moments on Route Triangle where, at times, it had been in danger of being consumed for instant morale. My decision to fight the temptation of eating the cake for expedient ends had proven wise as the anticipation of instant morale had thus always been there, whereas to have eaten it would have resulted in a subsequent low.

It was a privilege to celebrate my birthday with the troop. A Cheshire private soldier from the Officers' Mess had kindly agreed to bring tea to us at the house, which he served from silver service pots. The boys took full advantage of this rare pleasure by treating the Private, their equal, mercilessly. The boys scoffed the cake in short order, testament to my grandmother's culinary expertise, but despite an upbeat mood the troop were not entirely satisfied and Trooper Baker asked, "Sir, when will we get our first task?"

As intelligence had predicted, the BSA had seized Jajce, a Muslim town approximately sixty kilometres north-west of Vitez. Shelling of Turbe had started and was reported as heavy, albeit a meagre thirty to forty shells a day by general warfightings standards. The Intelligence Officer, Captain Chris Leyshon, had briefed us on the movement of Muslim refugees escaping or being driven out of Jajce and heading for safety in Travnik, our neighbouring town. A Soviet-built FROG-7 launcher was at large in the Jajce area. Intended targets included the Travnik ammunition factory, a little too close for comfort.

The Commanding Officer was to visit the HVO HQ in Travnik the next day, before driving to Turbe where a meeting had been arranged with the BSA. Our debut was the none-too-exciting task of company reserve, which included protecting an armoured ambulance and REME recovery vehicle supporting the Colonel's excursion. Only one kilometre out of camp Corporal Bremridge radioed me from the back of the convoy. His Scimitar had spluttered to a standstill because of a fuel blockage, but he said that he would be okay. Close to camp he would be safe and so we had little alternative but to continue without him.

Travnik was busy, mainly with local soldiers milling about the streets. Dishevelled people with eyes wide like Dickensian London urchins hung from every window of every house and flat to watch the United Nations, about twelve vehicles, drive up their high street. BBC Land Rovers were parked outside the HVO HQ, probably in pursuit of Colonel Bob who was fortunately in and out of the HQ in quick time.

Colonel Bob ordered me to stop short of Turbe while he and a Warrior platoon went forward to the BSA HQ. The ambulance joined them in order to collect some dead as part of a faction body exchange. All reporters were instructed to stay with us for their own safety, which was a bonus as we received plenty of attention.

Yozza, Elvis and I sat munching sandwiches with our heads out of our hatches while looking down a typically beautiful Bosnian valley for any activity, including the return of the CO and Lieutenant Alex Watts' platoon.

"*Bollocks*, what the fuck was that?" cried Elvis, dropping into the turret to take cover. Some 800 metres away a grey smoke plume rose, followed by a blast travelling up the valley, which noticeably hit my face. Prudently, I too dropped into the turret and looked through my periscope. Seven or eight rounds continued to land in roughly the same area over the next two minutes. The rounds were not hitting anything significant, just landing in fields, so the fire was speculative, its fall of shot not being directed by a BSA forward observer. At least, if it was directed, the observer was incompetent.

Turning around I saw the REME behind us very sensibly reversing their Warrior back around the road's last bend, a rocky spur in the valley offering protection from anything fired by line of sight. Mesmerised by the artillery fire, we remained in place for a while longer until a fresh volley of shells landed closer, a clear signal to move.

The Commanding Officer's party returned from its mission without the bodies for repatriation. Twelve bodies were too many for the armoured ambulance to carry, even in an undignified manner, so none were taken. On our return Travnik was teeming with well-wishers. Every window was crammed with women and children, faces now hopeful and hands waving vigorously, all trying to see what was going on. It was like a small victory parade. These people must have heard the Serb shells exploding and assumed our involvement. The attention was flattering, but I prayed that none of Travnik's people thought it was the UN firing or that any were counting on us to protect them. That was not what we were here to do and something we were unequipped for. From the spectacle of local support, there appeared to be a certain amount of goodwill and belief in us. How long this would last remained to be seen. These people were the BSA's next target and there was little anyone could do about it.

# 5

# KLADANJ

At the end of 1992 the majority of international humanitarian aid entering Bosnia was doing so via the Croatian ports of Split and Ploce. Aid was being driven unescorted by international agencies, often sub-contracted to local haulage firms and lorry owners, to distribution depots in relatively benign areas. By mid-November the battlegroup was escorting convoys from a number of these depots forward to the most needy people in this land-locked state. Inhabitants in beleaguered areas astride the Bosnian Serb front line were a high priority.

Tuzla was a town in one of these areas and had become increasingly isolated by Bosnian Serb military success. Its burgeoning Muslim refugee population, exacerbated by BSA ethnic cleansing of its satellite villages, was having a devastating effect on local resources. Consequently the UNHCR's emergency humanitarian aid operation in this region was overstretched and required immediate military assistance.

UNHCR aspirations to alleviate this overstretch included a plan to deliver aid along an internationally sanctioned overland corridor between Belgrade and Tuzla and, ultimately, to fly aid directly into Tuzla's military airfield. Locals feared that an operational airfield, albeit for humanitarian use, would make Tuzla a higher value target for the Bosnian Serbs. This ran the risk of dragging the town into a Sarajevo style scenario and so, not surprisingly, local people of influence were reluctant to support this proposal. BSA guns positioned on hills to the east of the airfield were already within effective range of it.

Directed to establish a staging point for convoys and their escorts, B Squadron was sent to Kladanj, forty kilometres south of Tuzla. This exchange point would also serve as a forward operating base for recces and humanitarian operations into this large enclave. The Squadron was ideally suited for such a pioneering task: self-contained, equipped with light vehicles, capable of communicating over long distances and manned by well trained, intelligent soldiers accustomed to operating independently.

After several days of B Squadron successfully escorting and

patrolling from Kladanj, Colonel Bob ordered the attachment of a Cheshire Warrior platoon to provide the squadron with extra capability and protection. There were, however, only two major routes from Vitez to Kladanj with bridges classified to carry such weight. Of the two, the northern route, via Zavidovici, was cut off by hostile BSA troops holding a deep enclave of land. The southern route passed through Ilijas, a Sarajevo suburb, then blocked by the BSA's siege of the city. The mountainous land between these two points, held by the BiH, was where my troop was tasked to find an alternative route on our way to join the squadron in Kladanj.

Studying the map before departure, to plan the most favourable route, gave me an indication of the challenge ahead. Closely drawn contour lines and an expanse of green paper, dissected by finely drawn black lines representing tracks, did anything but depict a Class 30 route. With no combat engineer bridging available in theatre, the route had only to be unsuitable for Warrior at a single point for this recce to fail, regardless of whether the remainder was a six-lane motorway.

The broad metalled trunk road, providing an artery along the Lasva Valley, was fit for an armoured division, a good start to our recce. Turning off this main route at the industrial town of Kakanj, we left the twentieth century behind and started a punishing climb into the Zvijezda mountains up narrow dirt tracks, in truth more suitable for mountain bikes and goats than the ageing Scimitars, although they fared well.

Our appearance at tiny hamlets and remote farms was a surprise to the local inhabitants who, as we sped past them, waved in delight. The tiny lanes had been built with the horse and cart in mind, not armoured vehicles, which, combined with the numerous obstacles lying in our path, could have posed a difficulty if it were not for the Scimitar's agility. It was not long before I deduced that the map was accurate and that the route would be unlikely to receive a recommendation for traffic weighing thirty tonnes.

Twenty kilometres from Kladanj this was confirmed when my armoured patrol became canalized in a steep-sided valley where the track, served by small wooden bridges, criss-crossed a wide stream. Sergeant Stubberfield of the Royal Engineers assessed about twenty or so bridges to be Class 10, strong enough to bear Scimitar, which at eight tonnes is less than one third the weight of a Warrior. Although only doing our job, Colonel Bob was unlikely to be pleased when we reported our findings to his headquarters.

Kladanj was a small town which had a distinct, failed communist, cottage industry atmosphere. Muris, an interpreter from Vitez, proudly told me that Kladanj had formerly been a ski resort, but as we entered the narrow dirty streets there was nothing that I could relate from my alpine experience that reflected this. The town was grey, unkempt, war-damaged and bereft of utilities. Worst of all, and like everywhere in Bosnia, it had an aura of the 1970s about it, but without the music. Tired Bosnian décor led one to believe that a killer plague had struck in 1975 and erased every painter and decorator. Patterned velvet wallpaper, worn-out shag-pile carpets and smoked-glass and chrome tables were the grim legacy. Elvis told me that it was this and not the civil war that was responsible for local discontent.

The troop was welcomed with empty streets, because it was raining again and presumably most of the men were at the front line! Employment opportunities in Kladanj were negligible. Hotels were empty, save for the occasional Non-Govermental Organizations (NGO) customer brave enough; shelves in shops were bare and services non-existent. On the positive side, the timber yard supplied a strong demand and soldiers told me that the abattoir next to the factory had recently emitted squeals of production. For numerous stray dogs it was a double-edged sword begging for offal at the abattoir!

The squadron base, a disused glass-fibre factory, complemented other architectural disasters of the town very well. Two Lancers wrapped in parkas stood on guard inside the factory's steel entrance gate. Accompanying them were two scruffy dogs, attracted by the burning brazier near their sentry box. There was something reassuring about arriving at a British base after twelve hours of driving across destitute Bosnia: security, familiar faces and warmth, not to mention the smell of cooking food wafting across the courtyard, even if it was compo rations.

The high-roofed and unheated main factory hangar not only housed the squadron's armoured vehicles but also doubled up as a communal area for dining, relaxing and washing under cover. The troops slept on floor space in a variety of locations around the factory. Most slept in shop-floor offices cluttered with unwanted filing cabinets and Neolithic typewriters. About thirty soldiers lived in an outhouse providing the most healthy, if not uncomfortable, living.

Officers and sergeants were allocated the bungalow-styled offices, separated from the factory by a goods courtyard, which roaming animals and mud made look more like a farmyard. A fortnight prior to the squadron's arrival a mortar round, most likely fired by the BSA, had landed and detonated in one of the offices. Fortunately the office had been unoccupied at the time but was uninhabitable afterwards. Consequently the roof had a gaping hole in it three feet wide, and yellow insulation foam, probably containing asbestos, was spread everywhere. It looked as if someone had gone out and left a puppy in charge of a huge roll of yellow foam.

Our Scimitars secure, I went to find an office to sleep in. In the next room to the aforementioned mess were two grinning ginger-haired colleagues, Billy and Ben, who greeted me. They thought I would be stupid enough to believe that the mortar-damaged room was reserved for me. "Monty, go and clean your room, it's a bombsite," said Billy in a high-pitched imitation of an old fishwife, while failing to suppress his giggles. To be within range of the BSA's indirect fire was most heartening!

Anything I had thought or said about the condition of our house in Vitez I now revoked. This place was a dump and, if the Bosnian Serbs did not get us first, giant rats, rabid dogs and the not insignificant factory hazards, such as potentially fatal glass-fibre dust and splinters of half-finished baths and basins, surely would. On the positive side, there were enough shells of pink, blue or white wash-hand basins for every soldier to have his own. Sadly the factory did not make plugs!

As usual Squadron HQ was established from the two Sultan command vehicles. It was here that I later received a brief from the Squadron Leader. He outlined likely tasks for the forthcoming week and updated me on recent intelligence. Abes quoted undisclosed sources, which claimed that only 5% of all aid distributed in Bosnia was reaching its intended target. At every stage of distribution, a quantity of humanitarian aid was pilfered, allegedly up to 95% at the point of final delivery. Most of this was assessed to be falling into the hands of the HVO and BiH, orchestrated by their brethren in associated local authorities.

There is, I suppose, little point in a nation having well fed women and children defended by soldiers too malnourished and weak to fight. Nevertheless, the difficult fact for many to swallow was that during this period only a small fraction of international aid, whatever the true percentage, was actually going into the mouths of those for whom it was intended, the helpless women, children and elderly of Bosnia. Their pathetic images screened on television had pulled the heartstrings of viewers across the world, who sitting back in comfortable armchairs, had relieved their consciences by dipping into pockets to do their bit. Well done them, even if they did not realize that they were actually feeding soldiers. These were alarming statistics if true, not to mention rather disheartening to think that UN soldiers were risking their necks for a 5% success rate.

*Friday 27 November: Colonel Bob, informed of our Zvijezda mountains route report, remains determined to push Warrior into Kladanj and eventually Tuzla. He and his team, including Miss Kate Adie, attempted the southern trunk road through Sarajevo's suburbs today, initially discounted because of BSA checkpoints around the city. They have been denied access through Ilijas and are now stuck in the ghostly mining town of Vares, 30Ks to the north of Sarajevo. 2Lt Tudor Ellis has somehow been pushed forward to Kladanj with his four Warriors along sections of the route that we had been unable to recommend. This evening he told me that the steel stanchions of one bridge visibly bent under the weight. The bridge survived so this obviously makes it OK! Tudor's platoon has been accommodated in the outhouse.*

The following night our camp suffered its first death. Cowering in the corner of the squadron briefing room was a mangy dog discovered in a feeble state. It must have come through an open door to shelter from the cold. Hearing the Sergeant-Major's voice, the dog scampered as quickly as his rotten legs could carry him, only to be chased outside and around the back of the building by a pistol-wielding Sergeant-Major . . . *Bang!* The dog was cleanly and instantly put out of its misery with a bullet to the head, a sorry sight, but the best course of action in Bosnia. Animal rescue centres are alien to the Balkan ethos, which, when you consider their record on human rights, was hardly surprising.

Hearing the pistol shot and believing the camp to be under sniper fire, a number of the newly arrived platoon bomb-burst from their outhouse cocking rifles. In so doing they became an immediate target when another shot rang out in the close confines of the courtyard, doubtless a Bosnian aimed shot. Everyone scattered for the nearest cover, for me back into the offices where I knelt down with my eyes just over a windowsill to see whether I could acquire the firer.

Most of us assumed the culprit to be a drunken local soldier firing from somewhere near the brothel across the road, but from the offices it was impossible to locate the firing point. Bizarrely, the silhouette of a man in a window of the brothel left little to the imagination. He was servicing one of its ladies in a broadly similar fashion to the way one conveys a wheelbarrow. One can only guess that this man's proud and overt performance was intended to ram home a point for the squadron, by now *de facto* monks.

Sergeant Gaylor found himself isolated behind the factory's oil storage tank when a drunken HVO soldier emerged from the shadows under a street lamp staggering in front of the factory gates with the butt of his AK-47 resting on his hip. "I've got him in my sights . . . I've got him in my sights, I can take him out," Sergeant Gaylor cried dramatically, his rifle tucked tight into his shoulder ready to despatch the drunk. "No ya' fukin' can't, now pack ir in," the Sergeant-Major shouted, stomping over to Sergeant Gaylor to prevent an incident. The drunk mouthed off something about his *pushka* before disappearing; the excitement was over.

The following day a suspicious Captain Ward assessed what had happened and suggested that the gunshot had not actually been fired into the camp. He suspected that it had been a Negligent Discharge by someone from within the perimeter, possibly a Cheshire soldier cocking his rifle while running out of the accommodation. Nothing could be easily proved, neither particularly wanted to be, and so the incident dissolved into the week's events, which included BSA mortar fire landing in the village at 1100 hours that morning.

The BSA front line was less than five kilometres to our east. Engineers had built a sandbagged shelter in the courtyard some weeks before, into which all one hundred soldiers now shoehorned themselves. Some shells landed in the town and one was heard landing at the T-junction 200 metres east of the camp. Fortunately none of the shells landed near us and so the squadron enjoyed a break in routine with a modicum of excitement while avoiding injury.

Once the firing had ceased the Sergeant-Major, Sergeant Clarke and I went to investigate at the T-junction, something that we would have berated inquisitive young soldiers for as irresponsible. The portico of a smart white-rendered house provided some cover for us, as well as two Croat soldiers, who had withdrawn from their checkpoint. One of the HVO soldiers pointed south along the road in the direction of further mortar shell impacts. A round had landed, followed by another even closer, but at only 300 metres away I didn't need the intro-duction. Small dark grey plumes of smoke rose a split second before the explosions' "crump, crump" reached our ears. Dropping to the ground as quickly as possible, without making a fuss, seemed an appropriate response. Sudden movements panic the men! Taking cover behind mock Graeco-Roman pillars and transfixed by the display, the three of us remained for a few minutes longer before withdrawing to the relative safety of camp.

Aid convoys of approximately ten trucks at a time arrived in Kladanj from Vitez frequently. The local haulage companies were frustrating to work with, having no convoy discipline and generally operating unreliable vehicles, which often caused delays or just failed to show up. Fortunately most convoys this far north were operated by UNPROFOR troops, their trucks being new and usually driven by Danish or Dutch soldiers. The escorting troops from Vitez were always fed and watered in Kladanj after their long journey before turning round, while a Scimitar section or troop from B Squadron took the convoys forward to Tuzla.

The first seven kilometres of the route from Kladanj to Tuzla was metalled road, sitting below the top of a ridge and in most places exposed from lack of foliage or hard cover. The HVO held the ridge, which overlooked BSA trenches and gun positions as close as two kilometres away on the opposite side of the valley. Several clearly marked UN convoys, led by the squadron, were engaged by BSA guns and mortars during December, not only I'm sure to prevent aid reaching their enemy, but as so often in the Balkans, a result of drunken sport. The first to be engaged was Lieutenant Mark Jones's section. As mortar rounds and anti-aircraft gunfire (fired horizontally in a direct fire role) exploded around his vehicles, the troop corporal, Charlie Ducker, was heard to say during a radio contact report, "This is like bomb alley". The media immediately latched on to this nickname and made it stick.

*Friday 4 December: The Squadron Leader has been ordered to put his plans into practice and receive the first UNHCR aid convoy travelling from Serbia to Tuzla tomorrow; Operation CABINET. My troop has not caught the selector's eye for this pioneering event, Billy Fooks's troop has. His troop and SHQ have been forward-based to an empty warehouse in Tuzla since this morning. BBC and ITN reporters and camera crews have arrived tonight ready to cover this internationally newsworthy event, most notably Mr Martin Bell, who chatted at length with me and said he saw the war continuing for many months yet. Tomorrow we escort them through Bomb Alley.*

The sun had not risen when the TV crews filmed Corporal Bremridge and me guiding our Scimitars from the hangar. A simple escort duty, but within 500 metres of the camp gates ITN's armoured Land Rover had broken down. Captain Lee Smart, the Public Information Officer who was hosting the crews, radioed to tell me to leave them, but we stopped and Yozza rectified the fault in seconds. Having safely reached Stupari at the end of Bomb Alley we released Martin Bell and colleagues to free-run on to Tuzla and the task of covering the Operation CABINET story.

On our return to Kladanj a blue civilian van made the mistake of overtaking my Scimitar but without the legs to pass Corporal Bremridge, thus becoming sandwiched between us. On hearing explosions while still four kilometres from camp, I dropped inside the turret and swung around to look through my rear periscope in a hope of catching a glimpse of whatever it was. Failing to see anything, I could only presume the BSA mortars were firing at us, confirmed that second by another explosion, but this time louder and closer. "Sierra three-two this is three-zero, that's mortar fire, put your foot down and get inside the turret, out to you; zero, this is three-zero contact wait out." In the Scimitar in front Trooper Kusbish could be seen facing backwards staring at us with his head and shoulders exposed, completely unaware of what was falling around him.

Curiosity led me to peek my eyes above the turret hatch opening while we sped along at over 40 mph. Something splashed the earth on a bank above eye level on our off side about ten metres behind the Scimitar. With some exclamation, Elvis expressed his concern that the Serbs were firing a large calibre automatic gun at us. I agreed, and assumed it to be something like fire from a 20mm anti-aircraft gun.

In these few moments the vehicles had travelled only half a click, but the Bosnian Serbs had our range and were tracking us accurately. Facing forwards and looking through the main periscope I saw the next round land not more than five metres in front of S32. The explosion kicked up dirt from the road surface and the familiar dark grey cloud of smoke engulfed the Scimitar as Trooper Sparkes drove on through it. Another round followed immediately, landing literally three metres in front of our vehicle, frighteningly close, and again we escaped without a scratch.

Viewed through the protection of the periscope was, however, falsely comforting, as nothing happened to us. Had a mortar round achieved a direct hit on a Scimitar it would have been opened up like a tin of sardines. It reminded me of television scenes where, inexplicably, the baddies somehow manage to be such bad shots that the good guys get away unhurt; we were getting away.

Back in camp the jubilant dusty-faced crews dismounted and started comparing versions of events. If nothing else the boys had been 'baptized', restoring some lost self-esteem from having not played a key role in the early days of the squadron's deployment. It was my duty to speak with Trooper Kusbish, for he needed to stay more alert. His answer was, "Sorry sir, I thought the bang was the blue van back-firing," which was an interesting notion.

Neither Scimitar appeared to have been affected by the close proximity of these blasts, sending the wrong message about our level of protection and apparent immortality. The Scimitar, being designed for reconnaissance and air-portability and fighting in self-defence, has aluminium armour, sufficient against fragments of indirect fire such as these former-Soviet 82mm mortars, but unlikely to protect us from any direct projectile larger than 7.62mm machine gun. The blue Toyota Hiace van between us, aware it had no armour, had sensibly found the necessary means to escape.

If the BSA knew the exact range to the road, something that can be measured from a map, then our only access road to Tuzla would continue to be along a potential bomb alley. Probability alone surely guaranteed the BSA a hit before long. Robust action was needed to show resolve and hopefully put an end to this intimidation before someone was injured, or, worse, a vehicle and whole crew were lost. The UN Rules of Engagement only permitted aggressive action in self-defence, and in immediate response, which would be extremely difficult guidelines to fulfil with a concealed enemy firing from over two kilometres away. Being reluctant to stick my head out of the turret for very long during the incident, I had failed to spot any Serb firing positions.

In between tasks the lot of the troop leader was less exciting. It was the troop sergeant's job to run most administration, but many gripes and complaints were targeted at the officer. A day later the Cheshire Quartermaster visited the factory to evaluate our living conditions, a morale-boosting visit, which resulted in an ordered reduction of funding for locally washed laundry. Moreover, the amount of showers taken by each man at the village's Bosna Hotel, then two a week, was to be halved. In the eyes of the soldiers there was only one reason for this measure, a cost-cutting exercise. They were right, but did not stop whingeing about it until a bigger problem surfaced a week later.

The troop's more vocal members also expressed their dissatisfaction by criticizing me for neglecting to pass on information. Soldiers are used to relatively smooth-running training exercises where a given day is generally pre-planned from a Main Events List. Bosnia was real life where information was not always available and the common enemy was quite often boredom. The soldiers needed to understand this pretty soon or it was going to seem like an even longer tour of duty. Whenever I received news it was passed on as soon as was practicable, but they were unhappy and right to raise the point, as it reminded me to make sure I briefed them every day, however inconvenient. It was important to have this kind of honest dialogue within such a close-knit team and one that I encouraged, as long as criticism was thought through, justified and constructive.

In every group of society there is a rank structure or pecking order, even if a rank is not visible on a sleeve or shoulder, as in the army. In the British Army the pecking order within ranks is well recognized too, by the years of seniority. Regardless of rank, you will always be junior to somebody, so in a way it is relative, unless of course you are at the very bottom. Climbing off the bottom rung and closing the gap with those senior and in authority must be the ambition of every new soldier; it is no fun being new. Those with sporting talent earn accelerated respect and are quickly accepted into the team; others remain the 'grey man' and avoid attracting attention to themselves in the first place and some will attract attention whatever they do. Kusbish was one of the Squadron's newest troopers and fell into the last bracket. He was hard-working and well-meaning, but, like many new soldiers, prone to lapses in concentration and judgement through inexperience. In barrack life such lapses are quickly forgotten, but on an operation of Grapple's magnitude they are not, because poor judgements carry far greater implications. Unless you have a thick skin or the ability to laugh at yourself, making a mistake can batter a young soldier's confidence, often creating a domino effect which sees mistakes develop into memorable blunders.

Unlike other troopers, a well-intentioned Kusbish offered to show our new and thankfully underemployed medic around a Scimitar. Parked up in the factory, where soldiers were watching the squadron's newly installed television and eating lunch, Kusbish showed Corporal Kinnair RAMC inside a turret. Having explained the sighting system and radios, he decided to demonstrate the electrical firing circuit test for the coaxially mounted 7.62mm machine gun. Trooper Kusbish turned on the turret's power using the master switch, selected Coax on the gunner's selector switch box, leant over to the commander's side of the turret and cocked the gun before pressing the firing switch on the elevation hand wheel. Amplified by the hanger's voluminous high ceiling, more than twenty soldiers watching television were paralysed by the deafening sound of a firing machine gun. More shocked was Kusbish who emerged from the turret ashen-faced, bewildered and head bowed, aware of the gravity of his offence. The most distressed man, however, was Trooper Sparkes who had been crouched down on the vehicle's engine decks just below the elevated gun. He was truly shocked and took a few days to return to his normal gregarious self.

Sitting on my bed writing a letter home, I disregarded the shots for the common stupidity of a drunken Croat; that was until I heard the Sergeant-Major's voice next door berating a stunned Corporal Bremridge. Why had he left a belt of machine-gun rounds loaded on the gun's feed tray? The GPMG is lethal and had it been pointing at a lower angle would almost certainly have killed a number of our men. As the commander of the vehicle, Corporal Bremridge was made partly responsible and never allowed to forget this event, which was tough to accept for a man so professional.

*Sunday 6 December: To keep up morale, troops tasked with convoys to Tuzla will occasionally be allowed to stop for a night in the Tuzla Hotel, which I'm looking forward to. Sergeant Clarke's section was due on the next task; however, a bolt has sheered off his suspension. So, standing in, I joined Corporal Payne for a convoy, which Corporal Bremridge was not happy about, but it is important to distribute work evenly.*

*After moderate privation the bath tonight was sensational. Changing into clean uniform, eating dinner off a plate and enjoying a beer are everyday things which, in just a few weeks, I have forgotten the pleasure of. It was good to see Mark Cooper (LO to BiH). His hotel bedroom is his permanent Bosnian abode and, as usual, is a tip. Sadly we could not just leave two Scimitars unguarded in the hotel car park and so a watch has been posted all night. Annoyingly the truck drivers are happy to leave their vehicles unattended so are not helping us. Tomorrow morning we are leaving the hotel after an early breakfast to avoid the swarms of children.*

*Tuesday 8 December: Today eleven Dutch trucks arrived to be escorted to Banovici. Just outside the village a police patrol met us to lead the way to the depot, unusually well organized. We sat on the turret hatches in the glorious winter sunshine, mug of tea in hand, while watching a handful of local workers start to unload enormous sacks of wheat. Before my brew had cooled down enough to drink, a UNHCR jeep screamed through the depot gates. A red-haired lady jumped out, stomped over, introduced herself as Irene, and told me that I was unloading into the ARBiH depot. So that's one method the armies use to intercept aid. She told me the correct destination lay a further two kilometres up the road. The Banovici children ran all the way in the hope of sweets. It is difficult to be friendly to the kids and keep them off your 'tank', so against my better judgement we ended up with Muslim sprogs clambering all over us. Everything had to be thrown inside the turret for security.*

Driving at the rear of the convoy from Banovici, our routine run was disrupted when Elvis spotted the orange glow of a large-calibre round arching through the black evening sky. It was some distance from us and about 11 o'clock in relation to our vehicle. Fired from the BSA lines into Bomb Alley, the round flew across the valley in a reasonably flat trajectory, rather like a tank round, and impacted on the hillside ahead. The only light was a nearly full moon, occulted by passing clouds, and thus with so many vehicles I had taken the decision to keep headlights on.

From the front of the convoy Corporal Bremridge acknowledged the firing within seconds by sending a contact report to Zero. Two minutes later and a kilometre further on, we found ourselves viewing the same orange tracer rounds, but now off to our left-hand side, at 9 o'clock in relation to us. "Incoming in a few seconds lads," I stated fairly matter-of-factly to Elvis and Yozza, only half believing the obviousness of this childlike mathematical coincidence of angles, while mesmerised by another illuminated shell flying straight towards us. Sure enough a few seconds later the round exploded, the initiation for several more following. Elvis counted eight in all, two of which sounded dangerously close. The trucks in front prevented us speeding up and so we dropped back, Yozza turned off the headlights, and I sent another contact report, but again with no acknowledgement from Zero.

Assuming no one to be hurt and briefing Captain Stuart Ward to that effect ten minutes later, it was a little embarrassing to be corrected when an injured Dutch soldier entered SHQ holding a field dressing against his blood-spattered arm. He was a truck driver whose window had been smashed by shrapnel from a BSA shell and had suffered lacerations to his forearm and face from the flying glass entering his cab.

Someone had to teach these Bosnian Serb cowards a lesson sooner than later, but exactly how best to target them remained a challenge.

The next day Sergeant Finlay and I drove back along Bomb Alley to see if we could identify any BSA gun positions. The opposite side of the valley was two kilometres away at the nearest point and afforded the Serbs a great deal of natural cover from fire and view. Sharing a turret, Corporal Bremridge and I took an intersection using grid references and bearings we had both taken the night before. Nothing military sat on or near either axis; BSA positions or weapons were nowhere to be seen. It seemed entirely sensible for them to hold weaponry further back and only deploy them forward for opportunity engagements.

Stopping at the HVO checkpoint, short of Kladanj, I was interested to pick the brains of its two soldiers. What did they know of the Serb mortars or firing positions? Showing them my map, the larger of the two, a man more than six feet tall, placed his thick and weathered index finger on to the spot in question. Pepici? This was in dead ground to Bomb Alley. The firing positions we had seen were on a forward slope and definitely further north. Maybe this was where Kladanj was being engaged from and not the alley; little had been achieved. Back in Kladanj we were warned off for Operation CABINET 2, a deployment into Tuzla to escort more humanitarian aid.

*Saturday 12 December: I hate five o'clock starts and breakfast in the turret on the move, which this morning was three dry oatmeal blocks. We had to be in position in the village of Caparde well before the Belgian convoy arrived at the BSA front line so that we could move forward into Kalesija to receive them and escort the aid into Tuzla. I did not quite understand the logic of this because it was supposedly coming all the way from Belgrade, hopefully without having been looted, so why should it be threatened then? It was most likely to ensure that the Tuzla mafia did not get hold of the aid in order to sell it on.*

*On the way out of town we experienced the normal suspicion and scrutiny at a series of Muslim checkpoints, which I found ridiculous considering what we were off to fetch for these people. Lieutenant Nick Costello, a British Army interpreter, was in a Land Rover in front of us and dealt with the bureaucracy quite happily, until we came to execute the hand over. My troop escorted the Squadron Leader and his party forward to meet with the BSA. The first Serb I saw fulfilled my image of the quintessential Chetnik. Standing guard over the negotiations in progress was a tall barrel-chested soldier wearing a brown woollen battle dress, musquash hat, with a double-headed eagle badge and a bushy and fierce looking beard. He reminded me of a bandit from the Khyber Pass.*

The Bosnian Serbs would not allow the fifteen Belgian Volvo trucks over their border unless unaccompanied, negating half the purpose for us being there. Withdrawing from our position, we patrolled back through Tuzla streets to the UNHCR depot. Consequently the trucks were way behind us, but we still received a very warm welcome from the local inhabitants.

At the depot there was nothing to do but sit and wait for the aid to be offloaded, which unfortunately meant fighting off more children. It was not our job to help the depot workers; we had armoured vehicles to look after and had to remain alert.

With empty trucks, the return was thankfully unopposed by either Muslim or Bosnian Serb. Typical Bosnian logic allowed us to escort the gleaming white trucks all the way into Kalesija, which we did with hatches battened down, irrespective of the lack of cargo. I remained at the rear of the column with my guns over the back decks ready to lead the team back into Tuzla once the handover was complete. While waiting for this ritual, which took far longer than it should have, we came under mortar fire, but landing a couple of hundred metres away, it was not directly threatening to us. Sitting in a Scimitar with the hatches closed does present a slightly restricted view of the world and, depending on necessary levels of activity in the turret, can cause the periscopes to become quickly steamed up. With only limited peripheral vision it is almost like having a sense removed and the need to look constantly about covering all of the arcs becomes essential. In the cramped compartment it is an uncomfortable experience and unpopular with crewmen.

Receiving the order to return to Tuzla, I led the column back over the front line. Once in Muslim territory hatches were opened before being caught amid a hail of small-arms tracer rounds which started at the rear of the convoy and worked its way to the front. The last burst flew overhead a few metres from the back of our Scimitar, missing everything, I believe intentionally, as a protest against UNPROFOR. Elvis traversed the Rarden cannon left, but a line of buildings blocked the view. There was no chance, nor justification, to engage. Such action, although tempting, would only make matters worse.

On returning safely to the factory at Kladanj we learned the welcome news of the Squadron's redeployment to Vitez for the Christmas period. The Cheshires were "bringing us back to guard the camp" was the chorus from cynical junior soldiers. Departing Kladanj in deep snow, we bid our relief, 'A' Company, farewell and looked forward to the change.*

* At the end of the year the Battlegroup's sub-units rotated. 'A' Company was deployed to Kladanj for Tuzla operations, 'B' Company remained escorting and patrolling in Gornji Vakuf, 'C' Company was in Vitez on operations and 'B' Squadron returned to guard Vitez camp and to conduct convoys when demand required it.

# 6

## SEASONAL MESSAGES

At the eastern end of Vitez the tower and belfry of the Catholic church was lit and prominent among the black and sleeping town. To its west stood the Mosque's striking minaret, both religions discrete yet mutually tolerated. The road was blissfully empty and its surface hard with packed snow. Travelling east, dark cliffs in the Lasva Valley soon towered either side of us, their craggy faces providing abundant options for human concealment. Near Busovaca a boulder the size of a small house blocked some of the route which slowed us down. It had been there for some time, its inconvenient position no accident of nature. This gorge was a perfect defile, ideal for ambushing a convoy. There were no exits or turning places and the cliffs were too high for armoured vehicles to elevate guns to return fire. Always in the back of my mind were the stories of the Wehrmacht's unwieldy panzer divisions suffering at the hands of Partisans in similar Yugoslavian valleys fifty years before.

Travelling in a Scimitar is a fairly uncomfortable business at the best of times. The commander's seat can be pumped up to provide a head-out-of-turret view, but its release mechanism is unreliable and so, with the risk of the vehicle rolling, is rarely trusted. Instead, crew gain the knack of wedging themselves in so that only one's head is showing, primarily to reduce the risk from snipers, and in this case mainly to minimize the wind-chill. This was severe with temperatures regularly as low as -15 degrees Celsius, compounded by travelling at speeds of up to 50mph. Our crewguard helmets fitted with headphones and black ski goggles, with which we had been issued, provided further protection from the bitter cold. Like most, I had invested in a balaclava, which my breath always made uncomfortably wet around the mouth. If pulled down, however, my mouth and nose were exposed to the biting wind and consequently the peculiar sensation of a runny nose freezing and licked lips sticking together. Every crewman had his own idea of how to be most comfortable.

Linking up with nine aid trucks of the Dutch/Belgian transport battalion in Busovaca was our first step before escorting them to Novi

Seher in the far northern sector of the Muslim territory. The trucks had relatively little protection against the potential threat, although their cabs were lightly armoured with steel-plate attachments and bullet-proof glass. In charge of the trucks was a Dutch officer, Lieutenant Lars Dayunger. The four Scimitars were organized evenly among the convoy to provide maximum security during the journey.

In Zenica a UNHCR representative called Samir, driving a Land Cruiser, joined our convoy as we drove past him sitting stationary in a layby. Zenica is a large predominately Muslim town and prior to the war had been busy in heavy industry. Now it was run down and at capacity with refugees. The town is surrounded by hills between 1000-3000 feet high, which are dotted with rural villages and farmsteads providing a contrast so close to the town. The River Bosna runs from north to south-east through this Muslim stronghold, its banks lined with dated office blocks, hotels and apartments, a façade to a large number of redundant chimney stacks on its periphery representing a bygone communist age of full employment.

Samir's job was to lead us to the depot and monitor the off-loading of food aid. B Squadron colleagues had told me that he was a delightful fellow, but not renowned for his sharpness. Samir substantiated this on arrival in Novi Seher when he told us that he was unsure which depot we were to deliver to, or indeed where any of the depots were. The UNHCR were paying him a generous salary for his talents! Fortunately Mark Jones had sketched a map, literally on the back of a fag packet, as a failsafe for me. It was difficult to understand, but Smeetz, the Dutch transport sergeant, related it to a previous visit and, his memory jogged, had us there in no time.

Once the trucks had been delivered safely I was free to set out on my next assignment, a mail delivery to the father of Muris the interpreter. Father and son had been unable to telephone or write to each other for several months and so the delivery provided a good excuse, albeit unofficial, to venture further north up to the Bosnian-Serb front line. Only Sergeant Clarke knew where we were off to, which on reflection was not that sensible.

On the envelope of this thick spongy letter was Muris's father's name and in capitals, Miljanovci, a village name that was on the map, but as popular in Bosnia as Sutton or Newtown is in England. Corporal Bremridge and I first set out towards Jelah, the furthest north ventured by anyone from the battlegroup; travelling beyond it attracted a health warning. At a prominent crossroads in Jelah I leant out of the turret and shouted to an old man, "Miljanovci?" while pointing straight ahead. "*Dobro*," he said, a reply distorted by a roll-up fag hanging from the side of his mouth. This was not so much a question about navigation but a need to see his reaction. Had he replied, "Miljanovci!" with raised eyebrows, we might have withdrawn the Christmas postal service there.

Several villages further along we saw a lad of about thirteen years old mooching and kicking stones at the side of the track. Leaning from the turret again, I showed him the envelope. He pointed ahead and then gestured to the engine decks for a ride. Slightly irregular but harmless enough, we drove at a steady pace for another mile until he signalled us to stop outside a small house. If this was Miljanovci then six houses was the qualification for a place name on a map.

An old man, who I naturally presumed to be Muris' father, walked out of the house and down a small path to investigate us. Like so many of his generation he wore a thick tweed jacket, a patterned pullover, shiny grey nylon trousers and worn-out boots. Handing him the letter immediately put a broad grin on his weathered face, confirming to me that my task was complete. He stuffed the letter into his jacket pocket without reading it and focused his attention on us, insisting that we toast this happy moment with slivovitz.

The house looked clean, yet had the familiar combination of Bosnian body odour and Balkan cigarettes. The old man removed dusty cut-glass tumblers from a glass-fronted cabinet, which was cluttered with ornaments and pictures of family. Necking back the clear but potentially lethal liquor, Corporal Bremridge and I manfully fulfilled our duty. The bottle was thrust out for a top-up, but I politely declined, "*Nema hvala.*" Signalling our exit in sign language and a loud mix of English and Serbo-Croat, we beat a hasty retreat to the Scimitars, now predictably crawling with filthy-faced young boys.

With our excuse for being outside the normal geographical umbrella gone, and some nerve lost, I realized how out on a limb we were, although not still without uses. While returning quickly to Novi Seher, we chanced upon three towed artillery pieces, Soviet designed D-30s, which, sitting in a field on a reverse slope, were being dug in by soldiers. The guns appeared to be in very good condition and were pointing towards the Serbs, which suggested we were heading in the right direction.

Back in Novi Seher I was surprised to find the depot workers only just finishing unloading, saying quite a lot for the speed they worked. Sergeant Clarke and Corporal Payne's crews were on their umpteenth brew as they sat on their hatches watching the spectacle of humanitarian aid delivery to the group of male 'civilians', extraordinarily all of fighting age.

On our journey home to Vitez we stopped at a small shop to let the crews buy cigarettes. On sale inside was an 85mm brass shell, probably fired from a T-34, a Second World War Russian tank. I bought the shell for 10DMs, cheap for an umbrella stand, but a rip-off in Bosnia for a piece of useless brass. The shop was also selling enormous sacks of wheat with WEU printed on them in bold letters. When I asked the shopkeeper to explain this, he said he had a shortage of bags and that the WEU bags were very strong and useful. They were factory-sealed and did not look reused, but it was nigh impossible to disprove him.

The accumulation of such episodes was slowly creating a deep cynicism in me against supporting international aid organizations. The situation was so bad that a number of UK-based charities operating in Bosnia had procured cast Army Bedford trucks in order to drive aid out personally and thus guarantee successful delivery, which had to be applauded. I had seen sufficient evidence to decide never to drop coins into the rattling tins of international do-gooders again. Charity should start at home was my conclusion.

After dropping the Dutch trucks and their drivers off in Busovaca at the end of a long and tiring day, Corporal Payne led the troop back for the home leg. Trooper Wiseman was driving his Scimitar at quite some speed, just too fast to be comfortable, but acceptable on account of us all wanting to return in time for supper. It was a challenge to keep up with him, which was fine until he negotiated a blind corner and drove over a wooden plank on which four anti-tank mines were sitting. It was one of those irreversible split-second moments when the blood rushes from your head as you assume the very worst scenario; in fact you barely have time to think about that. The Scimitar passed over the plank hardly noticing its existence. Left in its wake were two flattened green mines, which would have been no less effective had they been cake tins. They had been placed in front of the Muslim checkpoint to create a chicane, a simple and popular measure in Bosnia to control traffic. Following too close behind, I failed to deliver even one coherent word as warning for this potential danger. Despite searching for the correct sequence of words, including the noun 'mine', I only managed a strange and unintelligible sound. Fortunately Yozza was alert and had enough time to carry out emergency braking and a swerve before accelerating away from bemused and unimpressed-looking Muslim guards.

In the Vitez operations room I reported the day's findings, which included a sighting of three BiH M63 wheelbarrow multiple rocket launchers in a field that afternoon. The Intelligence Officer was grateful for the reports and remarked how the Lancers always brought home information for him, however mundane the task. Using a map, I showed Chris where we had been, which initially he found hard to believe. He was trying to piece together, more exactly, where the BSA front line ran. A penned red line marking the front line on his map had Miljanovci in the Serb area, which clearly it was not, so our delivery had not been in vain after all.

Returning to a pile of mail stacked on my bed was a welcome surprise, but turned out to be nearly sixty Christmas cards from my godson's infant school. Support from people in the UK had been overwhelming throughout the tour and we were grateful for it. Replying to them all became quite a task. B.F.P.O. 3000 was an address for public supporters to write speculatively 'to a soldier', most of which we gave to men with a poor record for receiving mail. Many letters had photographs enclosed, some quite immodest, in the hope of attracting pen friends or organizing meetings during R&R.

Responsible for guarding the camp, the lead-up to Christmas was one of routine for the squadron. Mindful of the likelihood that boredom would set in, it was up to troop leaders to invent ways of relieving this, but there was little scope in the circumstances. Soon, if not already, alcohol would find its way into the tents, however stringent policing by NCOs was, and discipline would suffer as a result.

The media was at large in Vitez busy filming 'our brave boys' away from their families at this festive time, as well as reporting the news. Both Mess and cookhouse provided havens of sorts for trusted journalists, such as Mr John Simpson, to whom I had the fortune of chatting in the Officers' Mess. Later, when entering my troop's tent, I found myself confronted by a camera crew and a journalist who gave me no choice but to attempt answering ridiculously broad questions such as, "What is it like to be away from home at Christmas and what do you think of the Bosnian war?"

On Christmas Eve the Commander of British Forces, Brigadier Andrew Cumming, late 17th/21st Lancers, addressed large groups of the battlegroup to congratulate us on our performance. His message was that our uncertain future was exciting, with many contingency plans being made. The implementation of an air exclusion zone over Bosnia had been put back a week and many nations were pressuring the British to intervene with force. The final message was to "dig deep" but into patience and hard work.

By the time I left the Mess it was midnight and the start of Christmas Day. There only needs to be a hint of an excuse for celebration in Bosnia before automatic rifles are drawn and fired skywards. As the chimes of midnight came, the black sky lit up with the celebratory fire of orange tracer bullets, most coming from the Croat Catholic quarter. It seemed to me that such a ritual was a useful yardstick with which to measure a country's sophistication!

Despite a radio stag for four hours of the night, I was up at 0600 hours to serve 'gunfire' to the boys. Entering tented accommodation to deliver this traditional concoction of tea and rum was not that pleasant, the odours of bodies, booze and flatulence almost visibly suspended in the air. The soldiers were not that impressed either, Officers and Warrant Officers invading their space at this hour on Christmas Day, their 'day off'. Gunfire is a tradition throughout the British Army on special days, including celebrating battle anniversaries. A regular outcome is a water fight, but, given the temperature, there was fortunately no danger of that. A number of camera crews recorded this Army ritual, which was a sure way of sending the wrong impression back to wives managing all the needs of their families for six months at home.

Before lunch a large congregation attended a Carol Service and Holy Communion, which was accompanied by the very fine Cheshire Regimental band. The Padre, Captain Tyrone Hillary, gave the sermon, which reflected on our achievements, families at home and, of course, the people of Bosnia who we prayed for. Spirits were high and the voices of two hundred or more soldiers lifted the gymnasium roof as we sung in unison Once in Royal David's City with the band to keep us in time.

Spiritually uplifted after a rousing sing-song, we repaired to the Officers' Mess to host the sergeants for pre-lunch drinks, another Christmas tradition common to most regiments. After a 'sherry' or two, officers and senior ranks of the battlegroup marched behind the regimental band to the main tented cookhouse where lunch was served to the soldiers. The chefs had worked very hard to cater for several hundred within a couple of sittings on the limited cook trailers. All the Christmas trimmings were included to make the occasion seem as homely as possible and the tables had been decorated with crackers and two cans of beer for each man.

The hierarchy queued up with two plates each to deliver steaming food to the soldiers as quickly as possible. It is not uncommon for a food fight to break out when these lunches are served back in Germany or the UK because the soldiers know they can fill their faces with burgers later. Not so here, and it would somehow have been inappropriate. The occasional empty beer can was used as a missile in brotherly banter, but the mood was generally subdued. Some soldiers were enjoying themselves, but there were many with distant stares, minds wondering to being at home with their families. A free telephone call home would give soldiers a chance to share a few minutes with their loved ones, but for unhappy soldiers the call was like a drug, the high wearing off quickly and followed by a low that could often only be made better by another fix at the telephone booth.

The Christmas spirit continued with the subalterns returning to the house to open presents in front of one another. I was fortunate to have been sent two stockings crammed with small gifts. One was from my mother and the other from a splendid London girl who had been a stalwart letter writer and friend. Having had the stockings for several weeks I had forgotten who had sent which stocking and was certain that I was unwrapping presents from my mother until discovering a glossy copy of Penthouse. Unwrapping silk boxer shorts from the other stocking, I was no nearer clarifying the situation!

When the Cheshire Regiment was stationed in India in 1935 the Sergeants' Mess hosted a group of Indian Army sergeants who presented them with a large wooden key, the 'key to the Khyber Pass'. By rights it was the property of the Sergeants' Mess, but every year, on a special occasion, the officers and sergeants fight for its custody. Boxing Day was the occasion, the battle ground the Sergeants' Mess in defence of their ownership.

One has to bear in mind the age and size of the sergeants compared to the officers, their greater numbers and some advantages of defence. The Cheshire sergeants have lost possession of the key twice since 1935, initially in 1956 and latterly in 1989 when the then RSM, David Sherlock, ran the Mess. A subaltern had used some form of Trojan horse technique to get within the ring of heavies that guarded the key. David was now a commissioned officer and captain, the boot was on the other foot, but he was still bearing the emotional scars from the shame.

In 1992 the key sat proudly behind the bar with about forty or so Warrant Officers and sergeants between it and us. Concentration of force, an important military principle, was as true as it had ever been. The occasional brave or stupid subaltern who attempted an independent raid at the target was always devoured by the defenders, stripped naked and spat back out into the front line. Our valiant squadron leader was to be one of these victims, but he had been selected as a high-value target from the outset. After a couple of hours of stalemate we all shook hands after what had been fairly rough play. Nursing bruises over a late curry lunch and beer helped a great deal.

On a more serious note, it was only later, after we had all had such fun, that we learnt of Justin Freeland's injury while on Operation CABINET. Waiting at the *rendezvous* point in Kalesija, three mortar rounds had landed when Justin was leaning out of his Scimitar while talking to two local civilians. Shrapnel hit him in the upper right arm, a cause for immediate evacuation to Tuzla hospital, there being no proper British medical facilities that far up-country. Lieutenant Mike Murdoch (Royal Irish Regiment) drove Justin there in a Land Rover.

In Tuzla Hospital Mike had to walk around saying "X-ray" in the hope that someone would understand him before eventually queueing for assistance among a line of injured and limbless Muslim soldiers and locals. Local doctors, already over stretched and under-resourced, dug metal out of Justin's arm using only local anaesthetic, which Justin said had not been very strong and had worn off during surgery. They had sewn his arm back up, while all along Justin had been too dazed to remember the syrette of morphine he carried in his smock. Justin was brought back to Vitez where our surgeon, Lieutenant Colonel Attard, removed a further nine pieces of shrapnel. In an unsurprisingly tasteless fashion, the media hounded Justin's distressed family at their home in Berkshire.

The majority of the battlegroup assembled in the Vitez garage to watch an impromptu show by the comedian Jim Davidson that night. The hangar was formerly a civilian garage that had been commandeered by the REME for vehicle maintenance. Sappers had built the stage at short notice and Jim Davidson gave what appeared to be an off-the-cuff performance wearing a pair of old jeans and a sweater, which made it so much more personal. Most of the soldiers were genuinely very grateful to the voluntary performers who had so unselfishly entertained us at that time of the year. A few, mostly Royal Irish, embarrassingly heckled Jim Davidson, but were shot down by a man who had heard it all before.

*

The end of the year was unspectacular, the troop, and I am sure much of the squadron, becoming bored with the routine of guarding camp and fed up with maintaining the Scimitars outside in temperatures rarely above zero. The lads did have the benefit of moving out of the tents into the school's main building. However, because of the increased threat from BSA artillery strikes, the outside walls had to be sandbagged, which the boys spent the last two days of 1992 doing.

Fortunately routine was broken by the need to take an aid convoy to the small Muslim town of Visoko, not far from Sarajevo. I was particularly keen to go, for friends in the UK had sent me a letter from a Bosnian woman called Nada, who was taking refuge in Brighton. Her father lived in Visoko, but she had not spoken to or heard from him in over a year and only hoped that somehow I would be able to deliver this letter.

Dab hands at mail delivery, we made the journey to Visoko and soon found Nada's father's flat, but nobody was at home. Having posted the envelope through the letterbox we turned to leave when an old man, escorted by several teenagers, arrived breathless at the top of the stairs. He was delighted with the letter and penned a reply immediately, writing furiously to make the most of the short time he had. Meanwhile, and no surprise to us, we sipped a glass of slivovitz and complimented the old man on the beverage, "*dobro, dobro*". He was therefore confused when we politely declined a refill, excusing ourselves, as ever, through mimicking the driving of a car.

On New Year's Eve our return journey to Vitez was made spectacular with celebratory fire dissecting the sky. The last two months with the troop had been rewarding and successful so, I joined the team in the Junior Ranks Club for a New Year beer. Having just plonked twelve beers on a table I was confronted by the Mess Manager, Sergeant Ingram, who asked me if I would kindly leave the club as it was for junior ranks and not officers. I asked him why, if this was the case, were there sergeants in the bar; surely they too had their own Mess to go to. "No Sir, those sergeants are on duty in here," he said very confidently. "Well in that case Sergeant Ingram, if they are on duty, why are they drinking beer?" I retorted. I was invited to stay in the club and was wished a happy New Year, but instead chose to see this in with Justin, whose spirits were up and who would soon be flying back to Woolwich to convalesce. When the clock struck midnight there was more tracer illuminating the sky than was sensible. The locals did not seem to understand that these bullets do fall to earth at quite a velocity.

# 7

# ZAVIDOVICI

As the Bosnian Serb Army had closed in on the Muslims and Croats throughout 1992, towns offering insufficient resistance eventually fell. Consequently large numbers of people were driven from their homes or fled as refugees into the centre of Bosnia and to relative safety. The shape of Bosnia that remained non-Serb, therefore, changed continually, albeit slowly. In October, before the deployment, it had been shaped like a fat stumpy tree with three thick malformed branches. Jajce was a 'branch' to the west that the BSA, through continued offensive action, lopped off towards the end of the year. In the north-east Tuzla and its environs remained a Muslim stronghold and in the centre, beyond Novi Seher where 3 Troop had delivered Muris's letter, the Serbs were nibbling away at this 'branch' although there was much resistance. This area of land in the centre was known as the Maglaj Finger. The ground between the Maglaj Finger and Tuzla was held by the BSA and remained an obstacle to aid convoys needing to travel west to east between Zepce or Zavidovici and Tuzla. The single alternative was to take a long circuitous route to the south, adding hours to the journey time. These extended lines of communication were more than an inconvenience to the BiH attempting to supply their defence and so it was viewed as vital ground they were determined to retake. Assuming the BiH to be some way off achieving this, the UNHCR hoped to broker a deal with the BSA to allow convoys safe passage.

Zavidovici was a small Muslim town sitting on the eastern edge of the Maglaj Finger. My section was tasked to visit the town's BiH headquarters to gain information on the area and to establish how far east we could travel along the Tuzla road before being stopped by the BSA. At midday I was to meet up with Captain Matthew Dundas-Whatley, an LO to the BiH, in Zavidovici town centre on a bridge which crossed the River Bosna. A gangly chap with curly hair and a plummy voice, who was rarely seen without a broad grin on his face, he was to be there to prepare the way and introduce us to the local commander.

On the southern outskirts of the town my legitimate journey was halted at a Muslim checkpoint. Technically speaking, local factions had no authority to inhibit the freedom of movement of UN troops, but too often did, a tactic that I was beginning to get fed up with. Stepping down from my Scimitar, I approached two guards dressed in the ubiquitous blue camouflaged police combat suits, one of who was manning the barrier. The other, holding his AK-47 by the pistol grip, took a few paces forward. The rifle looked well oiled and he had taped two magazines together for fast reloading, a habit that mimicked Muslim cousins on the West Bank. Quite deliberately he took a long last drag on a cigarette with squinty eyes, as if whatever I wanted would have to wait until he had satisfied his need. He then stubbed it out by grinding the butt into the road with the sole of his boot. It was plain to see that this guard thought himself important, common in some people if given a little bit of power, probably the equivalent mentality of the British traffic warden.

Knowing that Bosnian men are big hand-shakers, I thrust my hand out confidently. He slung the rifle over his shoulder and received my compliment with casual nonchalance. "*Dobro jutro moy colleager; Ja sam Britanski oficir.*" I garbled some nonsense while raising my arm like a barrier and pointed to my vehicle. "*Kuda idete?*" (where are you going?) he asked, blowing deep inhaled smoke out into the atmosphere. He shook his head in outright refusal to my reply, "*Nema UNPROFOR.*" Why did we have two armoured vehicles but no food convoy went the gist of his argument?

"Elvis, get the fags out; this one could be tricky," I called back. None of my crew smoked but we kept a carton of cigarettes on the vehicle as currency. For best results the cigarettes had to be Marlboro as these were the locals' favourites and were hard to come by. Not being a smoker, the fags would sadly never achieve their full effect, that of two opposing soldiers reaching neutrality and escapism from lighting up together. He gladly received my offer, in fact took three cigarettes, which I felt unable to tell him was rude. He indicated that he would have to telephone his commander, to which I childishly quoted my favourite useless Bosnian phrase: "*Moy Major iuvat velk sliva,*" (My Major has large plums). At first he did not appear to understand or find this comment funny, but then the soldier on the barrier started laughing and, I suppose not wanting to look stupid, his face too broke into a grin. "*Hvala liepo, dovidenja,*" I thanked them loudly above the engine noise as we drove through the barrier waving, only to hear Yozza say over the intercom "dozy clowns."

There was no sign of Matthew or his white Land Rover at the bridge and so we sat in the turret and enjoyed the warming effects of one of Elvis's coffees drunk from filthy mugs thick in congealed sugar, coffee dregs and unknown turret matter. Like eggs and bacon cooked in a greasy old frying pan, the coffee seemed to taste better the less we cleaned the mugs, so went his justification. Thirty minutes were spent waiting by the bridge, watching the relatively busy populace trudging through the snow-covered streets while going about their daily affairs. Most people shuffled along, heads bowed to avoid the miserable weather. One benefit from bad weather, at least, was the lack of children troubling us for sweets.

Losing patience I decided it was time to venture down the Tuzla road at least to achieve something of our task before we had to return home. Within one kilometre another Muslim checkpoint confronted us, this time stopping us leaving the town perimeter. All that I could understand was the guards repeated caution of mines on the road and that UNPROFOR had already been shot at along this stretch; that would be Mark Jones and his troop. I was sure that the issue could have been forced more, but it was not worth it. I had the grid reference of the checkpoint, which partly met my needs to estimate the approximate extent of the Serb front line.

When retracing our steps through Zavidovici to check for Matthew one more time, we caught sight of his Land Rover near the bridge. He had organized an escort for us down to the BiH HQ, so shortly after we were following a green Lada Niva crammed with five soldiers through the previously denied checkpoint. Matthew was already late for another meeting, so had to dash off.

The local headquarters was based in a disused school, a strangely familiar building, which on entering I discovered was exactly the same communist architectural pattern as the school in Vitez. As experienced elsewhere, I had to leave my rifle with the entrance guard, something I hated doing, but had little choice. Keeping my magazines, however, was a request they agreed to. They might have had my rifle, but at least they could not shoot me with it, something that would be really embarrassing.

The local commander was a young man, who was very welcoming and keen to tell me of his former service as a lieutenant in the JNA. Unusually for ex JNA, he spoke very little English, but was assisted by a rather incongruous-looking Arab, who also greeted me and explained in perfect English that he had lived in Colchester fifteen years previously. Despite having only ever been to Colchester once, to attend a District Court Martial, I claimed to know it quite well. He asked me if certain places still existed, which of course I had to say yes, but also said it had changed quite a lot in the past decade.

Using the Arab to interpret, I asked him if he would ask the commander to plot the Serb dispositions on my map. At this point I learnt that the Arab did not speak Serbo-Croat, so he conversed in Arabic to another man, who then translated this to the commander. To relay an accurate explanation of what I wanted seemed highly unlikely, but the commander agreed and, using my red pen, started drawing on my map. There were then various disagreements over the accuracy of the commander's plotting and a Chinese parliament ensued. Eventually a compromise was agreed, but I was refused any information regarding his own troops, who I assumed would be roughly 100-500 metres west of the Serb positions he had plotted.

Before we were allowed to depart we were coerced, most hospitably, into joining our friends for a spot of Bosnian lunch which, given their food hygiene record, aroused instinctive caution in me. Considering it an important cultural experience and heartened to see the section invited in after waiting patiently outside in the cold, I accepted. A large bowl of soup was placed down in front of me. Swimming in the centre of it was a piece of fatty and sinewy meat covered in pimply skin just recognizable as a parson's nose. Having soaked up the 'consomme' with bread, I chose to leave this Bosnian dish at the risk of offending my host. But the commander seemed pleased and did not hesitate in reaching across the table and scooping it up with his spoon. Chicken-bottom soup was clearly a delicacy during the war; ummm!

After lunch we met up with the boys who had been taken to the soldiers' dining room, which Sparky swore was more like a dungeon, where they had been served 'summer soup'. I enquired what this pleasant-sounding soup was, to which I was told, "som'r this and som'r that," almost better not to know. Muslim soldiers escorted us a little way east down the road to look at the front line, which they need not have done. We stopped near the Krivaja River by a hamlet called Hrkici. It was not a spectacular sight because I could not see any soldiers, trenches or equipment; in fact it could have been any randomly chosen part of the landscape, and probably was. However, it satisfied them that they thought they had satisfied us; all part of the diplomacy that I was learning.

Having been very well looked after, the section was escorted back to the bridge at Zavidovici and released to go on our way. Thinking only of a pleasant run home before dark, we were to be disappointed when several kilometres outside town my Scimitar developed a fuel

1. The Hay Wain – Saraci.

2. B Squadron forms up at Tomislavgrad ready to deploy.

3. 3 Troop's hide on Route Triangle.

4. A refugee's home in the Lasva Valley.

5. B Squadron camp at Kladanj.

6. A Scimitar near Caparde before Operation Cabinet.

7. Convoys arriving from Belgrade during Operation Cabinet.

8. 3 Troop, B Squadron, 9th/12th Royal Lancers, Tuzla Airfield. The author is standing in the centre.

9. Kacuni Checkpoint. A Scimitar replaces a logging truck which Muslims had used to block the road.

10. 3 Troop in Kacuni with Halema.

11. A convoy being unloaded at Lucovac.

12. A locally-manufactured BiH armoured vehicle at the site of the Scimitar crash.

13. The author and Trooper Baker lunch with Croats in Kacuni.

14. Mario and his friends play soldiers in Kacuni.

15. A woman in Ahmici explains to Ali the Interpreter what has happened. *(Giles Penfor*

16. A burning house in Ahmici.

blockage and spluttered to a standstill. With no means of recovery, it was important we called for assistance from Vitez. Our VHF radios, however, were way out of range and the HF, designed for long distance, was proving to be a bit of a black art, despite numerous attempts to tune it. Regardless of this there may have been Cheshire call signs in the area so it was worth a try. With the three vehicles – S30, S32 and 14B, the ambulance that had accompanied us from the start – nose to tail on the side of the road, I began to send radio checks to anyone who might be listening on the VHF frequency. "Hello any call sign, this is Sierra three-zero, radio check, over." I repeated this a number of times before the familiar voice of Trooper Kusbish answered up on the radio from S32, approximately ten metres behind me, "Sierra three-two OK, over." This was not very helpful but had everybody in stitches, answering the call for a much-needed outbreak of morale.

Failing to call for the REME to recover us, we were reduced to very few choices. I was forced to make the decision to use the ambulance to tow us within range of VHF reception to camp. Towing is easy if you have a rigid 'A' frame towing bar, but extremely difficult with ropes that are only designed for troop self-recovery over distances measured in metres. Our progress was snail-like and winter's early darkness was falling. With very little control, Sparky fought to steer the Scimitar and soon became exhausted, so it was no surprise when, not far from Zepce, the ambulance and Scimitar slued across the snow-covered road as easily as a couple of sleighs. Helpless in the turret, I thought our vehicles were going to roll over as we slid off the road into a snow-filled drainage ditch. Fortunately both remained upright, but, with a 30-degree list, had become very stuck, even when detached. Still unable to contact the Vitez operations room by either VHF or HF, I was forced to make the awkward decision to send Corporal Bremridge and crew back to Vitez alone. If *they* had an accident we would all be in a proper pickle .

Five of us piled into the back of the ambulance to keep warm while, on rotation, one man maintained a vigil outside. The engine was left running to circulate hot air around the vehicle, in what would other-wise have been an aluminium fridge, but after a couple of hours was switched off to conserve fuel. Just before midnight, after five hours of waiting in the bitter cold, the REME arrived with a Bedford 8 tonner to tow us home. Recovery was a simple operation for these experts so we soon found ourselves in Tiffy's Land Rover with the heaters on full. A night out in the snow was the last thing we had wanted.

The following morning my squadron leader gave me the news that 3 Troop was to take over from 4 Troop and be attached to 'A' Company for the remainder of the tour. This was well received and left us only a few days in camp to prepare for our departure to Tuzla. Regardless, the troop continued to be available for duties and was stood to for convoy escorts that would not then materialize because the local truck drivers, or 'choggies', would break down, be late or leave before we arrived at depots.

When not required for escorts I used the time to write annual confidential reports on the soldiers in my troop. This was an unglamorous but essential task that required proper concentration and took an inordinate time. Sitting in the Mess I attempted putting pen to paper, but regularly found my attention wandering on to the activities of the nurses who, because of limited medical demand, would quite often relax in the Mess, drinking coffee and gossiping.

With so few women living in camp the Cheshire subalterns insisted that our house cleaner should be young and pretty, which initially seemed a fair idea. Unsurprisingly this was not a success as the chosen girl, scared of getting her hands dirty, did nothing more than sweep the hall and landing each day. So before long a reluctant consensus was to release the said girl and look for a grafter. We found one in a middle-aged woman with a moustache, a promising beard and only a few teeth, just the antidote for the desperate Casanovas. With children to support, she was highly motivated and worked like a Trojan. She also took our laundry home, which would reappear the next day, one quarter of the time it took our laundry unit, and she ironed it. Unfortunately the laundry would smell a bit dodgy, a sort of Bosnian river-armpit combination, which nobody likes, but she needed the money and deserved to keep the job.

Any such employment in a land offering so little opportunity was keenly sought and readily snapped up. A job helping UN troops was a lifeline for those fortunate enough to be selected. For a few, such adversity brought great opportunity. One particular local man with entrepreneurial talent had quickly erected a wooden shack that happened to be between the camp gate and the front of our house. He was reaping the benefits of its prime location and the captive customer base. With his hands in all sorts of other pies, he was making a tidy profit out of a relatively poor situation and consequently was resented by much of the community. He employed a pretty girl called Marianne to run the store while he ran his other businesses about the village.

Marianne was about twenty years old and had a crush on Justin Freeland, who, when injured and convalescing in the medical facility, would receive visits with demonstrations of affection, mainly in the form of fancy but out-of-date chocolates. Marianne was often seen reading an English grammar book in the store, which she professed was so that she could speak more intelligibly to customers. It was easy to see that her motivation was a desire to speak lovingly to Justin. Justin spent his whole life avoiding her.

Marianne told me that the store made DM200 per day, at that time a small fortune in the local economy. Later in the tour rival stores popped up here and there, so I advised Marianne to wear an even shorter skirt with her long black leather boots, despite the temperature. She agreed that the UN were good for business but not for the country. This was a common attitude in Bosnia; you were only popular while you were useful. Even in the first six months we lost the consent of a number of locals who failed to see any progress in peace or personal benefit by the UN presence, only congestion and noise.

*Saturday 9 January: The mail finally arrived today and I received ten letters. This morning Elvis and Trooper Wiseman helped me boresight our gun in preparation for the move to Tuzla. Later on an artillery alert was sounded. We carried out the drill of getting under cover in one of the many large shelters now built in camp. Miss Kate Adie arrived at camp with loads of news and had lunch with the CO. Historically she is bad luck. Soldiers say that locations she visits are normally bombed afterwards; let's hope this is not true.*

*The sun has shone all day and the snow in the valley has gone, unfortunately leaving thick mud behind. With not much to do this afternoon I spent my time speaking with Major Andrew McDonald, 'C' Company commander. We discussed Bomb Alley and his knowledge of the BSA positions. I shared the little information I knew from the two Serb contacts we had in November. Andrew understood the main positions to be sited at the base of a broad forest firebreak, which he said was easily identifiable in the snow, rather like a chalk stripe. We will have to look out for this on our way up to Tuzla.*

*News tonight reported that the Deputy Prime Minister of Bosnia has been shot dead by Serbs at Sarajevo airport while under close protection of French UN troops. The APC carrying the Deputy PM was stopped by four tanks and forty men. A Serb opened the back door and carried out the assassination. Slobodan Milosevic, the Serbian President, has condemned the shooting and has claimed that the* assassin has been arrested. He now states that he will attend the Geneva peace talks. As a result nobody is allowed out of camp for the time being, unless absolutely necessary. The concern is that Muslims could now make reprisals against UN troops for this incompetence. Despite the curfew, Mark Jones made the short journey down to the Dutch/Belgian battalion in Busovaca where he is seeing a lieutenant called Veronica.

Abes had a word with me tonight and advised that I take my attachment with 'A' Company steadily at first and gradually win my spurs through hard work, so to speak. I have been a troop leader for nearly four years so find this rather patronizing, but it could only have been well meant.

A nurse who I have been spending some time talking to in the Mess grabbed me tonight outside and kissed me. I was rather taken aback and now find myself lending her my duvet while I am in Tuzla – she could have just asked. Lieutenant Alex Watts has invited three female interpreters to live in the subaltern's house. They claim to have been displaced from their own homes. Consequently I could not get into the bathroom tonight and when the electricity came on at 0600 hours the house fuses were immediately blown by Layla's hair drier. I had to have a cold water shave again. Thank goodness I am leaving tomorrow.

# 8

## BOMB ALLEY

Moving at speed, tracks whirring and clattering, our four white Scimitars skirted around sleepy Vitez which, sitting in a dip, was blanketed in early-morning mist. At the Dubravica checkpoint a local Croat police guard, wrapped in a parka, acknowledged my wave with a lethargic lift of his hand. Shadowed by rolling mountains the meandering journey north-east to Zenica was swift along the well-engineered twin-track road, giving us an important lead start to the long journey ahead.

Outside the Zenica depot ten immaculate white trucks formed an orderly line on the main road. Laden with sacks of wheat, they were destined for Banovici near Tuzla. These trucks, like most, were not fitted with radios; therefore, briefing the Danish civil defence commander, I explained our drills and signals, confirmed the route and recommended a number of pre-determined halts.

Our first stop was on the hard shoulder of the motorway near Kakanj so that one of the Scimitars could race into town and buy some fresh bread, which we ate while still shrouded in mist. There was very little traffic on the motorway, on average one vehicle was seen every quarter hour. Of these, common sites were tractors or horses with trailers carrying a family's worldly possessions or decrepit Lada cars. Occasionally an old Mercedes-Benz saloon would be seen. The choice of senior army officers and local mafia, these vehicles seemed never to have hubcaps and were always speeding.

At Visoko conditions were icy causing the trucks to slew and crab across the road, reducing our progress to a crawl. Regardless of the risk, the Danes were happy to continue and not stop to fit snow chains. Our Scimitar drivers, on the other hand, raved about the new studded track and the considerable traction it gave.

Improving weather allowed us to make up time along Route Acorn until we reached Milankovici where an old fuel tanker blocked the route. This was thanks to the far-reaching optimism of its driver who, with bald tyres and no snow chains, had tried to ascend a steep dirt track, which, in the shade of trees, was still covered by black ice. The tanker had ground to a halt near the lip of a small precipice, so not surprisingly the driver was reluctant to make further attempts for fear of disappearing over the edge with his livelihood. An unhelpful number of locals and other delayed drivers had crowded around the spectacle, all jabbering away with ideas, but failing to reach a constructive decision.

Each Scimitar carried two sandbags of grit, which we scattered under the tanker's tyres and in its path. This helped, but was not enough. With the track so narrow it was impossible to pass a Scimitar around the side of the truck in order to tow it out. At probably three times the weight of the Scimitar's eight tonnes neither did we really want to, a sure way to burn out a clutch. Just as I was contemplating pushing it with the nose of the lead Scimitar, a large and antiquated yellow bulldozer arrived up slope of us. It provided the fully laden tanker with just enough momentum to allow its spinning wheels to reach firm ground and gain traction. The onlookers cheered with relief. It had all been God's will!

By now it was early afternoon and wonderfully mild given the time of year. Continued tuning of the HF radio finally paid off when our sitrep to 'A' Company headquarters and estimate of our arrival time at their location was acknowledged. Before starting on the last leg of our journey my convoy halted outside the iron railings of the former glass-fibre factory in Kladanj. This had been deserted by our successors, 'A' Company, in favour of the former Yugoslavian Air Force camp on the outskirts of Tuzla, our final destination. Pausing here for a short break at the foot of Bomb Alley we ensured the Scimitars were properly prepared to run the gauntlet along this notoriously hostile pass.

In the hope that UN convoys would never again be attacked, the Commanding Officer had negotiated with the Bosnian Serb Army and agreed criteria, which, if fulfilled, would guarantee a convoy safe passage to Tuzla. Consequently we flew our sky-blue UN flags on top of the turrets; attractive to children, quickly soiled and in the way, they usually remained inside the turret. The vehicles' orange four-way flashers were switched on as further identification and I insisted that all gunners' and drivers' hatches were closed for protection. To have to go through this procedure was ridiculous and annoying; we were UN troops.

How the Bosnian Serbs could blatantly threaten our lives and, worse, the lives of truck drivers delivering humanitarian aid was beyond me. It was enough to make one's blood boil, but in order to keep a level head, emotion had to be suppressed. Already I knew that if fired upon I was going to reply robustly and had said as much in the Mess the night before. Not to do so would be a dereliction of duty and principle and this made me nervous. To have the responsibility for protecting lives and the means by which to do so, a loaded gun and rules of engagement, yet to take the easier and safer option of turning and not acting would be difficult to live with. It would also be more dangerous in the longer term. UNPROFOR, in the multi-national sense, was already known to be timid and indecisive. This position was risible in the eyes of locals and fast costing us their respect. The boy in the playground who had continually bitten his lip needed to give the school bully a swift right hook and show him for the coward he was. To put up with continued digs and snipes would only lead to others being bullied as well; it had to be stopped.

Our loaded Rarden cannons and machine guns were made ready and the working parts liberally oiled. It also seemed sensible to remove the green nylon muzzle covers from the cannons. Despite looking more professional and demonstrating our intent, that of safe and proactive protection, it would also prevent a bill being raised by the Quartermaster in the unlikely event of a scrap. There was not much that could be done directly to improve the safety of the Danish truck drivers, but partly to secure the route using a two-car piquet was a simple precaution.

Corporal Bremridge and I set off up the stretch of winding tarmac road to the start of Bomb Alley, the seven-kilometre section between Kladanj and Stupari. Advancing in a low gear to the top of the hillside road, a wonderful vista of the Gradovica Valley came in to view. From my open hatch I could see empty pastureland, topped with just enough snow for the black leafless woods beyond to be usefully in contrast. This was no man's land.

The nervous excitement of anticipating another run along here was all too apparent. The turret was quiet, broken only by attempts at jokes that would not have been funny had we not been about to imperil ourselves once more. For the last four weeks the troop had been unable to drive this stretch of Bosnian territory without being shelled by Serb mortars or direct-fire weapons. It was therefore probable that nothing had changed, even with the Commanding Officer's negotiations.

The two-car piquet was positioned off to the eastern edge of the road, the Scimitars about two hundred metres apart. Much of the roadside was covered by a berm, both natural and man-made, which, although afforded good cover, I chose to ignore, wanting our presence to be as conspicuous as possible. The piquet was a security measure, just a deterrent, and so to hide behind a fire position would have been contradictory. Therefore we sat track-up (the whole vehicle visible) and side-on making us even more obvious and vulnerable, but pointed in the right direction to be able to move off immediately to Stupari if necessary. Stupari was the location of my designated emergency *rendezvous* point should we get into a scrape and become separated. If nothing hostile happened this was also a safe location where we could later meet up.

Once in position, engine still running, Elvis traversed the gun off to the right in the direction of the Serbs so that we could scan for dug-in positions that might pose a threat to Sergeant Clarke's section and the convoy when they transited the route. The sun had dipped below the mountains to our rear, giving the sky a rich blueness, more like a cool autumn evening. Facing east into this clear sky, further illuminated by the ambient snow, there was still light available at a time of day when less ideal conditions would have seen it fading.

Both vehicles scanned the frontage constantly in order to identify any Serb positions that would pose a threat. Despite looking through x10 magnification sights, it was quite difficult to spot anything. The front line was between 2000 and 3000 metres away. The broad firebreak in the forest, which Major Andrew McDonald had mentioned, was prominent and, covered in snow, became a reference point known as the 'chalk stripe'. Once content that the threat from across the valley was covered, I called Sergeant Clarke on the radio, "Sierra three-one this is three-zero, there is no activity and the area to our front is covered; move when ready, over."

"Three-one roger out," Sergeant Clarke affirmed. Five minutes later the rumble of the convoy became louder until Corporal Payne's Scimitar (S33) could be seen leading the trucks towards me. With Elvis busy scanning in front I turned to count all ten DAF trucks pass on the road behind us. Convoy discipline was good, with cautious 200 metre spaces between each, and the drivers and commanders were wearing helmets and flak jackets. Counting the tenth truck confirmed to me that our good preparations and deterrent had been worthwhile and for once looked like keeping the Serbs silent.

No sooner had I dropped down into my turret than I heard and felt the shock of an explosion, which, from experience, I guessed to be a mortar round. This was echoed within seconds by another shell, followed by three further explosions in short succession, all within the area of an imaginary football pitch. Sergeant Clarke, who, behind

82

the tenth truck, was just passing my vehicle, quickly came to a halt. He claimed to have seen the signature from an active Serb mortar base plate. "Three-one, this is three-zero, have you seen a target, over?" I said immediately in a deliberately measured tone, trying to control my speech from speeding up.

"Three-one, the mortars are over to the right; reference chalk stripe, at the top of that, over," came Sergeant Clarke's unflustered but keen reply.

"Three-zero, roger wait . . . three-zero, no that's not clear to me, I can't see them, are you sure?"

"Three-zero, this is three-two, if the firing continues three-one can fire a sabot round onto the position to identi . . . ."

"Three-zero, say again."

"I've got incoming, I need to move, wait out!" A volley of mortar rounds had showered Corporal Bremridge. Our two Scimitars had been in position for far too long. We needed to extract ourselves as soon as possible, but, because we could not just lay down indiscriminate suppressive fire, this would be tricky. Furthermore, if the Serbs were left unchallenged it might lead to them tracking our withdrawal to our emergency *rendezvous* for an easier target. Essentially we needed to neutralize their mortars in the next few seconds or the mortar bombs would soon be ranged on to us, if not already on their way!

"Three-zero, this is three-one, permission to open fire, over?" came an enthusiastic request from Sergeant Clarke. At this time, despite the tactical problem being simple enough, there was a lot to think about. Furthermore my judgement was clouded by my UN conscience, that of engaging the Serbs under the restrictive rules of engagement. I don't mind admitting that I was also probably a little too hung up on trying to control every call sign rather than explaining what I wanted to achieve and letting them get on with it. Something needed doing quickly if we were to extract ourselves safely and it was my responsibility to think of it.

"Three-one, three-zero, if you can identify the target then go for it," came my reply after a mental appreciation of all the factors that lasted a very long ten to fifteen seconds, but seemed like minutes. Meanwhile Corporal Bremridge was telling me that mortar rounds had bracketed his position; we were still sitting track up on the road, fully exposed. To have moved behind a berm would not really have helped, but most likely have slowed us further and denied us the use of our weapons. The Serbs knew the range to the road, so the mortar fire could therefore have easily been predicted on to any small covered areas that we withdrew behind.

"Three-zero, this is three-one, confirm you will allow me to fire?" Sergeant Clarke repeated, making it quite apparent that operating as UN troops was inhibiting his normally forthright style; we could not just fire at will.

"Three-zero, yes, I order you to fire," came my unequivocal response, hopefully removing any further hesitation. The glowing orange tracer element of the 30mm sabot round flew at nearly 1200 metres per second across the valley to the Serb position. It fell short, so was followed by a corrected shot. As soon as it landed Corporal Bremridge spoke up on the air.

"Three-zero, three-two, position identified, I am putting down suppressive fire, withdraw now." As Corporal Bremridge's crew started to engage the Serb mortars, the whole valley erupted into an uncontrolled fire-fight. Five separate Serb positions were clearly identifiable and all now firing at us. The mortars landed around us in abundance, while closer positions at nearly 2000 metres were firing heavy machine guns, most likely 12.7mm DshKHAA. One position had what could only have been an anti-aircraft gun firing directly at us, I assessed 20mm. But the excessive fire was not just incoming. The glow of orange tracer rounds criss-crossed the valley so prolifically that it looked like a deliberate weapon effects demonstration. At first I presumed this to be the troop getting over-zealous and my concern was that I was responsible for initiating an uncontrolled turkey shoot. It was in fact the Croats who, enthused by the UN's response for once, had decided to come out of their trenches to help us. The situation that had been created must have given the Serbs the impression that we were anything but impartial, but then they had started the fight in the first place.

"*Shell*, top of chalk stripe, two thousand, mortar position," I ordered Elvis.

"Two thousand *on*," Elvis screamed back in a drilled response that, like all of us, had previously only ever been practised on the tank ranges in Castlemartin and Bergen-Hohne.

"Loaded fire," I yelled.

"Firing *now* . . . *misfire*!" Elvis said, quite surprised. The gun had not fired. There was no excuse for my poor gun drills. In the excitement, and thinking about everything else, I had forgotten to wind the cocking handle of my own gun, critical in the circumstances. With three vigorous anti-clockwise turns the round made a beautiful clunk

84

as it entered the chamber, confirmed by the green arrow on the gun condition indicator. "Loaded, fire," I cried out again, having quickly rectified the foolish and basic error.

"Firing *now*," Elvis shouted, glee beginning to surface in his voice from finally being able to return fire at the Serbs rather than sitting in the open like a lame duck. "Add two hundred," he reported, as gunners are taught to do when the round drops short of the target. In this case the round had dropped way short and two thousand metres was already the maximum range of the gun sights. The only way to increase the range was to judge every extra hundred metres needed by one turn of the gun's elevation hand wheel. I gave a commander's correction, "Add four hundred . . . loaded, fire."

"Firing *now* . . . *bollocks*," Elvis bleated in frustration as the round still went minus of the target. The mortar positions were eventually engaged at over 3000 metres, which could be regarded as ineffective, but a High Explosive round is a small amount of ordnance, which, if it reaches its target, has an effect: it keeps heads down.

The picture was now busier, but clearer because gloves were off and all we needed to do was keep the Serbs' heads down while the convoy completed the move to Stupari and we withdrew north to join them at the emergency *rendezvous*. Corporal Payne had not been heard from, most likely having the common sense to stay off a busy radio net. Hoping that he would soon be waiting with ten trucks in safety, I attempted to send a contact report to 'A' Company, but there was no reply. Communications among the hills were often hit or miss. The company would not have been able to do anything anyway and I had more pressing concerns than to keep trying.

"Three-zero, three-two, the next rounds are going to hit me; I'm withdrawing," came Corporal Bremridge's message that I had heard peripherally in my earphones before, but had failed to acknowledge due to our busy turret. Frankly, had I had rounds bracket my vehicle I would not have bothered asking! "Roger, move now, we're right behind you . . . Elvis, *travus left*, travus left, travus left . . . *on*, two thousand, mortars on snowy knoll," I shouted, bringing the gun on to a new target. It appeared to be a mortar base plate and a heavy machine gun co-located, much closer than the previous position. "Two thousand *on*," Elvis's screamed back with his face pressed into the rubber face pad of the sight. I inserted another clip of yellow tipped H.E. rounds into the gun, "Loaded-fire."

"Firing *now* . . . add two hundred. Firing *now* . . . add one hundred. Firing *now* . . . *target*, three rounds," Elvis said in a steadier voice, but clearly enjoying himself as he completed the full engagement. At this point Yozza piped up from his driver's cab in an eager scouse accent, "Shair, we're gettin' fu'kin' engaged, the tracer's comin' in, we've gotta fu'kin' moove." Sure enough through my periscope I witnessed a stream of large red tracer rounds flying towards us. Extraordinarily, the long bursts, very pretty in the closing daylight, did not hit the vehicle but were self-detonating a couple of hundred metres in front of us. Each one created a puff of black smoke as it exploded. This was anti-aircraft ammunition, designed to produce flak in the sky and also very effective against lightly armoured vehicles, if in range!

"Okay Yozza, let's get the fuck out of here, move now." No sooner had I said this when Elvis shouted, "*Stop*, I can see the man loading the mortars." Thankfully, the anti-aircraft gun had stopped firing so I went with it. "Stop there, Yozza; Elvis, range?"

"Two-two hundred," he answered. I turned the gun condition selector to R for Rapid and reported, "Loaded; *fire*."

"Firing *now* . . . add two hundred. Firing *now* . . . *target*. Firing *now* . . . *target*, three rounds." I loaded another clip of H.E. and cried out loudly, "*Go on*."

Elvis continued, "Firing *now* . . . *misfire*." Short-cutting the drill, I lifted the gun's top cover to look at the condition of the rounds sitting on the feed slide. Jammed at an oblique angle, I had not seated them correctly in the rush. Looking through my high magnification sight I could see that the man who had been loading the mortar tube was now running as fast as his legs would carry him down the snow-covered knoll towards a small village, which I later worked out to be Pepici. Seconds earlier he had been trying to kill us and so, still fired up, Elvis tracked his movement and I fired the GPMG. A stream of orange tracer arched through the sky, but, burning out at 1100 metres, denied us the ability to see the fall of shot. A guessed correction followed by another burst was wasted as the man ran into cover.

More than ever, I was aware that we needed to extract our vehicle as soon as possible, but it was proving difficult. Having had a couple of engagements, Corporal Bremridge and Sergeant Clarke were able to jockey from their positions while I covered them and had moved further down the road so that they could now cover our withdrawal. A second from telling Yozza to move again, a heavy machine gun engaged us from the bottom of the valley, about 1500 metres away. This was comparatively close, but the rounds were falling wide. Having not had the time to unjam the 30mm shell, I continued with the machine gun, which, with its solenoid not working, meant that I, not Elvis, had to pull the trigger manually. This situation required the fire orders to be reversed.

"One five hundred *on*," Elvis reported to let me know he had the target in his sights.

"Loaded," I replied. The machine gun sits in front of the commander and, like the Rarden cannon, is the commander's responsibility to load.

"Fire," Elvis ordered, to let me know he was still ready.

"Firing *now*," I pulled the trigger in a ranging burst of about ten rounds, half of which I could see by the orange tracer, which, now the gun was warm, were burning out even shorter. Elvis and I made a crew effort by predicting the fall of shot and corrected the gun accordingly. Once target had been established the engagement changed to killing bursts, sixteen to twenty rounds for each burst. One burst of fire was all that was needed to open a window for withdrawal and avoid further entanglement. Lines of orange tracer screamed across our front as Sergeant Clarke opened up with his GPMG at the same position in order to cover our movement.

Yozza had got the Scimitar ripping down the hill to Stupari at quite some speed, past Sergeant Clarke who was still firing his machine gun, and past Corporal Bremridge who was scanning for targets. By the time we were at the bottom of the hill the Scimitar was hurtling along at 60mph, which I would normally consider unnecessarily dangerous. The other two vehicles peeled off behind and followed us into the village; it was now dusk. Corporal Payne called me on the radio to let us know that all the trucks were safely in the lee of a row of houses on the main road and that we would see him if we continued along it.

Linking up with Corporal Payne was a relief. Once the three of us stopped I told everyone to check that guns were made safe and to dismount for a debrief and a pause to calm down before we continued to Banovici, where the trucks still had to be escorted. Elvis, a trained signaller, made further attempts to send a contact report but found the 10 amp fuse had blown. Sergeant Clarke tried to send the report for me but was strangely unsuccessful too. Nobody had been injured and 'A' Company was still in blissful ignorance, so it mattered not for the moment. We would press on and wait until within range of the VHF radio.

The Danish drivers were in good form and said that they had been very lucky to escape being hit. At least two had had dirt and shrapnel spray their armoured windscreens, but with no damage caused. Corporal Payne and his crew were, understandably, a little miffed at being the only ones not to be involved. I reminded everyone of the importance of his role and in front of the troop thanked Corporal Payne's crew for executing the orders correctly by staying with the convoy and protecting them throughout.

Workers at the Banovici depot had been expecting us and launched themselves into the task of unloading straight away. Meanwhile the crews continued to exchange accounts of the event again and again. The whole occurrence had not even started to sink in. I spoke on the radio with 'A' Company operations room, allowing me to report the incident to their second-in-command, Captain David Sherlock. He wanted me to go straight to the company base so that I could give a full account, something that would have to be recorded as a statement for the chain of command and reported as a press release for the media. The media were going to lap this story up after weeks of tedious convoys. While the food aid had been delivered, the Danes still needed escorting into the centre of Tuzla where they were to spend the night. Sergeant Clarke and Corporal Bremridge dealt with that while Corporal Payne and I headed off in the dark for the airfield.

The first thing I noticed was that 'A' Company's operations room was centrally heated. Dave Sherlock stood at the doorway and shook my hand with unbridled satisfaction. An Intelligence Corps corporal sat down with David and me to talk the whole contact through. David's main concern was whether I had had my UN flags flying and my four-way flashers on. When I told him that we had sat track-up for almost fifteen minutes with our flashers going while being engaged by everything the Serbs had to chuck at us he was surprised that we had made it at all, as was I.

The statement, which I was obliged to write, I later dictated down the telephone to a very pleased B Squadron Leader sitting in Vitez. On putting down the telephone receiver David stuck a pencil drawing of an oak leaf on my chest. Looking at this very accurate drawing I remember saying, "I certainly don't deserve one of those David, the whole thing was a bloody nightmare. Troop fire control went out of the window and I even forgot to wind the gun on; in fact I can't remember anything that went right." David's reassuringly paternal reply was most comforting, "Well Monty, you got the trucks and your troop to the depot safely. Mission achieved. What more could you want?"

# 9

# RIBNICA

"All rise," the clerk of the court ordered as the Judge Advocate entered the wooden panelled room in his red gown, accompanied by two senior officers. Wearing Service Dress, I stood rigidly to attention, my Sam Browne shining and medals gleaming. Family, friends and regimental colleagues were present in the gallery, as well as members of the media. Once the Judge Advocate and the senior officers had taken their seats the clerk of the court asked me to step forward and, passing me a brown leather-bound bible said, "Repeat after me . . ."

The Judge Advocate opened the proceedings by listing the charges against me: Non-compliance of the rules of engagement, provoking hostile fire, maliciously endangering the lives of civilians, and so on. The prosecution was then asked to present the case for the Crown. The Army's lawyer addressed the court, giving evidence for more than two hours. He called a number of witnesses, including the man who had run from the mortar base plate down the hill to Pepici. This spineless specimen, who had fired at civilians escorting humanitarian aid, stood grinning in the knowledge that he could hide safely behind the complex laws governing the rules of engagement.

This Army's barrister was dreadful, a figure unfit to be seen in uniform, and bereft of operational experience, who used the benefit of hindsight and weeks of examining the evidence to dissect actions that, during the incident, I had had only seconds to consider. Believing unequivocally in my innocence, I had decided to make my own defence. The time had come for me to stand up and justify my actions.

"Sir, the commander on the ground carries responsibility for his men and is invested with the authority to take whatever actions he deems appropriate to fulfil his mission, providing it is within the rules of engagement and beyond reasonable doubt. The action of piqueting the route prior to the convoy passing along it was not aggressive, as the prosecution has implied, merely prudent. The various agreed measures to identify the convoy as UNPROFOR were carried out in full. The decision to return fire was made in order to suppress the Serb positions engaging my convoy and thus improve the chances of safe escape of the soft-skinned vehicles and their endangered civilian drivers. Furthermore, on the basis of constant Serb sniping since arrival in theatre, it is reasonable to say that to have not confronted the Serb attackers would have been a failure to deter them from continued intimidation of humanitarian aid convoys. Had these robust actions not been taken and a Danish driver had become a casualty, then the charges against me might have been quite the reverse. My mission was to deliver humanitarian aid safely to Banovici, which is what I did. No one in my convoy asked to be fired at, but once endangered the appropriate response was made. Only time will determine the effect this action has on the Bosnian Serbs and their intentions towards peace keepers along the road between Kladanj and Stupari and elsewhere."

The Judge Advocate looked up from his notes. Peering at me over the top of his half moon spectacles his face and voice failed to mask the outcome. "Lieutenant Woolley, before passing sentence, have you anything further to say?"

"No Sir."

"Lieutenant Woolley, after consulting the bench you have been found guilty of the charges against you. You are to be dishonourably discharged with immediate effect . . . adjutant," he summoned, "take this man away." For some reason my old school House Captain was the adjutant. He walked across the courtroom and in an instant ripped the United Nations medal from my chest. Two school prefects, bizarrely Justin and Billy, dragged me, kicking and screaming, down the stone steps of the main hall. Friends in the gallery now looked at me with righteous disdain. My old school's cadet force commandant stared at me with disappointment and said, "You weren't meant to use the guns, they were for the fifteen metre indoor range only". Inexplicably the Serb soldier who had run to Pepici was also the provost sergeant. He threw me into a bare cell which had sterile white walls, slammed the door and let out a laugh from the depths of his belly.

Seeing my rifle with magazine fitted lying close by my camp bed was a comfort. Next to it were my boots and resting on top of them, like a trophy, my sky-blue beret. In the empty corridor I could hear David Sherlock's hearty laugh echo off the thick walls. The room was bare and newly whitewashed. The bad dream was quickly forgotten as I recalled that I had good reason to be happy. My sense of well-being reminded me of waking in a Mediterranean hospital after a tonsil operation, relieved to discover all my limbs still attached. The room was silent. All that could now be heard was the noise of a strong wind shaking the trees outside. The enormous office windows had no curtains to shield me from the bright winter sunshine. Yesterday had been real, but all was now well; I felt contented and free of concern.

The troop's Scimitars were garaged under a lean-to near the base's disused airfield. This was a walk of a kilometre from the company headquarters and accommodation. The troop's guns, which late the night before had been liberally oiled as a temporary measure, needed a good dig out ready to resume operational commitments. The boys cleaned the guns with renewed devotion, more than ever aware of the importance of such chores.

A change in the troop's mood was distinctly apparent. This was nothing as dramatic as them going to bed boys and waking up as grown men, but life had most certainly been given a dose of reality and perspective. After a good nights' sleep, the gravity of the previous day's event had been digested. The result was a bunch of lads who appeared very happy, more confident and far more interested in their job, having recognized that escorting was not just for show. Mixed with plenty of banter, this created a wonderful atmosphere of a properly gelled team whose collective experience to date was now harnessed by olympic morale and self-esteem that I hoped would remain in credit for some time to come.

Yesterday's contact was the first such event for the battlegroup since arriving in Bosnia and thus was the talk of the company. Praise was forthcoming from every quarter. While the troop and I cleaned machine guns in the sunshine it seemed odd to think that my family would be waking up in UK and, switching on radios, learn of the incident, yet probably not know who was responsible for it. When I returned to the block for lunch, however, the situation had changed. An operator in the company operations room said that there was a message from the Commanding Officer, which all personnel were to read.

ON THE MATTER WHERE WE HAD TO OPEN FIRE. DO NOT OPEN FIRE UNLESS CAST IRON CASE. YESTERDAY`S INCIDENT WAS AN OUTRAGE. MIGHT NOT HAVE HAD REASON TO DO SO. MUST NOT OPEN FIRE. ANYONE WHO OPENS FIRE MUST ACCOUNT FOR HIMSELF TO CO, ESPECIALLY OFFICERS AND SNCOS. IT IS NOT OPEN SEASON. WE HAVE NOT TAKEN COVERS OFF WEAPONS, ESPECIALLY NORTH OF KLADANJ. BEWARE RULES OF ENGAGEMENT.

The statement froze me to the spot as I had been anticipating praise in the wake of teaching the Serbs not to interfere with UN convoys. The morale I had been languishing in evaporated in an instant. After lunch I assembled the troop and read out the signal. Not surprisingly they were angry, more so than me, but I assured the soldiers that they need not concern themselves as the decision to open fire had been mine alone.

But this statement *was* their concern, for its tone would shape their future thinking and attitudes. Every time a troop or platoon deployed on a task from camp it needed to be confident of undeniable support from the chain of command for its actions. This message, on the other hand, was likely to infest the ranks with over-cautiousness and dangerous hesitation. The rules of engagement were already ambiguous and difficult to apply to every scenario and this knee-jerk edict could only make matters worse.

The more I reflected on the statement, the more my young head became angry. This was going to put us in an awkward position, and it was *us*, the young officers, NCOs and troopers, whose necks had been on the line every day. Troops needed to be trusted by senior commanders, and politicians, and it made me wonder just how some of them might react confronted with the same situation. It's not easy fighting a turret for real. Maybe I had stolen someone's limelight for a day!

Understandably the Commanding Officer was counselling his troops to be cautious. The last thing he wanted was for everyone to think that it was okay to shoot first. A hostile response in a situation when you can walk away might destabilize the peace process, or worse, get one of his soldiers killed. He had reason to be concerned, but I saw it differently. I did not want my action to be criticized.

The way I interpreted this response had taught me two invaluable lessons. Firstly, when my soldiers are trying to do their job in future, but may lack experience, I must always support their decisions, or better say nothing before examining the evidence. Secondly, if a rollocking is required, do it in private and be specific, do not give catch-all statements that may be difficult to interpret or may conflict with doctrine. If you don't support the boys when they have acted in good faith, but look to be worried for your own skin, then you may lose their trust, respect and confidence. The day had been a black one for the troop and me and for all the junior commanders who had read this message and were now being asked to do even more, to lead dangerous convoys and bite their lip if they got shot at.

Fortunately the Rt Hon Sir Malcolm Rifkind MP, Secretary of State for Defence, did not seem to think that our actions had been inappropriate when he reported the robust and successful action of the British Battlegroup to the House of Commons. There was a rumble of approval from The House.

My new immediate boss, Major Martyn Thomas, 'A' Company commander, posed a question in a conference that night: "When is a mortar attack ever a cast-iron case?" When mortar bombs drop around the armoured vehicles they are only a small threat to crews, but if a round were to hit a vehicle it would be likely to kill someone. With measured consideration he stipulated that Bomb Alley was to be avoided for the near future and asked that all commanders consider the alternatives before replying with bullets and shells. This was a sensible way of getting the message across without frightening soldiers into thinking that the consequences of using force could be worse from one's own chain of command than the actual life-threatening situation they are intent on evading.

The newspapers did not cover this newsworthy incident as fully as I would have hoped, due to scandalous news breaking at home over a high-profile marriage that was failing; Andy Warhol would be disappointed! My one chance for a famous fifteen minutes, my story of a skirmish in a neglected corner of south-eastern Europe, had been thwarted by a story that held greater intrigue and relevance with the British tabloid readership; right place, wrong time. A couple of days later, however, we received a copy of the *Daily Mail* which ran the headlines: **Ambushed Lancers hit back with cannon shells – BRITISH TANKS FIRE ON SERBS**. It also gave the name of 3 Troop B Squadron 9th/12th Lancers, a much needed fillip for the boys.

*Tuesday 12 January: Early this morning Sergeant Clarke and Corporal Payne went to Celic with an aid convoy. My section's vehicles needed maintaining, but the boys were late to the tank park. It is evident that they think themselves untouchable since Sunday and have been reminded that they are not. Today I had my first proper chat with Mayda, one of two female interpreters. She must be nearly six feet tall and is very slim. Her hair is dark and is styled in a bob, which complements her long and slender neck and pale complexion very well. She has a most composed and sophisticated bearing. She also seems to enjoy wearing black clothes, which suit her. The male environment is fairly straightforward and laddish, which I enjoy, but as soon as a woman comes on to the scene the situation changes and behaviour does as well. I can't deny that my concentration is being diverted from my primary responsibility of looking after the troop's interests, which is a dreadful thing to admit, but we are still enjoying a bit of a honeymoon. Mayda is 22 and her home is in Tuzla town centre. Her father is the town's mayor, which may have something to do with her getting the interpreter job!*

After two days of basking in our glory and getting bored doing it, I was very pleased to be tasked with a recce of a small village called Ribnica. Ribnica was twenty-five kilometres south-east of Zavidovici. Had 3 Troop been successful in passing the Muslim checkpoint out of Zavidovici, the road would have taken us through the Bosnian Serb controlled land and south east to Ribnica.

In the morning I found a note on my desk from Lieutenant Mike Dooley (Royal Signals). It read, "Not happy with recce plan." He wanted the six armoured vehicles grouped for security reasons in this very dangerous area. "Hogwash!" What did he know about recce?

Mounted in two Scimitars Corporal Payne and I led Dooley's platoon to the Banovici checkpoint, just short of Ribnica. Despite their superior engines, the larger Warriors struggled to keep up with us along the narrow winding lanes. On arrival Cooper disappeared to liaise with the BiH and ask them for permission to view their front line, which they allowed.

Half an hour later and sticking to the original plan, Cooper and four Warriors peeled off to the town centre. They were escorted by Muslim soldiers driving a clapped-out yellow Mercedes saloon. My section circled to the south of Ribnica taking with us Sergeant Stubberfield and his potentially useful anti-mine device mounted on the front of his armoured personnel carrier. Sergeant Stubberfield led the three vehicles and Corporal Payne brought up the rear as we headed off to gather information in the valley. The patrol arrived at a recently resurfaced track, which, due to the mine threat, was treated cautiously. This was the same road that Mark Cooper and Bob Ryan had had a fire-fight on during the initial stages of the tour. Mark had informed me that, further along, a Serb T-55 tank was parked by a crossroads with a crew partial to shooting anything non-Serb. I warned the section of the danger and the necessity to turn back well short of this point.

A scruffy and unshaven Muslim soldier stepped out of his sentry box, which stood at the side of the track. He shouted up to me, "*Mine, Chetnik, ne dobro.*" This seemed good advice, given the threat. Were they informing us because they actually cared or were they trying to divert an interest that they did not want? Turning to Corporal Payne and his crew I asked if they were prepared to take the risk, as it was not essential that we prove this route. Everyone was confident and keen to venture down the track in the knowledge that the plough was available to remove any surface-laid mines in our path. Ignoring the Muslim soldier's better judgement, we proceeded down this potentially hostile road with foolhardy British invincibility, always aiming to push our luck to the limits and come home with as much information as possible.

As usual my map was tucked under the sight cowling in front of me for easy reading. Due to its small scale it was easy to misread, so in such circumstances I relied on the GPS for confirmation. Leaning down into the turret to read our exact grid reference off the digital display I realized that we had driven 200 metres further north than I had intended. Before I could call Sergeant Stubberfield on the radio and tell him to turn around, I heard the familiar "Crump, crump, crump" of mortar rounds landing in quick succession, and simultaneously the rattle of automatic small-arms fire.

Houses on the edge of this small rural village were widely dispersed. My immediate response was naturally to quickly drop down into the turret for safety. Looking through my dusty sight, I scanned for a firing point but could not identify one. Elvis, having already been down in the turret, had initiated a fire order, normally the commander's job: "Coax on, two hundred, Serbs by house and they're fucking well firing at us."

"Seen, wait . . . no, stop . . . Yozza you're gonna have to reverse, we can't engage," I said, trying to assess the situation within three seconds.

"Sir I've god'em. I can cut the basta'ds in half frum 'ere," Elvis cried with his usual enthusiasm. Pausing for a second, I could see the detail of their faces through my sight. The two soldiers were standing quite openly by the side of a white house. One was using its wall as support for his AK-47 while the other was adopting the kneeling position, but neither was heavily armed. Elvis was right. At such close range a killing burst from the GPMG would have literally chopped the two Serbs in half.

Sergeant Stubberfield's vehicle was reversing towards us at speed. We could not escape until we had covered his extraction. Elvis had traversed our gun over the left side, blocking his exit and nearly causing his vehicle to strike our barrel. Sergeant Stubberfield was handicapped by a large steel mesh stowage bin mounted on the top of his vehicle, which was bulging with a surfeit of engineer paraphernalia. This obstructed his periscopic view and had caused him to stand three feet out of his hatch in full view of the Serbs, which demanded some courage. His vehicle's only armament was a light machine-gun, formerly known as a Bren gun, an excellent weapon in its day, but only holding a thirty-two-round magazine. Sergeant Stubberfield had, more than anyone, sensibly fought off the temptation to fire back, being more occupied with guiding his driver out of this precarious position. Meanwhile I was trying to send Cooper a contact report, but failed to receive any acknowledgement.

All this time the sound of mortar rounds crumping and small-arms fire rat-a-tat-tatting was all around us. On several occasions I looked through the periscopes and witnessed the dark grey clouds of earth and smoke pluming twenty feet high as the munitions exploded between our vehicles. Goodness knows how they had failed to hit us, but they had and it was adding enormous pressure for us to move, an operation that was not that simple.

Our cue to withdraw was Sergeant Stubberfield peeling past us. Preparing to reverse, I looked through my rear periscope and was disappointed to see only dried mud and the green canvas pouches of my old '58 Pattern webbing. Gingerly I stuck my head and shoulders out of the turret to guide the vehicle rearwards, but immediately heard the deafening report of automatic fire at close range, sounding very much as if it was aimed at me. My instinct to drop back in the turret was hugely exaggerated, the same type of reflex as when someone kicks a football at you from close range, just more lethal! Fortunately Elvis' better orientation and unclustered periscopes allowed him to guide Yozza back under fire without risking sticking his head out of the turret. His composure was appreciated. Relieved of this task, I was able to look forwards and further consider the situation. We had to avoid opening fire, we could not go forward; we had to reverse and no one was replying to my radio report. It was a frustrating moment, but one I knew I should not have driven into.

While we were peeling off, turning about and traversing our gun rearwards in the direction of threat, Corporal Payne was covering us and also crying to engage some Serb sitting ducks, which I was forced to deny him. Our three vehicles withdrew back down the track at speed, Corporal Payne leaving last. Keeping out of danger but wanting to record this hostile experience, I held my camera out of the turret and took some speculative snaps in the manner that a cautious American GI in Vietnam might have fired his M16 rifle out of a fox-hole.

Meeting Cooper at the RV point, we took a breather, letting the situation return to calm before continuing our journey. The incident had been an extremely adrenalin-pumping ten minutes, not so much from what was being fired at us, but because of how close we were and how difficult extraction had been. The proximity of rounds landing around us suggested that the BSA were either trying to kill us, but were inaccurate, or were attempting to intimidate and deter us and thus were extremely accurate.

While we had been busy thinking we were in the thick of it, hostilities between Croat and Muslim had broken in Gornji Vakuf where 'B' Company, 1 Cheshire, commanded by Major Alistair Rule, were based. The marked deterioration in the Croat-Muslim alliance was not, however, affecting our lives yet.

# IO

# TUZLA

The trouble that had fomented between Croat and Muslim factions first came to the battlegroup's attention on the 10 January when a Muslim man was shot dead at a Croat checkpoint in Novi Travnik. This murder created ill feeling in the town and as a result a tit-for-tat ensued with both sides each taking three or four soldiers hostage. The Commanding Officer reacted speedily with delicate mediation and secured an agreement for a subsequent hostage exchange.

These tremors of division between Croat and Muslim were mere preliminaries to a full-scale battle that flared up in Gorni Vakuf on 12 January. The situation had not been helped by the Vance-Owen Peace Plan. Still only a concept, and not signed up to by the Bosnian government, this plan had designated Gorni Vakuf a future Croat Canton, despite the town being home to a majority Muslim community. In view of this, Croat leaders decided that immediate action to take control of the town should be made and the unconditional surrender of all Muslims demanded. Gornji Vakuf's outlying villages were systematically attacked with prolonged tank and artillery bombardments before being used as vantage points to target the Muslim town centre and force this process on. With everything to lose, the less well-equipped Muslims were credited with holding on to their territory against the odds through shear tenacity and courage.

'B' Company's base was a few hundred metres from Gornji Vakuf town centre, an area of intense fighting, placing its soldiers dangerously in the line of fire. A proliferation of deadly ordnance – mortar, machine gun and even rocket – rained down around the members of 'B' Company daily; miraculously none were injured inside camp. It was on 13 January, however, during this inter-faction fighting, that Lance Corporal Wayne Edwards of the 1st Battalion, Royal Regiment of Wales (a Cheshire augmentee) was killed while driving a Warrior patrolling Gornji Vakuf. He was shot in the head by a sniper, believed to be a Croat.

A series of observations made during everyday events led me to suspect that the Bosnian people's confidence in UNPROFOR was shifting. Local soldiers used confrontational language, the mildest being "UNPROFOR *ne dobro*." Civilians no longer gave friendly waves to us with hopeful and trusting faces. Attitudes were more aggressive and less tolerant. I regularly had to lean on my British rather than UN status to gain the desired end-game at checkpoints and meetings, which was perhaps a touch deceitful. This tragic death of one of our soldiers was the crowning insult; a perfectly lethal shot to the head was unlikely to be accidental cross-fire. The honeymoon welcome enjoyed by us appeared to be over; we were clearly not equipped or mandated to fulfil the fanciful aspirations that some Bosnian people had had in mind for us from the outset. Nevertheless it was increasingly apparent that changing events were causing our conduct of operations to creep away from the original mission of humanitarian aid-escorting to more of a security role.

Despite numerous attempts and initial success by Colonel Bob in brokering a ceasefire, influenced by this murder of a British peace-keeping soldier, the guns did not remain silent long. Ultimately the hostility in Gornji Vakuf was not contained. Far away in Tuzla, however, the fragile co-operation between Croat and Muslim was still holding. Instead it was the Serbs who remained the faction posing the most immediate and significant threat to peace and stability there. This Serb threat was also the greater in Turbe, a few kilometres from the battlegroup's headquarters in Vitez; two operational prongs of pressure that, with other axes, enveloped the weaker factions and attempted to slowly strangle them.

In view of the increased and unnecessary risk to British UN soldiers, unequipped for fighting, HM Government continued with its contingency planning for a complete evacuation. The Royal Navy aircraft carrier HMS *Ark Royal* was deployed off the Dalmatian coast with light artillery and Royal Marine commandos ready to support a fighting withdrawal, in the worst case.

As a consequence of the conflict spreading and heating there was much international frustration. The Geneva peace talks looked set for failure and the UN's threat of imposing a 'no fly' zone over Bosnia a very real possibility. Sarajevo was also suffering a heightened period of activity. The city had not settled since the assassination of the Bosnian vice-president some weeks previously. Characteristic of this form of siege warfare, in January the Serbs shelled the city repeatedly from the safety of the surrounding hills. On one occasion the Serb guns fired 140 shells in to Tomislavgrad, fortunately missing the British National Support Element base. From some quarters came a theory that the Croats had made an unofficial pact with the Bosnian Serbs against the Muslims, an accusation that looked increasingly real. Whenever the HVO attacked the Muslim BiH there was more often than not a coincidental lull in Serb activity.

This inter-faction fighting was thwarting the flow of humanitarian aid into Bosnia. During the first three weeks in Tuzla 3 Troop escorted only two convoys, a fact that made the boys a little fidgety, but no less so than the rest of 'A' Company. The troop was, at least, fortunate to have morale in credit. Two brief skirmishes with the Serbs was enough action to sustain us through this period of inactivity.

Initially the troop enjoyed squandering time and being idle. Nevertheless, I was acutely aware of my responsibility for man management and, in the absence of anything meaningful to do, my remit to search for ways of training and entertaining them. Boredom in soldiers is a disaster waiting to happen. Motivation and standards can quite easily slip in the less well disciplined and with it professionalism, making a weak soldier a liability to the whole team when a task does finally come about. Boredom is not unknown for taking casualties; the foolhardy soldier fiddles with his rifle and ammunition once too often at his peril.

Potentially there was plenty that could be done as a diversion. One lesson a day taken from the core skills of vehicle recognition, first aid, HF radio training and so on, lasted for a period, but the resources to train properly were, in the main, not available, making it all fairly dry. Furthermore the skills that were relevant to operations in Bosnia were handled for real on a daily basis anyway, so did not need practising. Physical Training had not always been practicable due to the risk of being shot at, although in Tuzla the airfield was available to let off steam. Limitations, such as these, forces the innovative troop leader to invent methods of amusing the troop, which today's soldier quite often detects as nugatory and does not thank you for. Day trips and adventurous training were not options and after-dinner speakers strangely in short supply. Performing skits and holding quizzes did not seem to have the same appeal with young troopers as it might have had their grandfathers; the world has moved on. Army welfare books and gymnasium equipment, personal stereos and computer games, however, formed the basis of leisure time, individual pursuits that far from engendered team spirit.

Vehicle servicing was fundamental to keeping the Scimitars roadworthy, the staple of the contemporary cavalry trooper's daily schedule. But not even this could be relied upon to consume available working hours as it does so readily when trying to reduce them. Each Scimitar was clocking up an unusually high mileage compared to that allocated in peacetime. Such regular use was beneficial for engines and transmissions, but was paid for with components. Spares were on a high priority, but were not forthcoming at the rate our mileage demanded them, and so not only were the vehicles often unserviceable, but the much-needed employment that fitting spares brought also dried up. Sergeant Clarke waited three weeks for a new wheel hub, essentially keeping his section off the road during that time. The longer a vehicle was left unused the more susceptible it was to other components failing, a vicious circle. It was perplexing to consider how budget-conscious civil servants could permit such false economy while UK national papers continued to report on heroic British soldiers escorting aid convoys daily. My troop constituted some 4% of the battlegroup's front-line armoured vehicles and half of it was sitting idle. Sometimes three of our four Scimitars were unserviceable, which members of the company were not slow in teasing us about, their Warriors being much newer and far more reliable. The situation was hugely frustrating.

Notwithstanding our underemployment, there was little else to complain about. The accommodation was heated allowing the brain and body to function properly, the food very good; the weather was fine but cold, mail was arriving and 'A' Company were welcoming and friendly. Soldiers being soldiers, of course, will always find something to gripe about – duties from the Company Sergeant-Major! Least popular was guarding the Chobham armour. Bolted to the fronts and sides of every Warrior, its protective properties were secret and every plate was accounted for assiduously. Guarding it was a twenty-four-hour-a-day drain on manpower and so every man took his turn, a chore resented by 3 Troop, neither the Warriors nor its Chobham armour being their responsibility. But if it was this kind of un-demanding job that scored whinges it was not so worrying.

*Friday 15 January: Delivery of more aid from Belgrade was welcome news. The majority of 'A' Company deployed for Operation CABINET today, but due to recent sightings of three Bosnian Serb T-55 tanks and a ZSU 57-2 (anti-aircraft gun) in Caparde, 3 Troop was left on the bench. Although this Serb equipment is antiquated, it would virtually vaporize a Scimitar.*

*Instead I commanded my section to Kladanj and picked up a Danish* truck convoy that Billy Fooks had escorted from Vitez. Until today we hadn't been to Bomb Alley since the fire-fight. The 30mm brass cases, which would have littered the ground, were no longer there, probably picked up by Muslims to be recycled into their war effort.

While the truck drivers had a break, Billy and I ate lunch and caught up on news. He said that there were many versions of the Bomb Alley incident circulating Vitez, most of them cynical. The common theme apparently is why we used the cannons beyond the specified range. Unfortunately the ignoramuses are unavailable for me to enlighten them.

A 30mm H.E. round might contain less explosive than a hand grenade, but it works on the same principle of fragmentation. Both depend on Chemical Energy (bang) and not Kinetic Energy (punch) for effect. The velocity of the 30mm H.E. round bears virtually no relation on the round's effects at the target in the same way as a hand grenade dropped on the ground will have exactly the same effect as a hand grenade thrown twenty-five metres. The Scimitar guns were elevated beyond their range of 2000m, 'throwing' the 30mm rounds as far as 3000 metres. The disadvantage is that with increased range comes reduced accuracy, but then the Bosnian positions only needed suppressing for us to pass safely. I think that puts it quite well – the infantry should bloody well read this.

Once the Danish truck drivers had rested we escorted their convoy to Zivinice, a small village on the Tuzla road. Bomb Alley was once more reassuringly quiet and so I am glad our efforts have not, on the face of it, been in vain. The day's operation was completed without incident and we were able to return to the air force base before dark.

That evening Tudor Ellis, a Cheshire platoon commander, and I went out with the company's two interpreters, Mayda and Sandra. Far from unattractive anyway, the girls were becoming more desirable with every day we spent separated from our normal peacetime lives. Sandra drove the four of us in her car, an experience I can vividly recall as one of my most frightening in Bosnia! It was refreshing to escape the military atmosphere of the barracks, albeit still in a fairly remote Muslim enclave where most men carried an automatic weapon and sporadic fire could be heard echoing off the hills, but that was Bosnia.

Sandra took us to two restaurants in Tuzla, but at nearly 2100 hours neither were taking new orders. In both cases this looked to be something of a blessing! The only restaurant she was certain would be open was on the fringe of town and some way up a hill, hence its name

Panorama. Dressed in uniform and discreetly carrying pistols, we quietly escorted the girls inside. Conscious that local men would only see a picture of foreign soldiers dating Bosnian girls, I could not but help feel uncomfortable. Alas, playing down the situation was wasted on Mayda. Six feet tall, well known as the town mayor's daughter and with the sharp uninhibited voice of a siren, she advertised our arrival, helping attract looks of disgust in the third degree.

It was easy to see that Panorama had once been a venue for a smart set, placed advantageously on the side of the hill overlooking town. Yet on entering the restaurant I would not have gone as far to say it was worthy of any Michelin stars. The place looked run-down and dirty, enjoying authentic eastern European cigarette smoke that hung over the tables so heavily it appeared exempt to the laws of Brownian motion. Conveniently placed in a corner and out of the way, we were certainly very cosy, which at least meant that Tudor and I did not have to cover our 6 o'clock arc!

Surprisingly the restaurant was quite busy. The clientele was caught up in a war and yet they were attempting to continue life as normal. Muslim villages in the Tuzla district were being ethnically cleansed and, although the Serbs were some way from penetrating the town's perimeter, howitzers were not far from being in range of it. The burden of refugees and a general lack of resources or quality of life had a significant impact on the town's ability to function properly. Maimed and scarred war casualties wandered Tuzla's streets, a devastating effect on the community, and yet here were people out to dinner. It was the first time I have had dinner with a pretty girl and been able truthfully to say that the pistol in my pocket actually was a pistol!

The dog-eared menu had been in the wars too. Given the town's circumstances, I suspected that every dish was prepared with the same type of meat, just disguised by a variety of sauces. Wiener schnitzel was the only food I recognized and so was my choice. Copied by the two girls, it appeared to have been a wise decision. Four large *pivos* with frothy heads that filled one quarter of the tall glasses was an ideal aperitif to sterilize our insides for what was to come. When the food eventually arrived I was proved right. The meat was processed beef, coated in questionable looking breadcrumbs with a dusty taste that conjured up grave doubts about its source. Remaining ignorant of the meat's history or preparation seemed to me a sensible precaution against psychosomatic vomiting. Strangely, nothing was left to waste.

The evening finished at Sandra's pad, a flat in a tower block in the town centre. It had a strong Yugoslavian communist flavour to it:

architecture, furnishings, lino floors and a smell that reminded me of the old people's homes I had visited with my mother as a young boy when helping her with 'meals on wheels'. The highlight of the evening was Mayda massaging my back and chest with oil, a treat that came about quite effortlessly, but was where my luck started and finished. It may have been that I failed to read the signals properly, although to me there was no doubt that she was showing a red and green light at the same time – most confusing. The price for my lack of courage was an uncomfortable night spent top and tailed with Tudor on a musty sofa wrapped up in a shared home-made patchwork quilt. Gibbering with cold, I woke at 0500 hours to see Tudor snugly cocooned in it. It was a most unsatisfactory end to what had been an enjoyable night.

The morning's mission, and justification for being in Tuzla, was to buy some creature comforts for the 'A' Company Mess. Martyn Thomas had given this task to the cavalry, owing to our reputation for style and ostentation, an image I had to uphold. Trapped in a war, the girls were badly in need of some retail therapy, that female-dominated impulse that bridges race and religion across the globe, even with a less fortunate communist upbringing. The two of us were escorted to a row of local shops where the shelves were all but bare. In one shop there was an abundant supply of empty cereal boxes stacked into pyramids in the window. Faded from daily exposure to sunlight, their only value was to let us know what we could have bought before the war, which was unhelpful!

The ridiculously high prices of one store were a surprise to me. A very poor quality Persian-style rug was on sale for 1000DMs, about £300, extraordinary to think anyone would have the money for a luxury whilst in the throes of civil war. Even more extraordinary was the store manager's refusal to entertain the thought of haggling, again a hangover from communist days with all prices being fixed by the government. They had much to learn if they wanted to bump-start a free market economy, but then their inflexible technique, if that was what it was, worked well. Fifteen minutes later Tudor and I walked out of the store with the rug on our shoulders like a couple of deliverymen.

Before meeting Martyn and a few of the company at an orphanage in town we had breakfast in preparation for the work ahead. Mayda persuaded us to chose *cevapcici*, a local favourite of greasy meatballs and onions in unleavened bread. It was delicious and I became an instant addict.

The orphanage seemed very well organized and looked clean. In fact it was commented on that our help might not even have been necessary. Chocolates were handed out to the children and powdered milk and other provisions were given to the staff for the babies, who in some cases were as newly born as a few days old. After taking photographs of us with the children we left them and their chocolaty faces and headed for a refugee centre on the other side of Tuzla.

The best description for this haven came from a private soldier, "gopping". It was difficult to say what purpose the building had been designed for, but fortunately it had plenty of small rooms, at least allowing for some family privacy. Personal privacy was zero, with an average of six adults and as many children squeezed into a small bedroom. The adults and children were poorly dressed and dirty. The whole building was suffering from an overburdened sanitary system, which was quite evident from the stench.

Had I known then what I was to learn later I would have said that these people were the lucky ones. What I could not tell was how many had lost loved ones, scars you cannot necessarily see from the outside; but even so they were alive, sheltered and safe for the time being. Unlike the orphanage, the children here grabbed at the chocolates, which was very sad but spoke volumes. Judging by the faces of some adults, I detected resentment as we handed out the sticky bars. Was it because chocolate was of little nutritional value or was it the way we handed it out, jealousy of something, the fortunate, or were they just showing the strain?

This place needed aid directly and I imagine was the sort of centre that charitable Brits and Europeans thought they were supporting when making donations, not the front line! Martyn decided there and then that it was a good cause. Back in Germany the Cheshire wives were making a collection of the most basic and in demand supplies. This centre would be their target and gave us all a new focus while our core business was quiet.

Work did come our way on 20 January. The section was tasked to conduct a bridge and route recce to Vrazici, a village about thirty kilometres north-west of Tuzla. Our aim was to establish whether the route was capable of bearing haulage trucks laden with relief aid and identify which bridges needed upgrading. Three serviceable vehicles allowed us to take advantage of this legitimate day out and Sergeant Stubberfield joined us, once more providing expert knowledge on bridges.

Despite the early morning fog we made good time along the relatively fast Brcko road. Turning off, a minor road, marked in yellow on the map, wound up into the hills taking us deeper into this rural Muslim backwater and above the fog. Enjoyment of the blue sky, panoramic views and trouble-free day sadly came to an abrupt end when unceremoniously halted by three men at a makeshift checkpoint in Lepici.

The reader should be able to guess the events that followed. The checkpoint commander, a rather hawkish man with a modicum of presence, put his cigarette limply between his lips and took a notebook from his breast pocket. He waved it at me. "Papers, papers, no move," he mumbled through his fag. Dismounting from the vehicle I confronted him. "*Nema* papers *moy colleager, ja sam* . . . going . . . bugger . . . what's Serbo-Croat for going, Elvis?"

"Haven't a clue Sir."

"Thanks . . . *Ja sam* 'going' to *Vrazici* for *Pomoc* . . . I have special authority to use this road," I said using my hands as if holding a steering wheel, but just managing to get through to him without saying, "Vrooom". I can't think what he thought of me. "*Pomoc, dobro*," he said, then muttered something about the telephone and disappeared back into his hut, I assumed to call his commander. "Bloody villager can't make a decision," Elvis chipped in, standing up in the turret.

It was always wise to leave engines running so we waited in the sun being gassed by our own petrol fumes while the telephone call was made. "Right, I've lost patience with these clowns. This route's already been cleared for us. He's kept us waiting twenty minutes and he still hasn't got a bloody answer," I ranted, jumping back onto the vehicle and replacing my helmet to speak to the other crews. "Sierra three-three, I'm not waiting any longer, just crack on," I said over the radio in an exasperated tone.

"Roger, out." Corporal Payne's vehicle revved and could be heard changing through the gears as it pulled away. We followed him, but had not driven more than half a mile up the road, if it qualified as a road, before a Volkswagen Golf in blue and white panda livery squeezed past us on the near side in a dangerous manoeuvre and took the lead. It was evident that we were now being escorted into the local village so I told Corporal Payne to follow him, which he did until we stopped in the courtyard of a factory in Gornji Srebrenik.

The office of the local army commander was like every other I had been in. The bungalow's wallpaper was 1970s, the desk sported minia-

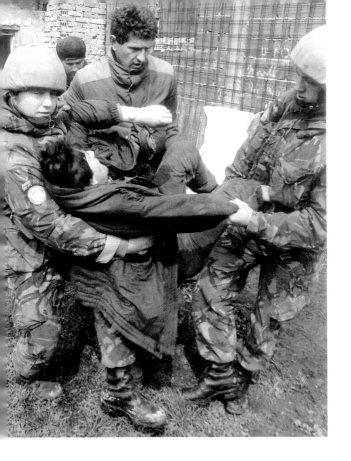

17. Soldiers in
    Ahmici carry a
    victim to cover.
    *(Giles Penfound)*

18. A casualty from the massacre at Ahmici.        *(Giles Penfound)*

19. A woman shot in
    the head is given
    first aid.
    *(Giles Penfound)*

20. Lance Corporal Priestley dresses the leg of a victim. *(Giles Penfound)*

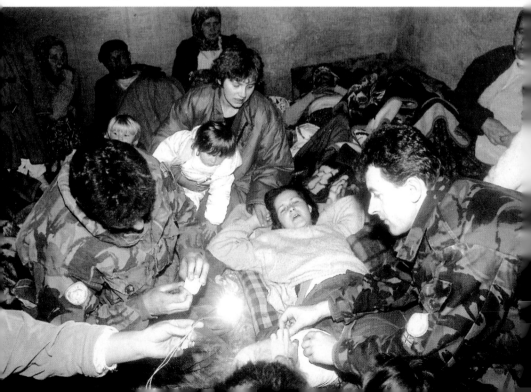

21. The minaret at Ahmici – still standing on 16 April 1993.

22. The toppled minaret – Ahmici.

23. A man lies dead on the steps of his burnt-out house in Ahmici.

24. Charred remains of Muslims are removed by British soldiers from a cellar in Ahmici
*(Giles Penfound*

5. Locals bury their families in a mass grave in Vitez.     *(Giles Penfound)*

6. Refugees being assisted by British soldiers.     *(Giles Penfound)*

27. The remnants of the truck bomb in Vitez.

28. Locals search for survivors after the Vitez bomb.

*(Giles Penfound)*

29. A soldier removes the remains of a victim of the Vitez bomb. *(Giles Penfound)*

30. Corporal Bremridge and his crew after being hit by an anti-personnel mine.

31. A BiH trench at Kula.

tures of the Bosnian flag and it smelt of stale eastern European tobacco. I met two ECMM officers (European Community Monitoring Mission), one Belgian and one a Dane who, both dressed completely in white, looked like a couple of lost cricketers without their bats. They tried to relax me, having adopted the attitude that one had to 'go with the flow' or stress would be inevitable. This was not going to calm me down. I was still wound up owing to the Liaison Officers in Tuzla having not cleared the route for us the previous day to prevent just this kind of delay. In this backward, bureaucratic country I was clearly unable to move freely, regardless of what the Liaison Officers did, but the last thing I needed was a Euro peace bloke in cricket whites, especially a Belgian, telling me to "chill out".

Eventually an explanation was given to me on a piece of notepaper, allegedly from the local commander, who was not available to see me. It explained his concern for our safety, etc, but I was sure it had just been typed up in the adjacent office by the assistant lavatory cleaner and was not official at all. With no way of winning, I had to accept the situation for what it was and left without a fight.

Outside, a local Bosnian television crew tried to interview me about my views on the conflict. With uncharacteristic sense to recognize a bad time for an interview, I declined, lest I tell the truth about the whole place being a joke and end up being disciplined for it. We were here to recce bridges for improvement and yet this bunch of hoods were not at all interested in me getting on with my job, even though it would be to their advantage.

The police escort returned us to Lepici where we were released. With time on our hands and the need to calm down I decided that the journey and this glorious afternoon sun should not be wasted. The four white vehicles snaked down a dusty track to a castle at Grabovik, which stood on an isolated knoll that protruded into the valley with a commanding view of the River Rijeka. The castle must have been Byzantine or Ottoman; whatever it was, it looked pretty old. Elvis asked whether the Crusades had come this way, a question I was unable to answer, although I thought they had. Local building standards had certainly taken a nose dive since the castle had been built.

No sooner had we arrived at the foot of the castle, which was in very good condition, than a multitude of children appeared from nowhere, in the same way as you come across a swarm of flies out at sea when sailing. Where do they come from, flies? Children had swarmed me many times before, but never while on foot and in these numbers. As I walked up to the castle I must have had thirty kids follow me, either hoping for chocolate or simply out of curiosity. I was followed into the castle and out again, which negated the whole point of visiting and spending some time in peace. It was like being a history teacher on a field trip in North Wales, really quite irritating.

Our return to Tuzla was fast, a journey of just over half an hour. My morale instantly peaked when I discovered I had received another pile of mail, mostly from family and friends with reference to the Bomb Alley incident eleven days previously. That evening the cookhouse was awash with new faces, all Gunners from 94 Locating Regiment Royal Artillery. They were in Tuzla to survey options for the use of 105mm light guns, war fighting equipment that remained on board HMS *Ark Royal*, still offshore with other British troops. Their arrival brought with it heightened speculation over our future and more "what ifs" than could be digested. The situation was changing politically and our role for humanitarian relief looked under threat. If conditions became too dangerous to continue we would have to withdraw or, rumour had it, change our role to war fighting in order to extract in good order.

# I I

# EAST OF THE DRINA

Kostajnica is a small Muslim village on the front line, a redoubt within easy range of hostile Bosnian Serb fire, but holding out. The village was to be the lucky recipient of some much-needed aid and 3 Troop, the advance party, had to prepare the way for it.

Just outside Srebrenik a policeman manning a checkpoint attempted to stop our four vehicles charging along at speed by holding out his traffic lollipop. However, three months of frustration spent dealing with inflexible officials made me ignore the policeman and tell Yozza to drive on. This was an impetuous stunt that I knew would only bring short-term entertainment, but seeing the policeman's face drop in horror almost made it worthwhile. I say "almost" because this errant behaviour was not very clever. Mike Dooley's aid convoy was a couple of hours behind us and our very purpose was to smooth such problems away to prevent his progress being interrupted. I had failed already.

The country was a web of checkpoints. I should have known better, and so was not surprised to be stopped a few kilometres further on. I suspect that the lollipop man had telephoned ahead and was having the last laugh. Indeed we now suffered the ignominy of being escorted to our final destination by three policemen in a Volkswagen Golf, a restriction on our freedom of movement that was impossible to argue. The police would often try to make us believe such precautions were in our own interest, but at least it meant we were protected from further delay.

The last few kilometres into Kostajnica were along a road that was as exposed and straight as a Lincolnshire trunk road. With black fumes belching into the cold air, the diesel Golf accelerated away, a manoeuvre we tried to copy, having been briefed by colleagues about the Serb positions covering this stretch of road. Fortunately the morning haze had not yet burnt off, so our slower dash was very nicely shrouded from view and made without incident.

The men led us to the *Pomoc* depot where, after dismounting, I was introduced to the town's president. He was a distinguished-looking, grey-haired gentleman dressed in a jacket and tie, who, wandering around, appeared to be at a loose end. I assumed the word president was just an approximate translation, as it was a rather grand title for the leader of a village. After greeting him with fluently delivered pleasantries, he seemed surprised to discover that I did not actually speak the language, and neither he English. Fortunately one of the Muslim soldiers did and positioned himself between us as interpreter. The soldier seemed to enjoy the opportunity to demonstrate his talent in front of his leader and helped us make polite, if not painful, conversation.

Having pinpointed the destination for Dooley's *pomoc*, I now had only to concern myself with identifying the extent of local Muslim and Serb front lines. Acutely aware that Muslim estimates of BiH dispositions would be exaggerated, I was well prepared to treat any snippets with a pinch of salt. The president spoke very generally about the war, avoiding my very direct question about the military situation in Kostajnica, and then at length about his wife, his children, his grand-children and his vegetable allotment. He could not understand why, at twenty-five years of age, I was not married with five children of my own. So obviously disappointed, I tried to excuse my marital circum-stances by telling him that this was perfectly normal where I came from, all of my friends being in the same situation. His raised eyebrows did little to hide his disappointment.

Having spent a good time buttering up the wrong man, I was lucky that the Muslim soldier was the enthusiastic type and keen to show me one of their front line positions. With the mist slowly lifting, he escorted me some distance between a series of buildings before we crouched low and jogged forward to a shallow trench. Although the trench had not been dug properly, it provided adequate cover for the two of us to walk another fifty metres forward before stopping behind a low stone wall that had been shot up to a pile of rubble. From this vantage point the soldier made various indications of his enemy's positions using his hand, leaving me questioning my own eyesight. It was easier just to agree and make the right noises rather than say that I could not see a thing and have him attempt a long-winded explana-tion. In fact, despite pointing out positions, he looked unsure himself and so I was not surprised when he asked to borrow my binoculars, a scheme that was sure to have been his intention from the outset, the wily old fox.

While still playing soldiers lying in the dirt and having finally seen a Serb position, the Muslim trained my binoculars onto the open road.

110

Like a shooting gallery of white ducks, a long line of trucks and at least two Warriors had come into view and were kicking up a deal of dust while rumbling steadily along it. Seconds later it seemed no coincidence to hear the report of several explosions and at sufficiently close range to make me jumpy. With a keen perception for genuine danger and self-preservation, I made no secret of my reluctance to lie in the open and so the two of us ran to a house near the vehicles for cover where I was ushered into a cellar from an entrance at ground level.

The president was standing just inside the doorway and welcomed me again as if we had never met. He was surprisingly upbeat, considering his village was being shelled, for which I could not apologize enough. The presence of our armoured vehicles and possibly the arrival of the convoy, if not the cause for the attack, had done little to prevent it. He shrugged my confession off quite magnanimously. The next time aid was delivered, I told him, it would be dropped off in Gracanica out of sight of the Serbs for everyone's safety, a plan he agreed to with a measured and statesmanlike nod of the head; either that or he simply did not understand.

While most sensible people had taken cover, Elvis was still standing on top of our Scimitar turret listening to his personal stereo and thus was unable to hear the first few shells exploding. Before I had the chance to shout to him, a shell, most likely anti-aircraft fire, detonated some fifty feet above Elvis's head, a sight that will be etched in my memory for ever. With people shouting at him, Elvis's attention was soon caught and he jumped down inside the turret closing the hatch behind with the urgency of a diving U-Boat skipper. Fortunately he was unhurt.

Most of the locals had not sought the safety of proper cover, but were cowering on the lee-side of a house not far from where I had just seen one of the rounds airburst. The small explosions continued while we stood quite cramped in the cellar. Most of the lads were still in their vehicles, so I hoped that the Serbs would limit their firepower demonstration to purely indirect systems. After fifteen minutes or so the firing stopped, a pause I decided we should take advantage of, lest we become prisoners of overwhelming hospitality in the village.

Having made swift farewells, we mounted up. Without cue, the three men boarded the worn-out Volkswagen Golf once more and soon had it wound up to an impressive speed as we collectively ran the gauntlet back along the exposed main road. Once past Gracanica the reduced threat allowed us to stop on the roadside for a spot of lunch, as there was no urgency that we knew of for us to return to camp. Oddly, we all nervously anticipated the moment when pestilent children would saturate the space and spoil our break, but after ten minutes or more Sparky commented how nice it was that for once we were being left alone. A minute later a jeep pulled up and a journalist and camera crew jumped out. "Do they ever bloody let up?" he whined with justified indignation. Taking my cue to speak up on behalf of everyone, I took to my feet and addressed the disturbance from the commanding position of the vehicle's front decks. Quite surprisingly, the reporter apologized and scurried away without need for coercion.

*Monday 25 January: This morning my Scimitar had to have a new engine, which will not help the B Squadron equipment reliability statistics. Once fitted by the REME, Elvis and Yozza ran the engine up and bled the coolant system. I later helped to change the vehicle's sprocket rings that had worn down to their 'tell-tales'. The troop seem to be in fairly good spirits considering that only two vehicles are getting out at any one time, due to a continued lack of spares.*

*Today Sandra learnt that her boyfriend has gone Missing In Action. She thinks he has either been killed, captured or has deserted – fairly perceptive of her! Needless to say she is very upset, so I spent some of the afternoon with Mayda trying to comfort her, which proved absolutely useless. She hopes he has deserted – I hope he hasn't because when they catch him he'll be in a real fix.*

*Martyn Thomas has negotiated with the Bosnian Serbs the safe passage of UN troops along Bomb Alley. They have apparently promised not to attack us as long as we do not use provocative behaviour. That said, the Royal Engineer section stopped along Bomb Alley today to shift a lorry out of the road and were engaged by Serb fire.*

*There is word that the fighting in Gornji Vakuf has spread as far as Travnik and Busovaca and even into Vitez. Never mind the locals, I hope that this does not affect our leave, but then if there is some action I rather hope we stay and get involved. In Busovaca there is fighting between Muslims and Croats all around the Dutch/Belgian transport battalion's camp, which apparently has led to the Dutch and Belgians not deploying for some of their convoy escorts.*

*I am enjoying Tuzla enormously, despite the lack of vehicle spares and work. There seems to be far less hassle here than when with the squadron. This may be because the company and Martyn see us as a novelty – the Cavalry factor – and the company is also a very happy bunch of well-led and motivated men. The central heating in the rooms is glorious and the interpreters are refreshingly amusing. All I have really missed from Vitez, except for a few mates, is the excellent food and the quicker arrival time of mail. Tonight closed with the fine weather breaking and a light sprinkling of snow covering the ground to remind us of where we are.*

In the next few days the monotony did not change, the only work to break the pattern being the collection of a Dutch convoy from Kladanj. At least the Dutch had been bold enough to get out of their camp. On 28 January the mixed Officers' and Sergeants' Mess held a drinks party to thank local dignitaries for helping us while in Tuzla. The chefs had prepared plates of pass-around food and a small bar was run by a couple of the company's soldiers. Our new acquisition, the red-patterned rug, helped give the room a warm and homely atmosphere, but, still new, we walked around it more than on it. Mayda's parents attended. Her larger than life father, who I thought looked a bit like the Bosnain Serb leader, Radovan Karadic, placed his Heckler & Koch MP5 sub-machine gun on a table with the everyday casualness of a briefcase. This compact and deadly piece of engineering was obviously coveted by every soldier in the room, a piece of hardware that anyone would have swapped for their troublesome and tinny SA80. Attired in blue service-dress, the airfield station commander was one of our more important guests to grace us with his presence. He told us proudly how before the war he had been a fighter pilot in the Yugoslavian Air Force, something he spoke about fondly with an occasional distant and nostalgic sigh. Having sunk several large glasses of beer, however, he snapped out of this and in a very jovial mood told me that I was welcome in his officers' club at any time because I had fired upon the Serbs, his enemy. Everyone laughed heartily, if not a little forced, as it was really quite embarrassing to be speaking in such terms. I shrugged the attention off, but this offer was clearly genuine. I thanked him for his hospitality and, reflecting on his comment, could not help but wonder what it would be like to go to war against people who had formerly been colleagues and friends. What would it be like to fight against friends who were, for example, officers in Scottish regiments? How reassuring to live in a United Kingdom. Yugoslavia killed more of its own people during the Second World War than it did Germans, quite an achievement, and here they were at it again. The Balkan fighting was not just territorial; there was too much hatred for that. The fighting was based on racism and not only on the battlefield, but one of the most vile forms of life-taking, human ethnic cleansing. It had become apparent that the underdogs, the most hated of all the tribes, were the Muslims, despite having shared the land for over 800 years. The worst of this form of racism was to come.

There were a few pretty girls at the party, including one called Edith, whose name I found unusual for a woman in her twenties on account of it also being the name of my grandmother. Edith was a Muslim who worked for the Tuzla Radio station. She made an impression on me that I will never forget, but nothing to do with romance. She was introduced to Richard, a large African man, whose nationality I never found out, but he worked for the UNHCR. Edith refused to shake Richard's hand because he was black. Obviously Edith's actions were not representative of all Muslims in Bosnia, but it did contribute to my increasing scepticism that every side was in fact as bad as the other.

Two days later another Op CABINET was co-ordinated by the company. There was no 'talking part' for me, but I went along as an observer so that I could join Martyn and a few others over to Serbia once the operation was complete, an opportunity that could not be missed. Sitting in the back of Cooper's Land Rover with my helmet and flak jacket securely fastened helped reduce my feeling of vulnerability very little. The vehicle's wafer-thin steel sides were my only other means of ballistic protection should the BSA start firing, which until now they always had. Worse, in the event of an incident my life was completely in somebody else's hands. For all its weaknesses I would have preferred, by far, to be in my trusted Scimitar.

In Saraci our group waited for nearly two hours. The convoy's delay was a simple case of the trucks being late and the monitors on both sides having to be given time to link up and co-ordinate. In truth it was hardly very challenging to chose a *rendezvous* point, ask the trucks to follow you and escort them into Tuzla, but it was made difficult because Balkan soldiers and aid workers were both involved, perfect ingredients for inertia.

Standing in shin-high snow, the officers gaggled around Martyn's Rover while we waited for the trucks to arrive. Most of the crews remained mounted up, drank brews and smoked. Captain Bob Ryan, one of the Cheshire Liaison Officers, found a black and tan mongrel puppy, which he immediately adopted as a pet. This was bound to end in tears. For the time being there was no policy to shoot dogs, but if they became a hazard to camp hygiene or just a nuisance they were on borrowed time. The calming and morale-positive effect of dogs around soldiers was only to be recognized a few years later.

Once called forward and having driven a little way, we stopped again. From the Rover's back window I could see that we were just short of the RV east of Kalesija and in No Man's-Land. The small village was a ruined shell that told a sorry story, but one that we all accepted as the norm. After a further delay we moved forward again for the arrival of the trucks, which, like the time before, were new and gleaming white Volvos. With an efficient hand over, Sergeant Clarke's section and a platoon of Warriors escorted the trucks away towards Tuzla, amazingly without hostile fire causing us to dash for cover. The operation had been simple and relatively painless.

With the formalities complete, Martyn was given the go-ahead for us to proceed in our two Land Rovers east into Bosnian Serbia. There were very few checkpoints and an escort was not required, which was so reasonable it was bizarre. One checkpoint we did come across had two BRDM-2 armoured vehicles and a ZSU 57-2 anti-aircraft system parked at it. This instantly illustrated the contrast between the two factions we were familiar with and this fledgling army whose roots were embedded in the former Yugoslavian National Army, once a powerful and well-equipped organization under Tito.

The BRDM-2 is a Soviet-designed reconnaissance patrol vehicle, which, being a reconnaissance soldier, I took a train-spotter-like interest in. During the Cold War, when similar vehicles were operated by our enemy, the Group of Soviet Forces Germany (GSFG), it was virtually impossible to get to see one 'in the flesh', or any of our enemy's vehicles for that matter. No surprise then that any kind of Soviet-designed military equipment held enormous intrigue and fascination. These particular vehicles, being former JNA, would have been built under licence in Yugoslavia well before this war. Being allowed to roam freely and witness such sights was peculiar and created a kind of 'behind enemy lines' buzz and sense of adventure among the group – quite a privilege.

Our first call was to Sekovici to meet a BSA colonel whose troops I had fired upon two weeks previously. His camp was a proper barracks, very well laid out and tidy with a professional military atmosphere, a far cry from most of the makeshift HVO and BiH camps we had seen elsewhere. As it happened the colonel was unavailable, so instead we were introduced to one of his captains. A charming man with military bearing and composure, his professional soldier status could not be hidden, something he was quick to tell us lest we take him for a wartime conscript. He had classic Slavic good looks and enough teeth to complete a smile, which he did a lot. Translated by Nick Costello, he told us with measured wryness how it was a necessity to have a good sense of humour in the Balkans, something we could not agree more with.

Sitting behind his desk in customary fashion, protecting his self-important image no doubt, we began what was becoming a set-piece conversation about English football. My enthusiasm for our English sporting heritage was completely artificial, my interest in football being zero, but still I smiled and laughed as the names of player heroes and clubs were recited. "Bobby Charlton . . . *dobro*, George Best . . . *dobro*, Manchester Utd . . . *dobro*, ha ha ha." The staccato Serbo-Croat dialogue, the thick cigarette smoke and the revolting slivovitz, again thrust upon us, were common factors whose subtle differences were wasted on someone who believed that he could have been sitting with any of the three Bosnian factions. Unlike any other office I had been in, however, this one had an enormous oil painting hanging behind the desk. Styled like a Soviet ideological propaganda poster, it depicted JNA troops with red flags mounted in T-34 tanks conducting some form of offensive action. It would have made a superb trophy for the 9th/12th Officers' Mess cloakroom in Germany, but he told me it was not his to sell.

Martyn delicately brought up the subject of Bomb Alley, mentioning that I was the officer responsible for giving the order to open fire on his troops. Completely without tact, someone then asked the Captain whether any of his troops had been hit. Firing from such a distance, I had assumed that none had and was not particularly keen to pursue the matter as a topic for discussion, but the Captain replied "*Nema*" with an enormous laugh from the bottom of his belly and refused to entertain even the thought of it. Rather than leave it at that he mentioned the subject a number of times making me think, "yes we got one of you bastards, didn't we?" but I was wise enough to keep these thoughts to myself, so laughed along spinelessly in case he had me shot for being impertinent.

As soon as an opening for a polite escape occurred we took it and returned in the Land Rovers to a crossroads a few kilometres away. The plan was to meet a Serbian LO here who would take us from this part of Bosnia held by Serbs and east across the River Drina into

Serbia. En route, however, we were delayed by a puncture, made worse by the spare wheel on the bonnet having buckled days before, but not yet having been replaced. Thereafter the ride was far from comfortable and by the time we reached the crossroads the Serbian Liaison Officer was nowhere to be seen.

Our solo journey across the broad Drina a success; the evening was spent in a hotel in Zvornik. Looking at the wallpaper and good quality carpets, it had clearly been an up-market establishment in its heyday, but, like so much in the Balkans, had been reduced to a musty-smelling dump in need of a lick of paint. Just as in Bosnia, hotel trade was the preserve of UN monitors and NGO officials, who at least kept the local economy afloat. The cost of each room was 20DMs, a tariff that included dinner and as much beer as could be drunk; the headache in the morning was free!

The evening was civilized, although surreal. Sitting completely at ease drinking beer in a Serbian hotel with several UN monitors, including a Russian Spetsnaz (Troops of Special Designation) officer, was weird. The front line that I had come to fear on my many patrols and convoys, the one where I was regularly shot at, was a veneer and behind it a country of welcoming citizens carrying on a far more normal life. None of it really made sense.

Despite having been in a hotel I had had quite an uncomfortable night as my duvet was similar to the type you get in Austrian ski chalets, about two feet too short! Strangely I could have telephoned home from the hotel more easily than when in Tuzla, but it was very early so I chose not to wake up any relatives.

It was extraordinary to drive quite freely out of Serbia and, at our convenience, stop at a greengrocer where we bought some fresh bananas and kiwi fruit, including a slack handful for the interpreters. The shop was well stocked and there was no queue. Clearly the UN embargo was having a devastating effect on the Serbians! I had read a newspaper article which claimed that Rumania was complaining how their inadequately resourced police were failing to enforce the UN embargo. Oil barges and other cargo vessels were navigating the River Danube largely unchecked and supplying the Bosnian Serb war effort.

Driving back into Bosnian Serbia was also no trouble. This time with precision timing, we waited at another *rendezvous* to meet a BSA LO who would escort us safely back over the front line. After some wait it was evident that he too would not be coming and so, at some risk, Martyn made the decision for us to proceed alone. As we drove through Kalesija, the village in No-Man's-Land, I saw a child's legs sticking out of a drainage ditch at the side of the road. Out of curiosity we stopped momentarily to discover that they were the legs of a small girl of about five years old. The thick morning frost lay like a shroud over her red dress and thick brown stockings. There was no need for a signpost welcoming us to Bosnia.

# 12

# MATERIAL WORLD

Boxes of second-hand clothes and toys, nappies, baby milk and food were dragged to the edge of the two Bedford tailgates for soldiers to carry into the building. Directed by the Company Sergeant-Major to ensure even distribution, soldiers trod the bare and filthy corridors in pairs, one holding a box, the other giving an item to a family member waiting at the doorway of each room. Targeting humanitarian aid to a specific refugee centre in this way, and handing it personally to the people who needed it most, was the only method of guaranteeing success and thus was considered extremely worthwhile.

Weeks before Clivena Thomas had co-ordinated this collection of everyday necessities with the other 'A' Company wives in Germany, while Martyn had been on the lookout in Tuzla for a worthy cause. Parlous in every respect, there was no question over his choice. The centre's fundamental problem was overcrowding and with it a greater demand than it had supplies. The stench from poor sanitation completed the atmosphere of a place that needed help. Nevertheless its comparative security was priceless for the many otherwise homeless Muslims sheltering there. These people might have initially looked forlorn, but probably considered themselves the lucky ones.

The Bosnians are proud people, but I suspect that most at this refugee centre had the good sense to take anything on offer. It was not difficult to see that their plight was genuine, if for no other reason than by their bright faces and grateful gestures. A great deal of thought had gone into what was sent in order to make valuable use of container space. At least that was almost entirely the case; catering-size packets of sugar puffs struck me as an unusual cereal to send. Having these without cool fresh milk would be comparable to the story of the man sent to Hell who had a magnificent feast spread before him but only six-feet long chopsticks to eat with. There was little evidence of noses being turned up; nevertheless, soldiers were conscious of the need not to appear charitable or patronizing. Indeed, knowing whether to be cheeringly happy or respectfully sombre was not easy to judge.

It was no surprise to find that our operation was attracting a large gathering of people outside, further encouraged by fine weather. The aid was for the centre and, although it was difficult to distinguish a person's status by his or her dress, most of the crowd looked suspiciously like locals, not refugees. At first the bystanders were milling around in small numbers, but as the soldiers became busier and more locals arrived, the Bedford tailgates were soon encroached upon until finally under siege. This made it difficult for soldiers to reach the boxes and continue the distribution. Before long we were experiencing the kind of overwhelming force one might expect from the audience at a rock concert. The soldiers on board despatching boxes were saved from being overrun by the stage-like elevation the trucks afforded them.

It was understandable that locals attempting to come through a war should try to pick up what spoils they could, but it made it no less annoying and typified the 'grab then criticize' attitude that those not actually starving were sometimes guilty of. It is easy to judge if you have never had to fight for your family's survival. Perhaps if placed in the same situation maintaining one's dignity and integrity might be an aspiration, perhaps not?

Martyn was on board one Bedford helping soldiers to unload. He handed me a heavy box of army compo tinned margarine, which I lowered to chest level before carrying into the centre. A few hands plunged inside the unsealed box for a lucky dip; within seconds I was engulfed by the weight of a shoving crowd and was being caught by flailing arms striking out in hope of a prize. It was truly overwhelming and so, using instinct before brain, I dropped the box on to the ground, rather than struggle to elevate it above my head. This opportunity, however, was the spark that lit the touch paper. The fight that followed embodied the survival instinct of wild animals, a ruckus comprising every age and shape of Muslim exploding in front of us. Children, old men and young mothers fought, grabbed and wrestled on the ground like hyenas over a carcass. With absolutely no care for others, the adults trampled children who, identified by their screams, were pulled free by Cheshire soldiers while the adults viciously fought on. It was an appalling spectacle, whatever the circumstances. Months of fading patience for a people I suspected were destined for self-destruction made me want to shout at the top of my voice and make them stop.

Breathless, having escaped the maul, an old and typical looking Balkan woman approached me. She was frail with a crooked posture and wearing a patterned headscarf, sleeveless cardigan on top of a jersey and thick wrinkled stockings. With tears running down her gaunt brown face, which was lined with deep furrows, she raised the back of her hand to stroke my cheek. Unsure whether she was over-joyed with our help or sad to see the behaviour of her country-folk, this emotional display from a woman I guessed had suffered a lifetime of hardship brought a lump to my throat and made me ignore the margarine incident for the side-show it was.

The Muslim people were watching their country slowly bleed to death through the selfishness of neighbours who had forgotten their conscience and lost all control in pursuit of survival. In the process the infrastructure had been destroyed or had completely collapsed. The few hospitals that existed were over-stretched, under-resourced and shelled regularly. There was no electricity, no sewage or refuse disposal and no public transport or postal service; in the cities food and potable water were not abundant. Inflation was sky high making the Dinar more valuable as lavatory paper, while only the Deutschmark or US dollar were acceptable currency. To think of voicing an opinion was a potential death sentence, if you could be heard, democracy being a distant aspiration. The police force was corrupt and, with people fighting internally for survival, nowhere was ever safe, even when the official enemy was at bay. If not this old woman, then many women like her, had lost everything: husbands, sons, grandchildren, homes, belongings, livestock and livelihoods, losses they relied upon for support in old age, losses that for most of us would make life look beyond hope. A sense of hope is a very strong pillar to support one's faith in such times, but not everyone can muster it when they have suffered this kind of mental torture. There would be plenty more tears in Bosnia.

The refugee centre experience had been a poignant one, most of all for those fathers with young children. Normally in such situations it would not be surprising to hear a thoughtless soldier open his mouth before engaging brain and say something insensitive, but not here. The atmosphere had been stark, concerning real people, not just pictures on a television screen taken in a distant and war-savaged republic. This was part of the wider Europe our grandfathers had fought to liberate and it had slipped back fifty years; nobody felt like joking.

Once our task was complete we left the refugee centre and drove across Tuzla to the town's main hospital, which had been shelled the day before. This was where Justin had been taken after being hit by shrapnel, a place of Victorian capability. The trucks pulled up outside the makeshift maternity ward that had been relocated in a cellar, affording a degree of protection from further shelling. Baby milk and nappies that had been put aside were carried inside, a small contribution to make life easier for the courageous doctors who were being asked to pull miracles out the hat every day. Conditions were indescribable and the rows of crying babies, many newly born, a desperate picture for even the most emotionally robust soldier.

In some respects this row of new life could have been considered as the future and hope, but taken at face value it appeared a grim and selfish piece of bad timing. Many of the soldiers went to witness the conditions for themselves, but, seeing that there were already too many camouflaged jackets and white gowns crowding the basement, I turned about at the doorway. The last thing I wanted to be guilty of was enjoying a freak show. If I told you that a soldier took a picture of a baby that had no arms or legs the reader will understand what I mean.

The day's responsibilities fulfilled, Mayda and I were dropped off at her parent's apartment. Carrying my bundle of *dhobi*, I sheepishly asked her mother whether she would be able to launder my dirty uniforms, something she was only too happy to do, despite the obvious health risk! Meanwhile Mayda and I went into town, as she insisted I had a haircut. The Tuzla Hotel charged 1DM for the benefit, expensive for Bosnia, but not for a UN soldier. I gave the heavily made-up hairdresser a 100 per cent tip, enjoying my relative wealth while I could. Being in no hurry to go anywhere, the two of us took lunch at a bijou restaurant nearby where we both unadventurously chose *cevapcici*.

Strolling back to the apartment I felt rather lucky to be alongside Mayda as she was dressed extremely chicly in a purple cape and thigh-length purple suede boots, which accentuated her extraordinarily long legs. She could easily have been mistaken for a catwalk model and drew much attention to herself, including a friend driving a Red Cross jeep, who stopped and offered us a lift. Owing to my carrying a pistol, convention forced me to turn the lift down, which for a moment I feared would mean Mayda abandoning me on a Bosnian street.

Mayda's father was at home sitting in a large chair when we returned. The first thing he said was that they were suffering another power cut, followed by a complaint that the BSA were concentrating their forces on a point along the front line for an imminent push. He then commented that there was little the BiH could do and anyway did not think that the BSA was so interested in Tuzla itself. It was fascinating to hear the concerns of the town Mayor and I wished I could have understood more, but Mayda was too matter-of-fact as she translated the gist of what he said while fluttering around the apartment more interested in our next engagement.

My 'fly on the wall' view of a privileged Bosnian girl's life continued as I sat on a chair outside her bedroom. With the door ajar, allowing her to rabbit on in a high-pitched voice about niff-naff and trivia, she got herself ready while I failed dismally to avert my eyes at appropriate moments. The special occasion was the re-opening of the Tuzla Hotel nightclub, a high point in the town's social calendar. After lengthy preparation she drifted elegantly out of her room as if on a conveyor-belt. She looked stunning in a long black figure-hugging dress that had a slit so far up her left leg it should have carried a government health warning.

A glimpse of suspenders tight against a shapely thigh, revealed while stepping into her father's staff car, had an unhelpful affect on my involuntary monk-like existence. What was even more frustrating was that she knew it. Dressed to kill and with a car at her disposal, she barked an order to the driver who chauffeured us a short way to her friend's flat. The car waited while we collected Ella, an obsessive fan of the singer Madonna who, when we arrived, was still making the finishing touches to her war paint. In her late teens, I was surprised to see that Ella's room was adorned with posters of her heroine striking various poses, a far cry from Bosnia's medieval rural community, but if that was an escape then it was no bad thing.

Ella had made every effort for this rare outing. Dressed provocatively, she had adopted the image that the world-renowned singer had ordained as a trademark in her early career. Her intentionally pale face was contrasted by deep purple lipstick, complete with a thick black border to define and enlarge her lips. She wore a black top made of netting comprising various layers, an excuse for a skirt, fishnet stockings, pixie boots and a hairstyle that looked to have been combed through with a hawthorn bush. The ensemble would not have been complete without a large crucifix suspended from a leather cord around her neck. Being a Muslim, this must have attracted one or two raised eyebrows, but then probably not; religion encompasses all natures of worship! To be frank I thought she looked rather silly and was in no doubt that, had she been going out in England and had stopped near a curb, at best she would have escaped with a police caution. She was ten years ahead of most people in Bosnia but ten years behind western Europe. Regardless, Ella was a lovely girl, spoke very good English with an American twang from too much television-watching and seemed to be enjoying life, which under the circumstances one had to admire.

Once deposited at the Tuzla Hotel's front entrance, the three of us made our way into the lobby and downstairs to the revamped and re-launched basement nightclub. A small number of soldiers had been invited to represent the company as a thank you from the Mayor for the work done and to bid us farewell; the company was to depart for Vitez in the coming days. With not many Bosnians in a position to spend a night out clubbing, I could only assume that the management was intent on drawing in some hard cash. Furthermore, there was a need to bolster numbers of eligible clubbers and to dilute the number of people with scrawny beards, check shirts and hill-walking trousers; NGO aid workers had been keeping the hotel in business from the start of the war.

Initially the atmosphere had been stagnant and appeared as if people had forgotten how to enjoy themselves or just dared not. As the beer flowed, however, the party soon picked up, the volume of music and chatter with it reaching normal nightclub decibels. The free beer soon ran out and so, without surprise, Troopers Blunt and Baker coerced me to buy a crate from the main bar upstairs. Common procedure for troop leaders, I obliged, which was fine until I was about to place the crate of bottles down on my troop's table. Mayda's father hoodwinked me, signalling for the beer to be brought to him and his table of guests. Too polite, not to mention too scared to say anything, I complied with a big smile and a loquacious repertoire of "*Nema problemas.*" The Mayor and his guests helped themselves to my beer, leaving the troop with a few bottles.

Prospects of the night developing into more than just a drinking session looked hopeful when a very attractive girl called Daniella introduced herself and effortlessly showed me an unwarranted scoopful of attention. She was so attractive that I was convinced someone had put her up to this; either that or she was a hooker. Unfortunately she spoke very little English and the music was deafening, so we suffered a stilted conversation sipping our drinks as a distraction while perched on stools amongst customers jostling around the bar.

Naïvely I still fancied my chances with Mayda during the closing days in Tuzla. She was playing it cool because she did not want idle gossip or awkwardness, or so I thought. With her father present, however, I had more chance of being hit by a meteorite painted in regimental colours, but still I did not want to jeopardize any chance I might have had later. This and the language barrier with Daniella became poor excuses for not pursuing what appeared to be a safe bet and so I detailed Trooper Kusbish to look after her. In hindsight this seems incomprehensible. Even worse, it was not long before she found me again, her first words being, "Mun-tee, I have looking every place for you now," and still I did not exploit her or one of the three hundred very reasonably priced hotel bedrooms above us. For an average-looking guy her persistence was flattering, but it might have been something more – my pistol perhaps, which she looked keen to handle.

Having entered the club dressed in my issue combats, I had stripped off my winter layers down to a black polar-neck top that I often wore to annoy the squadron leader. Strategically strapped around my chest was the black leather shoulder holster I had bought from a local man in Vitez. In it was my loaded Browning 9mm pistol. Needless to say I enjoyed this slightly surreal and certainly unique opportunity, even if I did look a pratt, and ensured the event was recorded on film. And that was what this was, just an opportunity for fun, not some sad childhood ambition to be the Milk Tray man, no certainly not, for at school I had had a pathological fear for the swimming-pool's top diving board!

At first I felt self-conscious because I knew what most were thinking, but knowing the chance was unlikely to arise again, I made the most of it. The next nightclub I was likely to patronize would be in London and not the sort where pistols are handed in at the door. The clubs that I frequented were in Fulham and typically the hunting grounds of city boys. They were easy to identify as they would arrive dressed in stripy suits carrying filo-faxes having continued from their offices to pubs then clubs; rather a sad highlight in the day of a young man. Nevertheless, as we UN soldiers slugged local bottled beer in Bosnia while swarming around only a handful of local women, they were in the same London clubs impressing girls with bottles of chilled Champagne and cocktails at exorbitant prices. They had GTIs and BMWs to drive girls back to their flats in; I had to share a Bedford truck with drunken soldiers then retire to a smelly sleeping bag. Nothing would have persuaded me to change places; this life, I believed, was much more fun.

As the party was thrown out of the club, and worse for a few beers, I insisted on kissing every girl goodnight, some sort of Casanova confidence-building exercise in compensation for blowing my chance with Daniella. Returning to camp standing up in the back of a 4 tonner with the lads was a little less ceremonious than my route out. Brave conversations on the way home, fortified by drink, suggested that the boys too had exceeded the 'two-can rule'. This was a healthy means for them to let off steam and raise issues that were bothering them. Troop leaders are wise to adapt to this wider pastoral aspect of the job, something I tried never to take too personally.

Back in the barracks I had hardly been in bed a minute when I heard a light knock on my door and then the unmistakable silhouette of Corporal Payne in the corridor. "Have you got a minute sir, we have a small problem?" he said in a whisper. He turned my room's fluorescent light on, which there should be a law against, and was followed in by Corporal Bremridge. Corporal Bremridge held out a Scorpion 7.65mm automatic pistol with folding metal butt, a lethal weapon and a favourite with the mafia. "Sir, Trooper Baker was brandishing this around threatening to slot anyone who told him to put it away. What do you think we should do with it?" he said, cradling it delicately in two hands.

"Where the hell did he get that from?" I exclaimed in shock at this stupidity.

"He took it off the reception desk at the hotel," answered Corporal Payne, smirking at Baker's unbelievable audacity and drunkenness.

"What, do you mean to say that some Muslim warlord's minder is now cutting around without his fucking gun and tomorrow will probably get shot for being careless? Bloody marvellous," I said, failing to mask my despair. After a moment's consideration I woke Cooper up. He had lived at the hotel for two months, knew most of the BiH and would be sure to have the answer. Cooper was equally surprised at the stupidity of this, but had no good ideas, so suggested we wake Bob Ryan for further advice. Bob, another Tuzla LO, saved us by saying he would return the weapon to the hotel in the morning and find its rightful owner, which allegedly is what he did.

The following morning Trooper Baker was embarrassed by his behaviour, although he did not remember much and was feeling too deathly to truly care. He was a very good soldier, just frightful after a skinful of beer. To have had him charged would have made the incident official and could have opened a 'can of worms'. For everyone's benefit, including the company commander, we kept it quiet. Not for the first time, I sat Baker down for a serious talk about drink, which was the least I could do, but unlikely to be the help he needed. Everyone concerned had been lucky.

*

126

*Wednesday 3 February*: Today we heard that there was a shooting incident in Vitez on 31 January. Apparently a white car, driven by Croats, sped past a group of Muslim men near the Garage and fired upon them. The Muslims shot back but the car did not stop. Opposite the Garage, the Bulk Fuel Installation guard commander, LCpl Byrne, took the initiative and followed up the incident by checking that the Muslims were all right. The car returned and was engaged with small-arms fire by him and two private soldiers. The soldiers fired 22 rounds but in the return fire Byrne felt his helmet being struck by a bullet. He was later treated in the medical centre for a graze to the head.

We also received reports today that up to 2500 Muslim refugees are stranded and homeless in the area of Mededa, a village near Kalesija and the front line. The people are victims of Bosnian Serb ethnic cleansing and tonight will be braving the sub-zero temperatures whether elderly or newly born. The company has offered to provide trucks to transport the refugees into Tuzla but the authorities have turned us down and said they can cope. As I write this tonight we hear that the refugees are still sitting in the open fields. I can only imagine the scene; families and friends huddled together underneath plastic sheets in the snow and dark, children crying and, with little or no medicine, any injured people fearing the inevitable. My suspicions lead me to believe that the Tuzla authorities are already overwhelmed with refugees and feel they cannot take any more. They do not want our help because they do not want the people and the problem.

Other local news was that two British mercenaries, Ted Skinner and Derek Arlow McBride, have been discovered dead in a stream near Novi Travnik. I believe they have been fighting for the Muslims and clearly this is the risk one runs when you become involved in someone else's war. It is one thing dying a mercenary, but quite another to be injured and subjected to hospitalization in Bosnia or be captured and interrogated.

Martyn came into the Mess this afternoon to tell us that two of the 'Options for Change' amalgamations will not being going ahead. The King's Own Scottish Borderers and the Royal Scots, the British Army's oldest foot regiment, have both been saved, as have the Cheshires and Staffords, which the company are overjoyed about. A full celebration is likely to follow.

The SQMS arrived in Tuzla this afternoon as the leader of the advance party ready to take over the accommodation and offices from

*'A' Company. This evening he was in the Mess with Sergeant Clarke, both catching up on news of Vitez and Tuzla. When I left the Mess they were having their last 'nightcap' while still putting the world to rights on subjects like, how best to run a troop and the danger of Bomb Alley. It sounded like a discussion that would never be concluded coherently.*

Our tour of Tuzla had drawn to an end. The troop had made a note-worthy entrance, I suppose a small place in UN history, but the activity rate had fallen from that day on. The troop and company needed a change and were looking forward to Vitez. However, they understood that this would entail a return to life under the watchful eye of battle-group headquarters and 'bullshit' from the senior ranks hierarchy.

The troop's last day in Tuzla saw the Scimitars all serviceable and 'back on the road' thanks to much hard work and the timely arrival of some critical spares. The long-awaited new rear idler wheel was delivered that very morning and was fitted by Elvis and Yozza in the following thirty minutes, which is cutting it fine.

Sergeant Clarke appeared at 1030 hours, looking rather fragile, and had missed GPMG cleaning. This sort of situation is embarrassing, especially when everyone else has managed to get up. It placed me in an awkward position, made worse by the fact that I also had enjoyed a lie-in or two during the tour. Of course, if you want to be able to do the right thing you have to set an example all of the time, which weak-ened my position. The worst thing I could have done was to be a hypocrite. I did not have to say anything to him; a look was all that was needed to achieve the effect without damaging a close working relationship.

The eve of our departure saw a number of us being invited to Mayda's home for a farewell supper. Her mother plied us with a feast that was brought to the table a plate at a time. Initially it looked like we might go hungry, but that was simply a lack of cultural awareness. Plates kept on coming, bringing a variety of Bosnian dishes, including my favourite, home-made *cevapcici*. Mayda and Sandra both inter-preted for the five of us, although Mayda's father, whose name I never learnt, spoke some English. The others agreed later that he seemed to understand much more than he spoke. The evening had been fun and the family very generous. It was another privileged insight of a family making its way through the war, even if more fortunate than most.

The following morning I led a long convoy of 'A' Company vehicles along the winding valleys and through the crumbling towns of a snow-covered Bosnia. A journey of some ten hours, it was not worth the wait. Vitez was unchanged: no electricity, a freezing house, filthy showers and a second-hand message from the operations room informing me that I was to take over a checkpoint in Kacuni the following morning.

# 13

# KACUNI

The morning was still dark when my section arrived in Kacuni, a linear village near Busovaca straddling the western edge of the broad Kozica Valley. A Warrior was stationary in the middle of the road blocking the route ahead of us; it was the checkpoint we had come to relieve. Parking alongside it, I jumped across onto the Warrior's decks to receive a hand over brief from its commander. I plugged my headset lead into the gunner's pressle box to hear Dooley speak above the rumbling diesel engine. Had I known that two Croat snipers lay a couple of hundred metres away and were accustomed to popping off shots at any target that took their fancy, I would not have positioned myself so boldly but asked to be briefed within the Chobham armoured compartment. Crouching lower behind the turret, the darkness covered me sufficiently for these few important minutes.

It was now evident that fighting between Croat and Muslim, which had started in Gornji Vakuf, had spilt over into much of central Bosnia. The battlegroup's immediate concern was the activity in between Busovaca and Kiseljak; Kiseljak was the location of the Headquarters of UN Forces in Bosnia Herzegovina (HQ BHC). Lines of communication between Kiseljak and Vitez were critical for the battlegroup, the UN headquarters and other units, thus needed to be kept open.

The trouble in Kacuni had flared up at the end of January. Croats in the northern half of the village had conducted offensive operations against Muslims in the southern half, although who had fired the first shot was officially unknown. In an attempt to thwart Croat attacks, the Muslims had placed a laden logging truck across the road at the bridge that essentially divided the village in to its two religious parts. Colonel Bob had tasked Major Philip Jennings, the new 'C' Company commander recently arrived in theatre, to clear the route to Kiseljak as an operational priority. Once this had been achieved a tacit agreement was made to replace the logging truck with an UN armoured vehicle in an attempt to deter either side from an attack, yet allow freedom of movement for UN and other authorized vehicles. For five alternate days in the next ten I was to command this checkpoint with Corporal Bremridge and my team to maintain this access while Sergeant Clarke's section took their turn to enjoy R&R at home.

It was on the southern side of the bridge, where the logging truck still sat, tyres flat and dragged to one side, that the checkpoint was established. Next to the river bank stood a house, the lee-side of which was a driveway, an ideal location to park our second Scimitar. Reversed in and used as an admin vehicle, its position gave us cover to walk about in safety when not manning the checkpoint. With the duration of each checkpoint tour spanning twenty-four hours – six men working three-man stags of two hours on and two hours off – this would be important for our sanity and well-being; unlike the Warrior crews, we had no rear compartment in which to take cover and live. Assuming the hand over to be accurate, it made sense to keep the house between the Croat snipers and us whenever possible.

Some of the other houses showed the hallmarks of fighting. At least one house nearby had a burnt-out roof, doors had been broken down and window panes smashed. The most prolific and revealing signature was the random pattern of bullet marks scarring house walls. Rubbish littered the street and domestic animals abandoned by fleeing people roamed freely. This even included a wandering pig, which must have been lost or wisely considered the Muslim half of the village the safer of two evils. Further south a few houses remained in tact, a delineation of where the remaining Muslim community sheltered.

The routine was simple, so it was not long before the section settled into this new post. Pleased with this comfortable set-up that sheltered us from danger and any potential horizontal weather, I sat in the turret of the admin Scimitar scribbling a bluey until disturbed by a voice I did not recognize shouting at one of my soldiers. Popping my head up, I discovered an irate Bosnian man standing at the foot of the Scimitar gesticulating wildly at Elvis. It was immediately apparent that he was unhappy with the Scimitar parked on the driveway, an imposition that had been made by accident due to the house looking derelict. Realizing that I needed to win him over quickly, I jumped down from the turret and introduced myself with an exaggerated manful handshake. Consulting every chapter from my charm manual I then reeled off as much Serbo-Croat as I could speak in the shortest time possible, an initiative that brought hope when a smile eventually surfaced. "*Mun-tee Musliman*," he exclaimed repeatedly, pointing a finger into the sky and raising his eyebrows as if he had had a revelation. "*Nema Musliman, Ja sam vojnik Ujedinjenih Nacija, ja sam British oficir, ja*

131

*sam . . .* Christian," I stated, wanting to make my position absolutely clear. The more I denied being a Muslim the more he joked that my Serbo-Croat was too good for me not to be; believe me it wasn't. How flattering of him, the charm was working and his mood completely changed within a few minutes.

Disturbed by the noise, a middle-aged woman, who I assumed to be the owner of the house, opened a side door and joined us. After a few words passed between them, the soldier gestured to me not to worry, adding the easily understandable staccato phrase, "*Mun-tee, tenk, nema problema,*" and shook my hand again, this time genuinely. His smile widened in to a broad grin that looked wickedly infectious and suggested that he was fun. "*Ja sam Kapral Zahid,*" he said proudly putting his heels together and presenting me with a pantomime salute. He had all the credentials of a heroic uncle figure and in his late forties was about the right age. My grandmother had always advised that to judge whether someone is trustworthy you should look at their shoes and into their eyes. Wise counsel perhaps, if you don't mind running the risk of being beaten up, and so I conducted this stringent litmus test and assessed him to be a good egg, despite his worn-out black boots being caked in mud.

Zahid tried to explain to us the need for caution in our new location, which included numerous hand signals and a discourse in Serbo-Croat, of which I managed to identify only the word sniper. He put his hands up to his face like a child does when pretending to use binoculars, indicating that he wanted to borrow a pair, and once I had handed him mine, he grabbed me by the shoulder as if to take me under his wing and led me away. Naturally I followed Zahid as the bill for a pair of army binoculars was £600. Moments later the two of us were lying behind a crumbling wall in the back garden, Zahid binoculars to his face peering over the bricks. "Mun-tee, shniperr," he remarked seriously with a professional evaluation, pointing into the distance while grunting with the exertion of holding up the binos. This was an alarmingly familiar scenario; we would surely get shelled next! It transpired that one of the snipers I had been told about was actually a kilometre away to the north-east and had our cross-field exit well covered, allegedly. After taking a look I was none the wiser, something that might have made me paranoid and question my choice of vocation as a reconnaissance soldier.

By the time we returned to the house the woman, who had been introduced to me as Halema, had brought out a pressed chrome tray with a pot of freshly brewing Bosnian coffee and tiny cups on it. To

132

complement the occasion and reinforce this new friendship I fetched a large fruitcake from the vehicle, made for me by Mrs Penny Robotham, the mother of a friend. With the instinct of magpies, Elvis and Yozza saw me remove the brick-sized object covered in tinfoil and so the five of us sat around the doorstep for a break and chatted away quite happily using a mix of languages to get by. The atmosphere was quite convivial, the sun now shining, and for a second I was removed from the hostilities, until interrupted by shots being fired in the street. Even a dog was taking it easy, basking in the sunshine by the bridge. It was a most civilized affair.

Halema and Zahid were quite different from other locals I had met, the first ones I felt did not have a hidden agenda. Grabbing my cheek between her finger and thumb, Halema said I was 'liep', meaning handsome. After a protracted explanation in three broken languages we understood that Halema preferred not to sleep in her house at night due to its vulnerable position on the edge of the village, so, ever the altruist, I suggested we protect it for her. At first she looked reluctant, not surprisingly, but my clean-shaven smile and son-like glow eventually won her trust and I was shown inside later that afternoon.

Her home was immaculately clean and looked like a period museum with hand-made cushions, bedspreads, rugs, dolls and lace curtains. In the corner, and most homely of all, stood a brown enamelled wood-burning stove that would not have looked out of place in a Yorkshire farmhouse kitchen. The heat from it could be felt at five paces, the real type, unlike the vector heaters we had become accustomed to.

Returning down the steep wooden staircase it was impossible not to notice the loosely hand-woven carpet made from multi-coloured pastels ending at the door next to a neat row of clean and assorted boots and shoes. My charm and audacity had paid off, which I was pleased with, as it is rewarding to recieve a dividend like this for the boys and would make us comfortable for a few days. It was, however, not the most compatible place for muddy-booted soldiers, which concerned me. We were going to need to be on our best behaviour.

Zahid and two other middle-aged soldiers stood outside the doorway waiting to escort Halema inside the village security perimeter for the night. Zahid introduced me to the soldiers, one of whom was called Jahid. With the knowledge that *zahod* means lavatory in Serbo-Croat, I pointed at the three men one at a time and said, "*Jahid, Zahid, Zahod.*" This was a dangerous and fairly rude joke to be making with someone I had never met before, especially as he was carrying an AK-47, but fortunately it was well received by Zahid and Jahid, who laughed at their friend and slapped me on the back. Alas, Bosnian humour incorporated play on words and the lavatorial crudity of the English people. Concerned that the sight of four squaddies trampling through Halema's house might turn her off the generous hospitality, I waited for the four of them to leave before re-entering in my socks.

All day we had changed stags every two hours by mounting the admin Scimitar before driving it out to the bridge, relieving the other Scimitar in place. By the time it was dark, however, it seemed sensible to short-cut this time-consuming routine and so, leaving the vehicles where they were, we simply changed the crews instead. This necessitated a daring thirty-yard dash from the cover of the house to the lee-side of the checkpoint Scimitar, protected to some extent by the dark. The oncoming commander would shout up to the gunner to jump out so that the outgoing commander could brief him. Shots were frequently heard in our general direction, reality prompts that achieved greater urgency during the procedure and so the need to slither in and out with a minimal silhouette became a well-practised art.

Everything had been flowing smoothly that night until 0045 hours when I was woken by a duel of automatic weapons in the street and wondered what the boys on the checkpoint would be making of this. They were well trained and had an armoured vehicle for protection; they would be fine; besides there was little to be achieved by lying awake worrying for them, especially with a stag an hour away.

By the time Trooper Baker, Yozza and I went on stag, the firing had quietened down. Yozza ran over to the Scimitar first and changed with the driver. Once in place Baker followed him, but as he did a single shot rang out, a bullet that was unmistakably intended for him. I waited a few moments in the hope that the firer, being a Bosnian rank amateur, would lose interest, giving me a clear run, but how would I know this? I might wait ages. Whispering the immortal words "fuck it" to myself, I took two paces back for a run up and sprinted across the thirty-yard gap like a greyhound that had received a cattle-prod to the testicles.

After a day in Vitez the section returned to Kacuni on 9 February, saddled with the prospect of an extended twenty-seven-hour duty. The boys were not at all happy, accusing the Cheshires of being unfair. This time I had difficulty in defending the chain of command because, although the maths added up, it meant that our relief would only be doing a duty of twenty-one hours. This contributed to a consensus that a two-man stag, (commander in the gunner's seat and driver) was the only pragmatic way forward if we were to remain alert for long periods. Changing just the crews and not the vehicles for each stag was extended to daylight hours as well.

Mid-morning Halema appeared at her doorstep with make-up heavily applied and hair brushed, grooming that looked most unnecessary and incompatible with our surroundings. With a lovely smile and a glint in her eye she requested our company upstairs, saying, "*cafee*," while pouring from an imaginary pot. My diary quite empty, "Ummm, stag 1200 hours," we were able to accept her invitation immediately and followed her in.

Goodness knows what had come over her, but Halema was being uncomfortably tactile with me, an experience I cannot deny was most unnerving, but one I dismissed for purely maternal instinct and friendliness. It was lovely that she had made the effort to entertain us properly, china cups and saucers and a plate of homemade biscuits that were scoffed in short order, but it was all rather peculiar. Without Zahid there to make fun of her, the conversation was stilted, so I was pleased when she insisted that she show us her brother's photograph album. Given the family's circumstances this was initially quite painful, but on reflection it provided me with a further insight to the communist Yugoslavia lifestyle in the 1970s. Her immediate family had all died in a car crash in Banja Luka four years previously, something she clearly drew comfort from sharing with us. Banja Luka was now a Bosnian Serb stronghold and a definite 'no go' area for both her and me. She had Muslim friends who lived in Banja Luka but had not heard from them for nearly a year and had no idea whether they were alive or not. With no communication, she feared the worst.

Seeing that I was uncomfortable, Elvis kept joking that he and Yozza would leave me with Halema so that they could get on with vehicle maintenance, an offer I replied to with a death stare. Fortunately the stag change was imminent, giving me an exit strategy without causing offence, which I took. The coffee and chat were enjoyable, but Bosnians are so hospitable they will entertain you far beyond what is sensible. It made me realize how shamefully inhospitable and busy English people can be, something I vainly resolved to better on my return home.

Thinking that Halema was hard up for provisions and wanting to repay her kindness, I offered her an unopened four-man box of army compo rations and some biscuits, which she gratefully accepted. I felt it important to explain what each can and packet of food actually was, for I had images of her preparing an 'all-in stew' with curried chicken, compo cheese and mixed fruit pudding. She had been a mum and would surely work it out, but very wisely she gave the rations to Zahid and the village militia, *de facto,* making me a hypocrite for showing favouritism. Nevertheless, the thought of Zahid and his friends being constipated for days brought a smile to my face and could have been argued as biological warfare!

Having switched to a two-man crew I sat in the gunner's seat with Trooper Baker in the driver's and watched up and down the quiet street through the vehicle periscopes. The rain was to thank for this peaceful lunchtime stag, but I did not appreciate it soaking me through the open hatchway. The dog I had seen lying by the bridge two days before was in the same position, but now getting very wet. I was beginning to suspect that it was probably not napping at all but dead.

Despite my vigilance while on duty I failed to notice Zahid approach the Scimitar and so was surprised when I heard his voice call out "Mun-tee". Looking up I discovered a frying pan hovering above my head. Zahid had run over to us, I think as much to avoid the rain as the threat of being shot at, and was offering me some freshly cooked meat. Taking a large chunk from the pan I had to juggle it before sampling. Wonderfully charred on the outside but tender within, it tasted like lamb, but was more likely mutton or goat. I took another piece and passed it down to Baker. Scarpering with his pan to offer the others some, Zahid looked like an English villager participating in a Shrovetide game. This man was very genuine and fast becoming our friend.

Hours later and on night duty the monotony continued, but at least with a heavy volume of gunfire flying in both directions to keep us awake. It was incredible that we were to just sit, watch, listen and report. Orange tracer rounds passing over the vehicle was not uncommon, which I considered ironically symbolic of the UN's overall position. There was a lot of time to think!

Kacuni was just showing signs of waking when we drew up to the house on Thursday. In the woods, just north of the river, I noticed that birds were already twittering. High ground, forming the valley's eastern watershed, was silhouetted by the rising sun, which had not yet shown its face. As I would not be needed for a stag until two hours hence, I decided to do what I am best at. Sleeping while my crew manned the checkpoint did not make me feel guilty for I had just

136

finished a four-hour watchkeeping stint in the Vitez operations room before climbing into my Scimitar and being chauffeured, slightly jaded, to another day's work.

Lowering myself down from the Scimitar on its safe side, I had walked around to the rear of it to collect my camp bed and sleeping bag from the boot bin. I untied the bin's cover and had just picked up the camp bed when I heard the "*thump*" of a bullet strike the road next to me followed within less than a split second by the slower "*crack*" of the rifle shot resound off the valley walls. The bullet ricocheted with a most authentic 'pee-yow-n' that lived up to my expectations from a comprehensive education in war films. The time difference between the thump of the bullet impacting on the ground and the crack of the rifle firing indicated that the bullet was travelling faster than the speed of sound. The shorter the delay the closer the firer was, an estimate I found easier to calculate than I had previously imagined from fieldcraft lectures. In this case the firer was close.

With a delayed response worthy of being called a Norman Wisdom impersonation, I dropped the bed and dived for cover along the side of the vehicle. Quickly turning around to face rearwards, I sat on my haunches level with the top of the tracks. My bed lay stranded in full view of this unknown lunatic whom I assumed, if not intending to kill me, must have hoped to at least scare me. I hated sleeping on the floor and so, with few alternatives, lay on my belly and extended an arm out just managing to reach one of the bed's metal legs. With finger tips I pulled it towards me, stashed it under my arm and did the thirty-yard dash to Halema's house without being shot at again. Halema's wooden summerhouse, superbly appointed in her back garden, was open and inviting. Sensible enough to have left the sleeping bag behind, I used my parka as a blanket.

Some hours later Captain David Sherlock and 2nd Lieutenant Gary Wright, the Company Operations Officer, came to visit us with the Company Sergeant-Major, Mr Banwell, in tow. They parked their Land Rover in the open about five metres from the end of Halema's driveway, got out and approached us. As they did, the CSM looked down at the litter around his feet and along the edge of the house and in his Lancashire accent commented that it was mostly army compo wrappers and tins, therefore our mess and a disgrace. He must have been bored. When we first arrived I distinctly remember seeing the second Warrior parked in the very same place, it being too wide to fit along the driveway. It had had its back door open and, although I had not seen the lads throwing litter, I suspected that this was part of the source, which, seeing the village a bomb-site, they had probably considered no big deal. My comments were not well received.

Meanwhile, David was demanding an explanation from me for not wearing a helmet and asked why the soldiers were sitting on the vehicle decks reading newspapers in the sun and not battened down. As I stood behind the cover of the house I suggested that he took three paces forward or risk being shot at by our neighbourly sniper and then went on to explain that one had to trade off the real threat with a twenty-seven-hour duty. Because we had bothered to converse with the locals and follow their patterns we knew more about the threat; our information-gathering was far more effective than had we spent our duty battened down in the vehicles, too worried to come out.

Later that afternoon the sun shone and, when sheltered from the wind, the temperature was most agreeable. Halema had two guests with her, both female and both doctors, providing an excellent opportunity for more local information-gathering. One doctor was pretty, slim, with long dark hair and wore tight jeans, whereas the other had a moustache that a seventeen-year-old lad would have been proud of and displayed the negative effects of the earth's gravitational pull. Both of them spoke English very well, giving me the ideal chance to ask Halema some unanswered questions while enjoying the complex ritual of Bosnian coffee-making. Zahid must have sniffed out the strong smell of coffee, as he soon joined us, as did my crew who sniffed out something else and it wasn't Halema's home-made doughnuts or hand-picked raspberries, "Don't fancy yours much Yozza," joked Elvis with a mischievous smile.

Good weather continued, the sun was shining and the dog, whose future we were uncertain about, was still sleeping near the bridge. When I saw a crow perched on the dog's side picking at its innards I was finally convinced that it was dead, the sniper having probably used him for target practice; he was only a mongrel after all! While happily chatting away, a Muslim soldier came creeping around the edge of the garden stooping in a half-hearted manner. His military attire, AK-47 at the 'carry' and tactical posture complemented the surroundings very well, unlike us, who having a tea party, so to speak, were quite out of place and made him look surprised. The soldier joined us for a coffee and seeing me cleaning my SA80, pointed to the oil and flannelette in a gesture that indicated he wanted to use them. "*Nema problema*," I replied. He showed his gratitude with a repeated, "*hvala, hvala*"; again I was guilty of helping the Muslim war effort. He took an interest in my SA80, as one would expect from a foreign soldier and, despite

138

my kindly token, was cheeky enough to laugh at the components of the stripped-down rifle. He pointed to the cheap pressed steel of the SA80's body and said, "*Ne dobro*". I suspect he had a point.

Seeing me offer my help to this Muslim must have given Zahid the confidence to ask for my help. He wanted the two of us to jump into a Scimitar and drive up the road to recce the Croat sniper's position accurately so that he could task a patrol to remove him. Again Zahid's earnest face showed that the request was genuine, which, not wanting to disappoint him, I had to explain would be impossible and so I made light of his request as if he had been joking.

*Thursday 11 February: Our close proximity is causing a deal of stress and tetchiness towards each other. Leave is over due after nearly three months continually together. Most vocal is Elvis who has expressed his dissatisfaction with the Kacuni duty, an attitude that I find unhelpful. This is a real job, not newsworthy, but it is a job that gets us out of camp and has its compensations, like a comfortable room at night. It is sometimes difficult to understand what will make the boys happy. It's not of course happiness that they seek, but fulfilment. Yes the tour is becoming turgid in places, but only because we have been spoilt by many exciting incidents and now they take everyday danger for granted, to a degree. Our Bomb Alley incident was probably as exciting as it gets for most people in an entire career. I wish they would be more positive at times.*

By the fourth duty at Kacuni we were becoming checkpoint experts. The UN vehicles came and went, often in a group for security, then none for hours, or more annoying, one every ten minutes. Incidents of shooting had become so common that we gave up reporting them minute-by-minute, instead consolidating reports on the hour. Detailed accounts were written up and handed to Captain Simon Ellis, the Operations Officer, at the end of each duty.

A small contingent arrived from Vitez that afternoon, not for any justifiable reason other than military tourism: Gary Wright and Dave Kelly, both Irish Rangers attached to the Cheshires, Sergeant Parrott and Catherine, who, being a theatre nurse, rarely escaped the confines of camp. It so happened that we were very well resourced to cater for tourists in our isolated and shot-up redoubt and so entertained them properly as cavalry are accustomed to do.

The garden looked a picture in the bright sunshine. The weather had been varied and inconsistent, but now it seemed as though spring would be upon us soon. Birds were early to be toing and froing and again the temperature was unusually warm when sheltered from the wind. Before long the impromptu visit had cued Halema's natural hospitality. The garden table was positioned in front of Halema's summerhouse to which she ferried teatime treats: Bosnian coffee, hot doughy rolls, raspberries, freshly made popcorn and corn on the cob, victuals that we far preferred to our Quartermaster's ration packs. The picture was complete with Trooper Baker sitting on a chair sporting a pair of Aviator shades, legs crossed and contented while consumed by the lurid stories of a *Sun* newspaper they had brought us. The moment was recorded on film, but as ever the peace was punctuated with a timely reminder of conflict, bored soldiers from one side or the other interrupting the occasion with rifle shots that echoed off the building walls. The scene was very British, one of understatement and coolness while all around was in chaos – unprofessional? Only to those who never thought of it first, or thought they had better not do anything that might get them into trouble. Sergeant Parrott, a fine example of a British Army senior Non-Commissioned Officer and a credit to his battalion, considered the occasion most praiseworthy. "Sir, I've gotta hand it to you, there's little that impresses me, but this just takes the fuckin' biscuit."

At 1930 hours I was back on stag sitting in the Scimitar when an enormous explosion virtually took my breath away. It sounded loud enough to be an artillery round landing nearby, although I was not well practised at judging the distance of impacting artillery shells. Baker and I immediately closed down the three hatches and sent a report to Zero.

Corporal Bremridge came outside to see what was happening, not what I would have done with artillery rounds landing, but he was also concerned with a clicking noise that he could hear beyond the valley and believed to be missiles being prepared. Goodness knows how he could hear this amongst the excitement and there was nothing we could do anyway, except report to Vitez that we could hear clicking sounds, a sitrep I was not prepared to send.

At 1950 hours I went inside the house to wake up the next stag. The boys were sitting on the chairs and were most adamant about not getting inside their sleeping bags because of the shelling. Given how important sleep is, I did not see how not being in one's sleeping bag was going to help. If they were that worried and wanted to be safer they should have been sheltering under armour in the other Scimitar. Like a drill from a field training exercise, they were worried that in the

140

event of having to 'bug out' they would not have time to stash their sleeping bags away. This was quite right, although the relative importance of losing a sleeping bag against being caught by an artillery bombardment seemed to have been forgotten.

While this conversation was going on, I was needlessly delayed from rejoining Trooper Baker who remained alone outside and must have been fairly concerned, which was negligent of me. Three months in Bosnia had hardened us to all manner of dangers and I was being dismissive of the explosions, and the concerns from the section I had misjudged. Seeing our relief nearly ready and wanting to continue as if it was no big deal, I prepared my sleeping bag and camp bed. This was a catalyst for Elvis who exploded into a tirade at the same time as a number of artillery rounds landing near enough to the house to visibly shake it, although in truth they had probably landed a couple of kilometres away. The mood was very tense; artillery rounds make a frightening noise, one of their by-products, but there was actually very little that could have been done. Our options were limited; leave the checkpoint all together for everyone's safety, which seemed somewhat drastic; get everyone closed down in the vehicles or just sit tight in the house and only move if the shelling appeared to be rolling in our direction. Within thirty minutes the shelling had gradually subsided.

At dawn the scene was as calm as a sea the morning after a storm, in fact so quiet I wondered what all the commotion had been about. It had been an important lesson in leadership for me, expensive in credibility, but best taught by a real situation when soldiers want leadership and are not scared of voicing their opinions. Clearly the episode demonstrated that I needed to re-evaluate my priorities and, more than anything, that we all needed a break.

*Sunday 14 February Valentine's Day: I enjoy returning to Vitez in the darkness with the prospect of a few hours in bed, but only after indulging in a fat boy's breakfast. Unfortunately today Sergeant Mason required us to carry out a 100% check of our vehicle CES (Complete Equipment Schedule). It was a nice surprise to be told that the troop had the least kit missing in the squadron, thanks to Corporal Bremridge's efficiency. Corporal Payne's Scimitar, however, did let us down being discovered in a bit of a state and with rusty ammunition. He is not present to defend himself.*

*Tonight I relaxed in the Mess by the fire chatting to Gary and Catherine. Catherine complained of being tired and so rested her head on my shoulder. She then lied her legs on top of mine before her arm reached round my waist, enjoyable but a little embarrassing in public. The two of them persuaded me to join them at the Sappers' house for a farewell drink, some of the engineers being due to leave Bosnia tomorrow. With an early start to Kacuni in the morning I did not want to stay long so after one swift drink I made my excuses and left. Catherine insisted on showing me out, raising my suspicions. Walking down the steep flight of concrete stairs I could sense her intentions and knew what was coming. At the door I turned to say good-bye, went to kiss her on the cheek but her movement towards my mouth resulted in half-contact with both. There was a brief pause before we kissed again. She gave me an innocent look with big brown eyes. Not quite believing my luck, I went to bed.*

Two mornings later the section left Kacuni, but did not get a chance to say farewell to our Muslim friends. It was sad to be leaving them, but Halema, Zahid and the others we had met seemed in good heart. They were a close lot, had the necessary fighting spirit and had enough provisions to survive, more than I had imagined. This was borne out when, before departing, I threw a large chunk of compo rations corned-beef to a stray dog that had been snooping around the vehicle. The dog gave the corned-beef a couple of sniffs and trotted away without even sampling the offering. Harmless enough, but it spoke volumes to me. The troop's effort was now to be turned to assisting the Croats.

# 14

## FALSE START

The white Catholic church, breaking the village's low skyline, and the abundant Croatian flags flying from buildings made the Croat quarter of Vitez easy to find. On entering the Hotel Vitez, regional Croat HQ, through its smoked-glass doors, I asked for Mr Kordic at reception. A man dressed in an ill-fitting suit with an effete manner, who appeared well-suited to reception work, looked up from his desk and in broken English told me to take a seat and wait.

Feeling more vulnerable sitting down in such places, I chose to stand and then paced up and down the entrance hall, making my impatience obvious. Unhappy with the lack of progress, I returned to the Scimitars to update the section on the delay and discovered two black limousines with matching blackened windows and red and white chequerboard pennants mounted on the wings parked by the front door ready to convey my VIP, which was a positive sign. Already past lunchtime and edgy to get on, I walked around outside just as impatiently while looking at my watch and studied the map on the Scimitars engine decks to estimate the time of our journey to Jablanica.

After a wait of more than an hour the glass doors of the hotel were opened. Three or four men stepped out into the afternoon sunshine dressed in dark suits and sunglasses, none of them distinguishing himself as my VIP. Following them was a thin man with a crew-cut hairstyle, also wearing a dark suit. Walking confidently, holding a briefcase and satellited by flunkeys, I assumed this to be Mr Dario Kordic, Deputy President of the HVO and an HVO commander. The flunkeys, who were behaving in a professional manner, if not a little over-the-top, opened car doors and acted respectfully, one man signalling to me with a wave of his hand that I should proceed.

Our armoured 'motorcade' moved unrestricted down to Busovaca, past Kacuni and along the valley to Kiseljak, the Scimitars having no problems maintaining a lead ahead of the dated black Mercs. The road was wet with slushy verges. Dwellings set back in fields looked cosy, brown smoke pluming skywards from their tin chimneys mounted on the ubiquitous skeletal breezeblock structures. A common sight was rows of chopped logs stacked perfectly around outside walls and on this occasion laundry hung in gardens attempting to dry during this fleeting spell of sunshine. At every village the ripple effect of children running out to see what was passing was as commonplace as lamp-posts in England.

The motorcade was stopped only once, not surprisingly at a Muslim checkpoint. Halting short of a red-and-white-striped barrier, next to a makeshift sangar, the commander checked my papers. A conscript Muslim soldier stood yards away with fists clenched ranting in the direction of the two limousines. The Croat pennants were somewhat conspicuous; Kordic might have removed these and done without us. After some hesitation from the checkpoint commander we were waved on. The upset soldier lurched forward to assault the first limousine, arms flailing, insults flying and, despite his colleagues restraining him, managed to spit on an off-side window of Kordic's car.

A few kilometres further south the journey was stopped again because of traffic congestion in a small town called Kresevo. The town was very high up and with deteriorating weather, was covered in deep snow. Unforgiving mountains stood between us and the end of our task, the route blocked by snowbound trucks, no doubt the same decrepit wagons, driven by foolhardy locals that had snarled up Route Triangle four months before.

My patience was running low after standing in my vehicle for an hour without moving forward one inch. There was complete chaos ahead and it was not about to be solved. At 1600 hours it was getting dark, snow was falling and the temperature was dropping. A French aid worker, who surprisingly answered me in English, said there was no prospect of the mountains being cleared that night. Fortunately he also spoke German and was therefore able to interpret between Kordic's chief flunkey and me. The Deputy President's aide wanted us to stay until the morning so that Kordic could rest up safely in a village guesthouse. Pacing along the traffic queue, I wrestled with my conscience to do the right thing, an assessment that took all of two minutes. Although we could survive quite easily in our bivis in minus 15 degrees, I did not see why we should do this for an HVO commander. There were no allowances available to us for hotels and, even if there had been, we would still have needed to guard our vehicles all night. Furthermore, the prospect of the troop eating a hot dinner was fast fading, the allure of a spam sandwich and kit-kat biscuit being decidedly unappealing after a long day in sub-zero temperatures. Kordic's aide compromised by asking me to stay for a further hour in the hope that the traffic might clear and the journey be concluded.

The French man translated my apologies to the aide; Mr Kordic would be safe in Kresevo. My decision was well received by the section and positively lifted morale. Humanitarian tasks are rewarding, the very reason we were in Bosnia, and longer tasks with night stopovers were popular too; any change from the norm always attracted volunteers. The concept, however, of UN soldiers being used to escort a faction commander and politician, one who amounted to not much more than a warlord, through high-threat areas merely to reduce his journey time, rather than take the longer safer route, was simply wrong. Whether or not I was ignorant of the bigger picture, the need for political leverage or diplomacy, made no difference to my perception of a situation that appeared to be just a favour and more mission creep. Minutes later we were manoeuvring around an array of old trucks and cars, jockeying for an escape and causing a disturbance to the queue.

With few aid convoys to escort, effort for the week was focused on local patrols. A programme of four patrols daily in the Lasva and Kozica Valleys and environs was mapped out each night. This high-profile presence was intended to act as a deterrent to Croats and Muslims in order to build local confidence and attempt to contain or even turn the inevitable tide of full-blown fighting. This patrolling was the very 'bread & butter' of UN Peace Support Operations.

It was still dark when my patrol stopped to check the battlegroup's observation post responsible for monitoring the HVO's roadblock on the Zenica road, a roadblock that had been poorly disguised as a checkpoint. One of the Commanding Officer's aspirations was to have it removed by diplomatic means, a process that would take some time.

Moving on to Kacuni we were spotted by Zahid at the bridge. He was camouflaged in a snowsuit, which, he proudly told us, Halema had made from bed linen. Unable to turn down the offer of a coffee, not to mention an update of the war according to a Bosnian corporal, the patrol parked up. Zahid was not his cheerful self but sighing and shaking his head. Picking out words that I could understand, "*Croat, ne dobro, pushka,*" illustrated well by dramatic animation, was all that was necessary to appreciate which faction had the upper hand. Cheering himself up, he explained how an HVO sniper had mistakenly shot a fellow Croat near the border. But Zahid's solemn face showed the strain and the severity of the intensifying situation. His people faced annihilation and at forty-something he was too old to be running about the countryside being shot at in a tailored bed sheet.

At 1100 hours we departed Vitez for a second patrol, this time all the way along the important Kozica Valley that linked us with UN headquarters at Kiseljak. This multi-national headquarters was established in a large hotel built for the Sarajevo Winter Olympics in the early 1980s. Part of the Olympic village, it stood on the side of a hill, its modern alpine design, like most things in Bosnia, looked dated and run down. This was a popular destination as facilities in this former hotel were relatively luxurious; indeed the officers and soldiers of the headquarters were far from suffering. Every soldier had their own bedroom, and amenities, such as saunas, were in regular use and a lounge with satellite television was a comfortable and warm place to relax before and after lunch.

The food was not as good as the English stodge in Vitez, but the continental-Scandinavian style buffet, with its cold meats, cheeses and salads, was a welcome change. Soldiers need and enjoy carbohydrate, especially in cold weather, and so the French, Spanish, Danish, Dutch and other European contingents, who occasionally visited Vitez, would marvel at the quality of British Army food. Who, on a snowy February day, would honestly swap steak & kidney pudding and chips with cold herring and a tomato salad?

The week passed slowly and finished with the notable return of Sergeant Clarke's section from R&R. The troop was still attached to 'A' Company and was to be switched to guard duties for seven days. Life took on a new dimension as activity revolved around manning four sangars, conducting regular foot patrols, manning the operations room with runners and signallers and providing the RSM with fatigue men. Other routines included the maintenance of vehicles, when time and the still ridiculous shortage of vehicle spares permitted. Consequently still only two of our four vehicles regularly remained serviceable.

Other daily activity that passed time included writing 'blueys', reading and re-reading blueys, until the next batch arrived; eagerly anticipating the next meal, then feasting to capacity; taking a shower in one of the new blocks, praying that you caught the hot water; cleaning and oiling rifles; reading books and out-dated newspapers and watching television. I was not aware of any troop reaching the desperate stage of swapping each other's blueys to read.

But there were other means of changing the routine pattern of life. On one occasion a number of us were sent to represent the battlegroup at a Zenica school drama production. The musical production was fairly uninspiring to listen to, being performed in Serbo-Croat, but it was extremely rewarding to watch, with happy-faced children and brightly coloured hand-made costumes and stage props. Clearly the children and the audience of parents had been continuing life as normally as possible, their smiles and laughter and applause suggesting that they had lost themselves in the show for an hour or so and had forgotten the reality that awaited them when the curtain went down.

The reality and the contrast with Bosnian lives were highlighted on our return when Billy Fooks told me about his day. Up to 2000 Muslim refugees from Banja Luka had been sent across the border near Turbe. Billy had monitored this event at the exchange point and said that, from what he could see of their clothes and belongings, they looked no different to people in UK, not the simple rural folk that we normally saw portrayed on television. Apparently a lack of male adults led to women, children and elderly struggling with belongings. The UN had again been criticized for assisting ethnic cleansing by providing the transport and help across the front line – you can't win! Surely by the time the border is reached the ethnic cleansing has been done? The UN is simply ensuring their safety. Soldiers able to help refugees carried belongings from the Serb coaches to the UN trucks, bags, babies and all. Land Rovers were weighed down with people holding on to the bonnets, literally for dear life. Many soldiers could not hold back their tears. One old lady had to be lifted into the hollow of the spare wheel on a Rover bonnet and made as comfortable as possible. Even some of the journalists helped carry belongings. As night fell the ceasefire that had been negotiated for this crossing broke and the Serbs shot over the people, but it was not clear whether anyone was killed. Each Muslim had to pay DM80 to be transported to Turbe, in other words pay to be ethnically cleansed.

Billy also told me that the regimental doctor, Captain Mark Weir, had found a bullet lodged in Lance Corporal Byrne's head. Lance Corporal Byrne had complained that three weeks after being shot at, his graze had not healed. During the Bulk Fuel Installation shooting the bullet that had struck his helmet had actually penetrated and lodged under his scalp – easy mistake.*

*Monday 8 March: It is fantastic to be going on leave. I am fed up with starts before 0500 hours to find convoys failing to turn up by midday.*

---

\* Lance Corporal Byrne was Mentioned in Despatches.

*Where these locally sub-contracted trucks carrying food aid are doesn't bare thinking about, and these are not one-off situations – is it worth caring any more? The journey to Split, four months to the day since arrival, was a long and painfully cold one in the back of a canvas-topped Land Rover. The quality of Route Triangle has improved immeasurably, thanks to the Sappers, helping speed up the journey. The polarity between life in Vitez and life in Split is stark. Split being the port of entry for all UK supplies has newspapers and mail arriving more quickly and they enjoy the benefit of welfare equipment, such as gymnasium running machines and bikes. Most significantly the temperature is much milder. It seems odd and a little patronizing to have lived such a hazardous existence to then be lectured on health and safety and tortured with peacetime bureaucracy by military staff, who in many cases have not ventured north of Gornji Vakuf. (Without knowing it, the regime was developing for an operation that would last at least another ten years.)*

*When the RAF VC-10 jet landed on Split's runway a huge cheer rose from the balcony. Its passengers were the previous tranche of soldiers returning from R&R. They walked from the aircraft wearing civilian clothes and queued to enter the terminal. Homebound soldiers lent over the balcony and laughed at this line of returners. Hanging their disconsolate heads, they had the non-too-pleasant prospect of putting their musty uniforms back on and a freezing eight-hour journey in the back of a Bedford truck. In fourteen days time we too will suffer the same.*

*

The stark "rat-tat-tat" of automatic fire from very close by woke me abruptly. I sat up and peered cautiously through the thin frost-covered glass to see a local soldier below proudly pointing his rifle into the air demonstrating a 'Beirut unload'. He was not the only jubilant man in Vitez, the chorus of distant automatic fire echoing off the hills in reply being clearly in evidence. It was as if the firers were communicating to one other using the assault rifles as a medium, in the manner that dogs bark across a neighbourhood. The only significant event on the Muslim calendar was Arab League day. There not being any Arabs living locally, it was obviously just another excuse for any bearer of arms to release their joy into the sky.

What goes up must come down and so, somewhere within a half-mile radius of this firer, thirty bullets would be raining from the sky with lethal potential. It was commonplace to see rounds being fired skywards, but by the Grace of God I never received any on their way back to earth in this pseudo-artillery fashion. Had none of them heard of party poppers and didn't they have a war to fight and resources to consider? Raising my eyebrows in matter-of-fact acceptance, I flopped down and pulled the bed covers up and considered it strange that a day earlier I had been in London. Refreshed from my break and back to work with only two months of the tour remaining, I expected life to resume its previous routine, as the situation would surely bubble away until our relief arrived.

Tension between Croats and Muslims in central Bosnia, however, had increased further in my absence, recorded by a number of house burnings and skirmishes, but still only a simmer by Balkan standards. An effective ceasefire that had survived beyond two days was, to my recollection, yet to be achieved and the situation did not look to be going the right way. When on patrol during official ceasefires I had often witnessed automatic weapons being fired, and not just in the air. The Bosnian chain of command was not as robust as professional armies would expect, making passage of information unreliable. Once information had percolated to troops on the ground, the risk followed of a drunken or ill-disciplined soldier re-igniting the situation with a shot at an opportunity target. Deep-rooted hatred, ethnic differences, local vendettas and corruption were some of the other factors fuelling the situation, which, simmered in slivovitz, made this *status quo* extremely fragile.

*Thursday 25 March: The tour is being shortened by a week. We shall now be leaving on or around 10 May. Although I enjoy being here as much as anywhere, the inevitable routine ahead makes me not mind this news. Despite the other section's intention to look after the Scimitars, they are in a poor state after our R&R and so this morning was spent at the Garage. Had a dig around in the turret, which was absolutely minging, and noticed the GPMG ready-rounds box was full of water and the ammunition link rusty, as are the 30mm base clips. If we hand in the ammunition rusty at the end of the tour I will get castrated by the RQMS, but neither is ammo meant to be dismantled, the only way to properly clean it – problem!*

*Later on I had to do some ethnic cleansing of my own in the house. Mice have finished hibernation and have been busy spring-cleaning. First sighting was a brown bum and tail behind the wardrobe. I managed to corner a very sweet little chap but he scampered off down Billy's end of the room. I have found three prominent holes in the floorboards, all possible homes, and have placed talcum powder*

*around the edges of them so that I can monitor any room incursions.*
*Still, it is said where there are mice there are no rats and they give me*
*fond memories of school dormitory days. About three inches of snow*
*covers the ground at the moment, which is fine, but it looks like*
*melting again bringing with it days of mud, or should I say clay, which*
*sticks to boots better than dog shit.*

Today's situation brief in battlegroup headquarters stated that the UN
is finally about to impose a 'No Fly' zone over Bosnia, which the Serbs
are unhappy about. They are the only ones with any aircraft to speak
of and now run the risk that any aircraft or helicopter caught flying
can be shot down. The report is referring to engagements by UN
combat air patrols, but after my experience engaging factions, I would
like to see a troop leader brave enough to give the order to open fire
on a Serb aircraft.

The briefing also extended to discussing the Vance-Owen Peace
Plan. Cyrus Vance and the former British Foreign Secretary, Lord
[David] Owen, had long been trying to achieve peace in Bosnia and
had made a plan that was designed to divide Bosnia-Herzegovina into
ten cantons, while preserving the multi-ethnicity within internationally recognized borders. Despite the plan being largely supported in
western Europe and amongst most factions, it had not got off to a very
good start, the United States and the Bosnian Government having
reservations, whilst the Bosnian Serbs would have nothing to do with
it at all. If it was finally accepted by all parties, there were to be a
further 50,000 UN troops to implement the plan on the ground, half
of which were likely to be American.

It was not long before there were signs of the Vance-Owen Peace
Plan failing. The simple conceptual plan to solve a complex practical
problem was being blamed for the increased hostility between Croats
and Muslims. The fact that areas had been so clinically designated
Croat or Muslim for the future was causing a considerable ruckus;
there was a mix of ethnic groups in every proposed canton and
troublemakers within them wanted ethnic purity. Faction commanders had told us that it was not military offensive action but illegal
civilian activity that was upsetting the fragile alliance.

*Monday 5 April: Today we were tasked to establish a standing patrol*
*in Turbe to monitor the latest Croat-Serb ceasefire, an eight-hour duty*
*sitting in the turret watching for any incursions or violations. Despite*
*being on the Serb front line, where incidents are normally quite*

frequent, the duty was actually rather dull – sitting looking around for eight hours is.

B Squadron has returned from Tuzla and so Justin and Ben are back in the house. They told me Mayda has a new job with the UNHCR. Found a bundle of newspapers unopened in the Mess this evening but they are already seven days out of date. Shocked to read on front page that the MoD wants to cut the Royal Armoured Corps from eight tank regiments to six – there were fourteen two years ago! The 9th/12th Lancers were also mentioned as a possible amalgamation – that will improve morale no end!

Early this evening in the Mess Gary Bellis and I drew names out of a hat for the Grand National. On 3 April we had had a sweepstake going at DM10 a horse, 36 riders, but the race had a false start and the signal to stop the race was either not heard or ignored, so the race ended up null and void.

This evening the Chief of the Defence Staff, Air Chief Marshal Sir Peter Harding, visited the Mess. Getting the opportunity to talk to him, he said we should not hold back but tell him of any problems. I told him about the vehicle spares availability and how it keeps many of the wagons off the road for days, even weeks at a time; he was surprised. The subject of losing 70% of our German Local Overseas Allowance while in Bosnia also came up. Instead we receive 30% LOA and Bosnia pay of 77 pence a day. Can't think what I shall spend this on when I get home! The boys had a number of their tent poles snap today due to the weight of snow. When do Balkan winters end?

Easter Day 11 April: This morning Tyrone Hillary gave an Easter Day Service outside the Sergeants' Mess. His sermon was very funereal, punctuated by the timely chorus of automatic fire nearby; obviously the Croat quarter of the town celebrating that Christ had risen; any excuse! Tonight we had drinks in the Mess followed by a dinner in the cookhouse for seventy people, mostly local VIPs from Kiseljak, Vitez and the surrounding area. The tablecloths were white sheets and the wine, which had screw on lids, was served in paper cups, which, when Mark Jones and I proceeded to childishly screw up and throw at nurses, got us death stares from the Squadron Leader. Colonel Bob gave a speech thanking the outgoing medical staff and welcomed the incoming. He said, "I must remark on how pretty the new nurses are. Isn't that right, Monty?" to which I replied, "No Colonel".

151

# 15

## TROUBLE AT MILL

Learning of the troop's checkpoint task in the Croat half of Kacuni village, north of the bridge, was disappointing. The UN has to be neutral and so this is what we would be, although the order did underline how friendly we had become with Zahid and Halema; I felt moderately disloyal to them. The up side was that we would not have to dodge the HVO 'snipers' who should have no cause to shoot at us from within their own domain; if they did it would be a very tricky duty. My section took over from Sergeant Ryan's half platoon under the cover of mist, which was so thick we were separated from Corporal Bremridge's vehicle during the fifteen-kilometre outbound deployment, or, should I say, I allowed Yozza to drive too fast and needlessly left them behind!

After establishing the checkpoint about 500 metres north of the infamous Kacuni sniper, my initial assumption appeared to be correct; we were on safe turf. At least that was almost entirely the case but for a rather territorial German Shepherd dog whose penchant for bodily extremities was a very real threat. He had several successful attempts at nipping the hands and legs of a couple of the section, bringing memories of my childhood and growling Alsatians flooding back. The dog was too well nourished and groomed to be a stray and had a leather collar. Its legitimacy was proved within twenty minutes of parking up when a Croat man in his early thirties, dressed in quintessential pseudo-military garb and unshaven for two days, came from a nearby shed. He gestured that the dog belonged to him and that it was only playing. With a welcoming smile stretching across his face, he spoke that ubiquitous Bosnian phrase, "*Nema problema*," words that solve all apparent ills and consoled us that this dog only had good intentions.

The houses in this part of Kacuni were only built on the eastern side of the road. The river ran behind them and to the west was a steep wooded embankment tapering in to the hills beyond. Our checkpoint was next to a smart chalet-style house similar to ones I have seen in Austria with white-painted walls, strangely unscathed. Having done the first two-hour stag I got my head down in an adjacent garage until more than an hour later when I was disturbed by the noise of voices. The voices became louder and closer until, through my green sleeping bag, I could sense a presence in the garage. I pulled the sleeping bag's hood back and looked up into the barrel of a gun. An AK-47 was aimed directly at my head; I did not know how to react. Not caring, I flopped back on the camp bed and told the intruder to "sod off." Fortunately this did not matter as the rifle belonged to a boy of no more than ten years old and was barely three-dimensional, having been cut out from a piece of chipboard. The boy, whose only other military accessory was a camouflaged peak cap, gave a cheeky grin, displaying neglected brown teeth as if he was proud of them and, laughing, hurried off to rejoin his mates.

Within seconds of turning over to enjoy another half hour before needing to get up, I was disturbed by adult Serbo-Croat chatter from very close by. Peering from an opening in my sleeping bag I was surprised to see four middle-aged men pulling up seats around an orange steel garden table in the mouth of the garage. Feeling a little awkward, I quickly rose, realizing that I was in fact the intruder, having not asked any residents if we could park the Scimitars in front of the house. I supposed these men were sitting down to make a territorial statement in a similar fashion that the 'war dog' had.

Always pleasantly surprised by the hospitality of locals, I soon found myself sharing a mid-morning *pivo* (beer) with them. The sun had burnt through the mist, bringing a fine spring morning and so the table was dragged outside for us to enjoy the rays. The three lads not on stag joined us for a beer, far more desirable beverages like tea or coffee having not been offered. We sat around on beer crates and boxes, as usual exchanging banter. Most of it was one way about the size of British ammunition and the poor quality of the SA80 and we received defamatory remarks about UNPROFOR and Vance-Owen, which were predictable. There was also, not surprisingly, much to be said about the Muslims, "*Musliman, ne dobro*", much of which I could not make out, but sounded vitriolic about their Muslim neighbours. If only I could have had an interpreter in such a situation. It would have been interesting to have learnt their honest views while their guard was dropped.

As I have said a number of times before, it is hard to say no to a Bosnian, especially when the subject concerns drinking alcohol and when you, the young officer, are trying to build a rapport so that you can benefit in some way. On this occasion the motive was using the owner's driveway as a checkpoint and any other hospitality that might come our way. It was bad enough that I did not smoke, so turning down drink as well was made even more difficult.

I often felt uncomfortable in such situations because in some respects we were being far from professional, and yet sitting in the Scimitars for twenty-four hours was not only unpleasant but completely unnecessary. As previously stated, to have done so would have prevented us meeting the locals, showing them we were human, building friendship, gleaning information, or at least moods, and demonstrating to them we were not scared of their environment. To batten down with helmets and flak jackets donned would have been counter-productive. It makes soldiers vulnerable, subjects of ridicule, and might have created ill feeling, the sort of false professionalism I would expect from armies who do not have the same experience of 'hearts and minds', but simply maximise 'force protection'.

It is one thing turning down Bosnian hospitality and another inferring that you have had enough. I made it quite clear to the section that if they thought it an easy option they could have the two pips on my shoulders. Sitting making very boring small-talk with Croat drunks while sipping locally bottled *pivo* and having to accept the odd shot of slivovitz mid-morning was not particularly enjoyable. I would gladly have gone on stag immediately. Trooper Baker had the opposite view and was quite happy to support my wider role and keep the British Army's side up.

A middle-aged woman brought a large plate of cold meat out and laid it before us. The men had barely noticed her and immediately offered me some of the pork. Undoubtedly it would have been fresher than meat from English supermarkets, but the fat and sinewy bits and their food hygiene record did not whet my appetite or fill me with confidence. I was sure they were making a religious point – "look at us, we can eat pork" – either that or they had nothing else in the larder. I did not feel guilty in declining this generous offer and do not believe that I offended them.

During my stilted conversation I joked that they might have beds we could use for the night. One man who, wearing a pair of slippers, faded jeans and a camouflaged cop-vest over a grey and black diamond patterned sweater, pre-dating the Winter Olympics, replied, "*Nema problema!*" Trooper Chambers, infamous for his resourcefulness, was left to sort out the details with a young teenager called Mario. Once complete, we collapsed the checkpoint, which only had a monitoring purpose, and drove a couple of kilometres north to Busovaca for a well-deserved lunch at the Dutch/Belgian transport battalion. Always keen never to push our luck, we stayed for forty-five minutes and, properly fortified by a quality cold meat salad, returned to our duties in the village.

What we returned to was far from desirable, however. Burning houses, two hundred angry refugees or a road strewn with mines would have been no problem, but the four men still sitting in the garage, a little merrier, had brought us six lots of fish 'n' chips. What's wrong with that, you might ask, and, keen on his food, Trooper Sparkes did ask. He enthusiastically unwrapped pages of soggy newspaper, clearly a benefit from not being in the European Community, to discover actual fish, the silvery sort with head, eyes and tail. Sparky might come from Grimsby, but a northerner set in his ways still likes a bit of batter. We sat at the table, this time politely forcing down a few watery chips, but making a very poor attempt at the fish. In landlocked Bosnia the sea was inaccessible, especially in these turbulent times, so I was fairly certain that fresh Bosnian fish – an oxymoron – could only have been caught in one of the nearby lakes or rivers. Those who have seen the Balkan waterways will know that even the most adventurous traveller might prefer to err on the side of caution before attempting what lies beneath or floats on top! Untreated effluent from back garden long-drops, prolific quantities of litter, industrial pollution and probably radioactivity made up as many parts of a river as did water. At least we were not being offered cigar fish!

Late afternoon Mario invited us into an empty house, which despite the ubiquitous Bosnian musty odour, was clean and fully furnished. Mario had borrowed his brother's television and video recorder, which, top-loading, was the size of a large suitcase. He also had a selection, or more accurately 'a collection', of X-rated European pornographic films whose quality was particularly questionable, but ideal to keep the morale of the troops up. This was an unexpected distraction, something that Trooper Chambers must have influenced very closely, but well done him for showing initiative.

At dusk I came across a group of eight HVO soldiers outside the house preparing to go on night patrol. They were very well equipped and dressed, faces heavily blackened and acting in a professional manner. They were young, twenties and early thirties, and had none of the 'village idiots' to carry as passengers that one so often saw masquerading as soldiers. One of them, frowning with a particularly menacing look, carried an RPG, quite something to be taking on a patrol unless you are hunting armoured vehicles. The only armoured vehicle I knew of was the BiH bus I had seen driving around the

Muslim side of Kacuni. It had half-inch steel plate welded all over it and looked like a Da Vinci invention or an armoured Dougal. Although it would have been a kind gesture, I could hardly drive a mile down the road and warn Zahid that he should avoid parking his car outside that night. Troopers Chambers and Baker took the opportunity to handle the RPG and AK-47s and, being the only one to have a camera, persuaded me to take snaps of them in various warlike poses, as is the habit of soldiers.

The village was moderately active that night, with bursts of automatic fire resonating off the buildings and valley walls. This was a little bizarre as four of the section watched pornographic movies in the front room of a Croat house while the deadly glow of orange tracer rounds could be seen from the window for anyone interested enough to lift their eyes from the television screen. Trooper Wiseman and I did two stags in the night, including the dogwatch of 0200-0400 hours. Hostilities were certainly rising, something the battlegroup watch-keeper sounded ambivalent about as our reports were recorded, "Roger out." The intelligence cell would be interested in the activity when we submitted a full report the next morning. When I did, it concurred very well with heightened activity reported elsewhere in the Vitez – Busovaca area. My expectation of eight weeks of routine was fast fading.

*Wednesday 14 April: The day was hot; is springtime finally here? I have been told that spring lasts no more than a week in the Balkans, with change from winter to summer a metamorphosis. Handed over our cleaned ammunition today with no problems. Captain Jez Morgan the ATO (Ammunition Technician Officer) was there, which helped. We received a brand new batch and will hand this over to the incoming Light Dragoons squadron in less than a month now.*

*Mounted a patrol in Travnik tonight where reports of increased tension, and even fighting, between Croats and Muslims has been made. A presence was required to defuse the chance of any overt hostility, the task of my section, supported by Sergeant Kujawinski's two Warriors. Before departure I briefed everyone and we carried out a radio-check, but Sergeant K had no comms. We had not gone more than a mile down the road before we were told to return to the School. Just after turning the four vehicles around I was told to go back again and take only my two Scimitars to Travnik. Martyn Thomas spoke on the air and informed me that there had been reports of HVO reinforcements entering the village, which I was to monitor and report on. Also I was to provide an overt presence outside vulnerable Muslim establishments. We drove straight to the BiH HQ and pointed the two Scimitars facing outwards in a defensive posture, which was probably not a neutral act, but our role was peacekeeping. I dismounted and spoke to a Muslim soldier who spoke excellent English. He was the Muslim LO for Travnik and liaised every day with Captain Dundas-Whatley.*

*I went inside the HQ with the LO and was sat down in a board-room and presented to a Muslim man called 'The Bird'. He explained that the HVO and BiH were working together and that the trouble had been caused by civilians dressed in combats. Isn't this what all their army is? When I came out of the building, at least an hour later, I could hear Warriors racing around the village, apparently trying to find us. Corporal Bremridge had not done much to direct them, although it may have been Tudor Ellis making a systematic search. I spoke on the radio, which was ridiculously busy with all the call signs and the Ops room waffling, and told them to drive east out of town where they could not miss us.*

*Martyn had sent me reinforcements and so I sent two Warriors to the old JNA barracks, had the other two patrolling the village and my Scimitars sat by the music school. We were to rotate every hour. Such an undisciplined radio net forced me to tell everyone to be quiet and only send a sitrep every quarter hour, which did bring my ears peace and my mind concentration. There was not much activity and it was raining quite hard. Foolishly I forgot my waterproof, but the weather was mild so it was no bother. The only activity all night was a couple of shells landing somewhere in the village, I did not think it wise to go and find out where. We withdrew from the town at 0200 hours and sat on its outskirts with engines turned off to listen for any activity – nothing.*

The situation locally was overheating and so it was no surprise to find ourselves fielding a fast ball early the next night. Martyn had radioed the Operations room from Zenica and asked for us to meet him as soon as possible at a *rendezvous* near Putis, a predominately Muslim village that had experienced some trouble, including reports of several murders, in the past day or two. He hoped to quell the incipient bubble of hostility in co-operation with a BiH commander by showing a reassuring presence on the ground.

The instruction gave us precious little time to collect a section and so we found ourselves running from the cookhouse to the Scimitars with anyone that was available, ending up with a hotchpotch of crews including Elvis as the commander of S32. Tearing around a quiet Vitez, we broke all the recently imposed tracked vehicle speed limits that were intended to stop accidents, but mainly to give the Military Police a reason to be unpopular. The Scimitars were driven east along the Lasva Valley, past the Busovaca junction and on to the Zenica main road where we stopped in a layby and waited ten minutes for Martyn, who arrived in the company of Zenica's BiH commander.

Martyn quickly briefed us on developments in Zenica where new trouble had ignited that day. The catalyst for this had been the kidnapping of a senior Croat figure called Totic. He was the HVO brigade commander and had been grabbed as he drove along the streets of the predominately Muslim town. This had created a volatile atmosphere and put serious questions above any hope for short-term stability. Some believed that the Croats might have engineered this themselves as propaganda in order to create an excuse for hostility. Whoever had done it, the situation was likely to explode as a result and consequently the shockwaves were felt in many of the surrounding Muslim villages. The situation was intensifying.

Moments later I was escorting Martyn's Warrior up a windy and narrow track to Putis with orders to secure its centre and shoot anyone who posed a threat to us. RPG was a particular concern, it being handheld, readily available to all factions and very effective. Not halfway up the hill, orange tracer rounds lit up the night's sky, arched like fire from a hosepipe, but luckily flew many feet above our heads. This display was only small-arms fire, obvious to all four crews and probably only intended to intimidate. Unlikely to be fired at by Muslims, did this mean the village was occupied by Croats?

Short of the houses the firing stopped, enabling the vehicles to form a ring of protection around the Mosque where the village centre was. Martyn and the BiH commander dismounted to speak to locals about the details of the murdered victims. Having parked the Scimitar next to an old building with a paddle-wheel attached to it, some sort of mill, we sat, listened and observed. Trooper Baker scanned our arcs of responsibility with the antiquated and ineffective image intensifying night sight, whereas I preferred to sit with my head out of the turret. Although vulnerable from sniper fire, this gave good local protection. You could hear things better and, once one's eyes adjusted to the dark, you could cover all angles of approach.

Trooper Baker spotted some activity in the woods, about four hundred metres away. Due to a cloudless night and plenty of ambient light, he was easily able to identify three armed men who were walking slowly between the trees. He was uncertain whether they were friendly troops maintaining a watch outwards or a hostile group looking inwards. Having monitored their movements for nearly an hour, he said he thought the latter. It was unlikely that while we kept armoured vehicles in the village they would try anything. Martyn had been gone ninety minutes. Later, when given our report, like us, he agreed that there was little we could have done. Baker wanted to put down a squirt of speculative coax fire to be sure, but this did not really comply with the rules of engagement and so we withdrew from the quiet village.

Hopefully the people of Putis had been reassured to know that UN troops were taking an active interest in them. They might have only regarded their humble hamlet as an insignificant number of homes unworthy of attention, but, whatever the scale, it had been threatened and was now our interest. Sadly we could not visit every village potentially at risk in the valley. As well as being a fact-finding mission it was hoped that our brief appearance might disturb the perpetrators of violence and cause them to delay any further plans, but the threat would be the same the following night and the night after that. With the other sub-units fully committed elsewhere, it remained for 'A' Company to patrol Travnik and Kacuni by night and now Zenica; the battlegroup had insufficient resources to monitor anything more; Putis would have to look after itself.

Had the resources been available to deploy an armoured car outside every home in central Bosnia little would have changed. Who were we to look for and how should we recognize them? They would never show their faces while we sat there with bigger guns. I had heard of HOS, but the intelligence cell was unaware of them operating in this area. Unaware of the fate that would confront them the following morning, the people of Putis, and many other village communities in the Kozica and Lasva Valleys, would tomorrow know the identity of the murderers. They were no evil group with masks and machetes, they had not been brought in from outside to do the job, but were the same people who opposed the presence of Muslims in a canton that had been selected as a future home for Croats. The efficiency of ethnic cleansing achieved the next day could not have been managed were it not for the people who had the motive to help. Targeted Muslims would be staring death in the face and in many cases it would be their life-long neighbours who would slay them.

# 16

## AHMICI

"It's like the fuckin' Wild West in Vitez, there's stiffs everywhere," Tudor Ellis unintentionally reported quite matter-of-factly as he walked into the Mess. Covered in dust and diesel fumes, cheekbones lined and red from wearing goggles, his young, slightly chubby face was a mixture of colours and showed his tiredness. Commanding his Warrior platoon since dawn, his kevlar helmet had made the curly hair on his head sweaty and matted and his baggy combats were in need of a wash. The flak jacket he was wearing flapped open like a cowboy's waistcoat, complementing Tudor's portrayal of burning Vitez on its first day of full-blown hostility very well. It wasn't yet NAAFI break, but already he looked like someone who had earned a full day's pay.

With the situation so volatile, all of 'A' Company was on patrol, whereas I was restricted to camp, my troop temporarily grounded due to the local area being assessed as too dangerous for Scimitars to deploy. But Tudor's subsequent colourful description of Vitez was not the shock it might have been. The pressure had been building for long enough and was due to burst, like an electrical storm on a blistering summer afternoon. Many of us had been woken before first light by the noise of sustained gunfire echoing off the valley's sides, a disturbance now registered as significantly more than the normal daily exchanges.

The benefit of hindsight made last night's activity in Putis fit the jigsaw. Having heard Tudor's first-hand account of Vitez, I wondered how widespread the hostilities were and whether Putis had also been targeted in the ethnic cleansing. If the streets in Vitez were so dangerous that people were unable to recover loved ones from where they fell fighting or running, then the problem was likely to be more widespread.

Having been increasingly bored in the previous weeks, almost waiting for the tour to end, I was now envious of Tudor's extraordinary assignment among the flames and gunfire of a town at war while we sat in the Mess with only a milieu of smoke and the sound of gun shots to quench our curiosity. But with only my troop remaining avail-

160

able for tasking, this jealousy was short-lived. In less than half an hour an out-of-breath runner arrived from the operations room to deliver a message from Captain Sherlock. My troop was needed to investigate activity in a small village called Ahmici, five kilometres east of Vitez. Being further down the Lasva Valley, it was away from the centre of fighting and so would be less of a risk for the Scimitar crews; at least, that was the rationale.

Although the request was urgent there was enough time to brief an *ad hoc* team of soldiers found available and ready. When I arrived on the tank park they were preparing the vehicles to go. From the task description I assumed that two Scimitars would be sufficient, Yozza and Kusbish joining me, and Elvis commanding S32 with Troopers Bertie Blunt and Billy Wiseman. David Sherlock, however, had wisely wanted us to take a Warrior for support. A Royal Irish Regiment crew was selected with Lance Corporal Connor commanding and two foot soldiers as dismounts. It may have been telepathy when, for good measure, we agreed to take Corporal Penfound, the battlegroup photographer, and Ali, a Muslim interpreter in the back of the Warrior.

After initiating a radio check I led the way to Ahmici, which, just past the Dubrovica checkpoint, was a mixed Croat and Muslim village we had driven past many times before without bothering to remember its name. A peaceful agrarian settlement with what appeared to be simple folk surviving a conflict through subsistence farming, Ahmici was bracketed by Vidovici and Nadioci, no different, yet not our problem that day.

With the familiar sound of Scimitar tracks whirring beneath us, I continued to make myself comfortable in the turret, as for any patrol. The added threat, however, made me double-check the condition of our weapons, clean dust off the periscopes and off my goggles and check the map, even though I knew the way; probably distractions for any apprehension. Over our right shoulder, and a kilometre across a field, Vitez houses could be seen fully ablaze or burning out and smouldering. Still standing prominently among them were the white minaret of the Mosque and the belfry of the Catholic church, symbols of a previously tolerant community sharing a town, but now polarized by irreversible hatred. The whole valley was shrouded in white cloud, but not like the beautiful mists we had enjoyed on many early morning convoys, instead, pungent man-made smoke that suspended itself above the small town like a suffocating blanket.

Further east, palls of black smoke could be seen pillaring skywards and then dissipating in the wind. A glance at the map all but confirmed my impending fear. Seeing Vitez burning was unbelievable, yet by driving past it from a distance, we were saved from the horror and reality of its detail. Moreover, set within the context of five months living in Bosnia, it gained the level of recognition relative to a smouldering volcano observed by a tourist from a coach seat; "Look everyone, a town being ethnically cleansed!"

As we drove closer to the source of black smoke to the east, the possibilities of a place-name were narrowing. The black smoke looked like it was about to be our problem. Within minutes I could see that the smoke was pouring from Ahmici, merely the symptom of a burning village. It was identified easily, as roughly every fourth house was a beacon showing us the way, the flames bright orange, almost yellow.

I directed Yozza to take the first left turn after the cemetery, which was already cluttered by many new flimsy wooden headpieces marking the resting places of young men. The proximity of the dates of their deaths could only be explained by one cause. Doubtless more wooden coffin-shaped planks, stuck vertically in the soil and inscribed in black marker pen, would soon record the current inflammation; the next tranche dated 16 April 1993.

Despite the burning houses being a distraction, I immediately recognized Ahmici. It was the only hamlet on this side of the valley that I had seen with a minaret. A striking white construction, this marked the position of its Mosque, a focus for the Muslim families of the surrounding hamlets and an easy navigational reference for its flock of god-fearers. For the Croat population, who had had to accept its presence and whose antipathy for the Muslims was no longer in doubt, this was now an aiming mark for both direct fire and the more pusillanimous, thus popular, indirect fire of distant mortars.

Next to the road was a smart detached cream-coloured house. It was either Croat owned or had so far been spared the fate of others. Opposite was a lush field of grass, bordered by a fence made from wooden posts and wire. This was still intact, making the entrance to the village look untouched by fighting, although a little unkempt. Indeed there was nothing tangible to suggest that Ahmici had been a deliberate battleground. There were no defences of coiled barbed wire, trenches, sangars or ditches, and certainly nothing as sophisticated as an armoured vehicle present. Ahmici was just a village inhabited by civilians. At this stage I had only made broad assumptions about what was happening; it was important to remain as objective as a young man can be.

162

To gain perspective many pictures are best viewed from a distance, just as the landscape of burning Vitez had been minutes before. But now we were in the picture, in one of the many burning villages, and it was exhilarating. The detail could be seen close up, real and three-dimensional; the scars on the buildings were already visible and getting larger; the smell of smoke, the definition of flames and the roar were not our imagination; burning timbers could be heard cracking as the fire consumed them. The modest would understate it, but it was in fact extraordinary, out of this world, or surreal as some like to say, so much so that it was difficult to accept. It was so bizarre that as we made the turn into Ahmici I approached the village, with its obvious challenges, as I would a training exercise, or that was how adrenalin was managing my brain. Ever more prudent from a bank of hard-learnt Bosnian experience, I slowed the pace of my three-vehicle patrol to a crawl.

Yozza brought our Scimitar to a standstill level with the second house in Ahmici where a woman in her mid-thirties beckoned me from the relative safety of its porch. I did not give more than a second's consideration to continuing without stopping to investigate, her display being animated and urgent. The road could have been mined, or an ambush, set for UN troops, might have been further along. Speaking on the radio, I told the two other vehicle commanders to move into all-round defence on the T-junction by the Mosque and for Ali to accompany me with the two Rangers.

Unexpectedly, the woman shepherded me into the house with a guiding hand on my shoulder and a few incoherent words. She had a western European look, her dark hair fashioned into a long-bob-style and secured by an alice band. She was dressed in blue jeans, a trendy black jacket and top, and pearl earrings. She was in a panic, speaking quickly, very shaken with dried tears crystallized on her pale and drawn face. I never asked for her name.

The house stank. The first room off the short hallway had its door ajar which allowed me to glance inside as I passed. Huddled within, and screened from outside by curtains, were at least four adults sitting on a bed. There was an elderly man and two large elderly women and, I think, a couple of mature teenage girls. A number of children sat between the adults for protection, mute from the shock of the events they were witnessing.

The woman showed me into the living room where a man in his late thirties was lying on a large sofa. His clothing was more the local rural style, so I guessed he must be a brother, but I never did discover the

163

relationship. In fact the woman appeared quite out of place, as if she had popped in from Zenica on the wrong day, rather like someone walking into a bank during a robbery to become a hostage. To all intents and purposes this woman was now a hostage, as were the terrified elderly civilians and children she had taken charge of.

At a glance from the doorway the sofa looked to be a rich burgundy red and it was immediately apparent that the moaning man recumbent on it was injured. My first indication of just how badly injured was when, standing next to the sofa, I discovered that much of its colour was in fact his blood. From the darkness of the blood and the extent it had spread, I assessed the time scale for this injury to be several hours previous. This was confirmed when I asked Ali to question the woman gently who, still nearer hysteria than calm, described with great emotion the events as they had happened after first light. Sadly there was no time for Ali to translate her story as my priority was focusing on investigating the man's injuries. As I was looking over the man I asked Ali to fetch Elvis and a first aid kit, who disengaging from the woman, made me the target for her grief and outpourings, a distraction that was unhelpful.

The casualty's arm was in a makeshift sling, his elbow tied up with cloth. Carefully removing this to take a look, synchronized by a suppressed yelp from the man, I revealed a hole that was bleeding slowly. The surrounding flesh had a cauliflower-like formation. It was his elbow that was causing him so much pain and the complaint that he and the woman obviously considered the most life-threatening. The flow of blood and the size of hole, however, did not seem commensurate with the blood on the sofa.

For the first time since being in Bosnia I reached for my field dressing. Taking it from the pouch on the arm of my jacket, I applied it to what was an awkward position, every wind of the cloth bringing forth a wince from my patient. As I did this I returned to reality, a consequence of actually doing something rather than watching with glazed disbelief. We were in a hostile village that had been ethnically cleansed and these were real people whose lives were about as bleak as it gets and yet there was little or nothing we could do about it. Worse, their only hope was that I had taken charge.

While I fully appreciated the urgency, I was aware that this man had been bleeding slowly for several hours. Believing there to be no immediate panic helped me maintain perspective and kept me calm. Had the man lying in front of me been one of my own soldiers, or if the injury had just happened and the urgency was thus greater, I believe my attitude would have been different, less distant. After six years of medical scenarios where pretend casualties had to be dealt with in time measured by seconds, this first real-life experience was not how I imagined it would be when finally tested.

The man, who was very weak and pale having lost so much blood, rolled over slowly to let the woman show me his back, in a sort of "Oh and by the way I've got this little nick as well" manner. He groaned as he did this and with a grimacing face murmured a complaint, but returned to remind me of the pain in his elbow. With no first aid kit and less first aid knowledge than me, his relations had made a poor attempt at stemming the bleeding with rags for improvisation. Although his bandage was saturated with blood, and therefore theoretically helping stem the flow, it was a piece of unhygienic clothing ripped up and applied ineffectively. Removing it carefully from the right side of the small of his back, I revealed two tidy red holes each the size of a penny about four inches apart.

Although I had never seen a real gunshot wound in my life before, it was obvious to me that this was what I was looking at and whoever had taken the shot had only managed to 'wing' him. The bullet had literally skimmed through the side of his back and exited below his ribcage. There are no main arteries in this part of the body to sever, but the trauma of a gunshot had caused a great deal of bleeding. The sofa was covered in so much blood it was astonishing to me that he was alive at all, let alone capable of moving and murmuring. From both holes blood oozed, which in some respect was a positive sign, but the rate was still enough to warrant concern. His condition did seem to deteriorate in the short time we were there, a problem I attributed to him relaxing his willpower on our arrival. He must have been thinking that he was about to be saved.

Elvis arrived and helped me apply his own field dressing to the man's back and then he took over while I dashed outside to send a situation report to the battlegroup operations room. Regardless of not yet knowing the scale of what had happened in Ahmici, it was at that point that I might have tasked some soldiers to deal with the first aid while I focused on the real priority, the military aspects, the safety of my section and the situation as a whole. This was even clearer to me, having realized that I had completely lost track of time while in the house.

The three call signs outside were informed what was happening, but only from my sitrep to the operations room, as it was not convenient or safe to dismount the crews for a specific briefing. In a hostile area, where houses were still burning and prolific automatic fire could be heard close by, I failed to appreciate how six junior soldiers were feeling, isolated in their vehicles and vulnerable. Having undergone five months of Bosnian civil war, I assumed that this would be sufficient to inoculate them from what was happening. Adrenalin from dealing with the first aid was, of course, helping me overcome the not insignificant danger. Wandering around this village was hazardous; 'stray' bullets could so easily have mistaken the identity of an UN soldier, despite the pale-blue helmet! The boys were unlikely to have had the same levels of protective adrenalin, which also comes from leadership, as they just had to sit in the vehicles and scan their arcs conscientiously for several hours. Static, and targets for belligerent factions, they had a right to be concerned. Before jumping down from my Scimitar to return to the house I told Trooper Kusbish that if he felt seriously threatened he should just shoot and we would ask questions later. He nodded and gave a hesitant smile. Frankly they needed a bit more leadership than that.

Elvis was doing a sterling job. With the injured man in shock, he had attempted to administer an intravenous drip, a procedure he had practiced only once before on a healthy and unenthusiastic soldier in a classroom six months previously. In this real situation, for which it so difficult to fully prepare, Elvis could not get a line in, despite several attempts, which the man, although weary, found energy enough to display misgivings about. From my basic knowledge I understood this to be the blood vessels contracting to maintain blood pressure and thus making the task near impossible. The man was very cold to the touch, he was not in a stable condition and we had done about as much as we could, short of evacuating him. I held out very little hope.

It was not until later that the penny dropped as to how he may have been injured. With his elbow against the side of his body, it was my guess that he had been shot from behind, probably running away. The bullet had passed through his side and embedded in his elbow. With the bullet lodged painfully inside his elbow this had become the perceived medical priority, when he was actually in danger of bleeding to death from the injury in his side.

The need to report our situation to battlegroup headquarters had me returning to the Scimitar a couple of times in the space of an hour. Outside the house I listened to the woman retell her story to Ali. She was pleading for us to evacuate the man and I was repeating the message that we were not equipped or authorized to do so. She also

166

wanted more first aid kit. It was difficult to explain that we could not afford to give her any more dressings and, even if we did, could she make effective use of them? Each field dressing was personal issue for one's own injuries in the event of becoming a casualty. We had already used up a box of spares. The emotionally charged atmosphere won my deepest sympathy and this small dilemma was tougher than one might imagine.

Later, having returned inside the house, while Elvis was busying with first aid, I looked out of the sitting-room window and noticed the Warrior creeping further up into the village, not what I had told Lance Corporal Connor to do. He was trying to be helpful. At the danger of being too spread out, I rushed outside and shouted to one of the crew to stop him by radioing, but I could not be heard over the engine noise. Running over to my Scimitar I called him on the radio, but he did not reply. I had no option but to return and tell Elvis that he should tidy up, remount and follow us up the hill as soon as possible.

Yozza drove us up the track in pursuit of the Warrior. Either side of us were homes, some with pyramid-shaped roofs, many burning and others the alpine design. We reached a small white bungalow with eau-de-nil coloured woodwork near the village limits. Outside it a balding man wearing a black anorak beckoned me. He looked quite elderly, but was probably only in his late fifties. Not wanting to be distracted from my primary purpose again, I ignored the man and told Yozza to carry on driving.

Fifty metres further on we came to a turning circle. Through my Scimitar's sight I could see activity in the woods about a kilometre beyond. Of course at this range it was almost impossible to positively identify which faction the men were, although, given their position and orientation, I suspected HVO. Separating us was a steep drop entwined in trees, bushes and brambles and an open field. To negotiate our way through this in pursuit of something unknown, and that we had not been tasked for, would have been irresponsible.


Q. Major Woolley, are you able to tell the court from which military group those soldiers belonged to, despite the fact that you didn't see the badges on their sleeves?

A. Well, first of all, I knew they were soldiers as they were carrying Kalashnikov rifles. I would say that they were HVO soldiers, and this assumption I concluded as a result of their position. They were looking into the village. The village is predominantly Muslim and they were on the periphery of the village and they were looking into it. It would seem that if you were a Muslim soldier, you would be looking out in order to defend the village, and their position was at the bottom of what is called a reverse slope, this slope where the wooded feature is here (indicating). So if the men were Muslim, they would either need to be closer into the village in order to defend it or need to be out, up on this high ground, in order to gain a good field of view in case any further aggression occurred from the Croats. However, if a Croat force had come through this village, clearing it, it could very easily have formed up at the edge of the village in order to observe prior to any further attack or to assess the damage that it actually had achieved.

Q. Major Woolley, everything that you saw that day or any significant events that you saw that day, did you record them in a diary?
A. Yes, I did. I had a diary that I filled out at the end of every day, throughout the whole of my tour.
Q. In relation to producing a statement that was requested of you by the Tribunal and coming to court today, have you used that diary to refresh your memory as to what you saw?
A. I have.
Q. And in relation to your conclusion about the HVO soldiers being at the edge of the forest, was that fact recorded in your diary?
A. Yes, it was recorded as HVO soldiers at that point.
Q. At that stage, were you aware of a War Crimes Tribunal in operation or going to be in operation?
A. No, I was not.


I settled with monitoring their movements for about ten minutes, hoping, unashamedly, that they might initiate a firefight and we would be given the chance to brass up the murdering bastards. Nothing happened and so I about-turned to see Elvis driving up the hill towards us. He had been in radio contact and gave me an inconclusive report on the injured man's state. He had done his best.

Stopping in front of the white bungalow, I looked over my left shoulder to see the anguish of this desperate man who was willing me to assist him. Elvis and I jumped down and I told Yozza and Kusbish to move back up the road some fifty metres to cover the area where we had seen the HVO. Inside the bungalow and immediately in front of us was a body lying on a makeshift stretcher constructed from tree branches and old sacking. Kneeling down, I took a look at a face that was red and swollen. The left eye was bruised and puffed up so badly it had closed. The other eye was glazed over, but I suspected there was some life looking out from it, despite its apparently unconscious condition.

The casualty looked like a man and only minutes later did I realize that this was in fact not the case. Wrapped around the woman's head was a multi-coloured stripy hand towel that was applied very badly to an injury at the back of her skull. Loosely tied and caked in blood, it was achieving very little. Removing it to investigate the nature of the injury, I was physically shocked to discover a huge part of her skull missing. Everything beneath was revealed, which I disbelievingly recognized as brain. My selection of profanities was on a par with the severity of the situation and helped suppress my own shock from what I was engaged in. Some people die from a single knock to the head, but this woman appeared to have been shot in the head and was still breathing Bosnian air. It was unbelievable, but I thought there was hope as she had guts to have survived this long.

Removing another dressing from my pocket, I applied it to the wound and, needless to say, did so very delicately, although, given her state of unconsciousness, this seemed to be more for the benefit of the helpless family and spectators watching our every move. The field dressing went on easily and I checked her body for other injuries through her thick rural clothing, but there seemed to be none.

Elvis had checked the woman's breathing with the back of his hand. It was very shallow, with long pauses between breaths and her pulse was also very faint, so she did not require resuscitation but did need her airway opening further. I was tackling this casualty in completely the wrong order despite all of our training.

Hoping to insert a plastic airway tube into her mouth, I pulled down hard on her chin, but only revealed a bottom row of teeth, her jaw being clamped tight shut. Eventually I managed to open it enough to push the curvy plastic tube in an inch, but, only ever having received theory on its application, had forgotten which way to then turn it and how hard to push.

The woman's right eye was open and staring at me in such a piercing way that I was convinced she was trying to communicate the horror to me and beginning to wonder whether in fact she was unconscious at all? "Stop bloody well doing that, you're going to make me vomit," is what I would have been trying to say. Fearing that I would push her tongue down her throat, I turned around for guidance from blank faces. One of the riflemen, Ranger Farmer, who had been assisting with supporting her head during dressing, took the airway tube from me. With a twist and some weight he pushed it home with appropriate Northern Irish encouragement, murmuring under his breath, "Ged'n thur' y' fok'rr," until the flange was half a centimetre from her lips. Exhaling air could be heard and felt quite clearly, which gave everyone hope.

Elvis then removed a new intravenous drip from its cellophane cover in the hope of making it work. The same situation befell him. The woman's arms were stone cold to the touch and not one vein was visible. We were not experienced enough to try and insert the cannula anywhere else and neither did we give it consideration. Throughout my years of first aid training there had always been mention that in such an event one can attempt to administer the saline solution through the rectum, although this only achieves a thirty per cent absorption rate. Looking at Elvis, I mentioned the option as a nervous joke, which I needed to do to soften the atmosphere. He stared back at me in disbelief, not just imagining the physical challenge and lack of dignity of such a procedure but picturing the family watching our every move and then us trying to justify our actions as "sound medical practice". "Sir, don't fuckin' joke."

With only one hope remaining to save the woman, I told one of the boys to radio the operations room for an ambulance. Surprisingly, the reply came back that an ambulance would not be available. The UN had already been accused of assisting with ethnic cleansing by removing people from their homes and so this was the official line. I left Elvis and Ranger Farmer with the woman and the spectators, and Corporal Penfound, who was taking plenty of photographs as evidence. Using the radio, I explained the situation to the battlegroup Second-in-Command, Major Bryan Watters, telling him that if this woman was not evacuated she would definitely die. The Second-in-Command ignored the red tape and, with a good dose of common sense, authorized one of the battlegroup's ambulances to be despatched immediately.

Meanwhile there was very little we could do but monitor the woman and ask her family to comfort her. The man in the black anorak, who I assumed to be her husband, knelt on the concrete floor and, with welled-up eyes, spoke to her, knowing that hope was all he had. Five men stood outside. Two were of fighting age and wore combat clothing, one middle-aged man wore a khaki coat and cap and two elderly men, dressed in farm clothes, smoked roll-up cigarettes. One of these had his trousers tucked into his cream woollen socks and was wearing a pair of slippers. The rubber boots that stood on the steps among several other pairs of footwear must have been his, which, considering the circumstances, was taking care in the home to an extreme.

There was time to get some feedback from Ali. Being a local Muslim he was most uncomfortable in this mixed village. Half of its inhabitants were his enemy and the other half were neighbours that his well-paid job had distanced him from. He was uneasy, highlighted by his poor concentration when interpreting. With little else to do, it was a relief to get some fresh air and reflect that what we had done was our best effort, given our level of training and resources.

The roar of Warrior engines could soon be heard at full throttle and was closing. Two Warriors, commanded by Tudor Ellis, came racing over the crest of the hill and in characteristic form stopped 'on a six pence' by a breezeblock house. Following behind came the familiar whine of an FV432, the armoured ambulance, which eventually came to a standstill. The ambulance was then reversed unguided with such haste that it brought down twenty metres of garden fence. The padre was commanding and jumped out to assist the stretcher-bearers by opening the large steel door at the rear. With a few words of explanation and a very obvious dressing around the woman's head, Tyrone was soon on his way to Travnik hospital.

After an exhausting couple of hours it was time to leave Ahmici. Having only been sent there on an investigative patrol we had seen and done enough. The three of my vehicles, however, had got no further than two hundred metres before being targeted again by more villagers in distress. The circumstances looked safe and so Elvis and I jumped out and ran down a steep grassy bank to another breezeblock house that was built into the side of the hill. Guided by a woman, we were ushered around the back where, due to the slope falling away, the cellar was accessible at ground level.

Already I could hear the moaning of injured people and crying infants and, before opening the cellar's rickety wooden door, I could smell the inside. The door was ajar, revealing a gathering of ashen faces in what was a dank and desperate refuge. The darkness inside prevented me from properly seeing how far back the faces went and

171

so I used my pocket torch, but this was not very effective. My conservative estimate was that at least twenty people were sheltered in this small room, mostly women and children and at least two men of pensioner age. Many were sitting on blankets and mattresses tucked around the wall's edges. One woman was breastfeeding a child that was at least two years old, which looked strange but made sense.

The odour in the cellar was distinctive and strong and was dominated by Bosnian cigarette smoke. Illuminated by the shaft of light from the door, the thick smoke could be seen hanging in strata four feet high, its main source belching from two old women. Sitting on top of a table puffing away, they looked ambivalent to their surroundings, probably triggered by the shock and hopelessness of the situation.

It was obvious that we were going to need a first aid kit so I ran the fifty metres back up to the vehicles to fetch one, our last one. The crews had sensibly spread themselves out, with Yozza in S30, the furthest down the hill. Crouching on the engine decks, I sent another sitrep to the operations room letting them know our progress.

At about 1400 hours the afternoon was dry but overcast, although much of this may have been the thick screen of smoke from other villages burning in the valley. It was so bad that, despite our vantage point on the hillside, we were unable to see the valley floor. Activity on the periphery of the village was evident by the high volume of automatic fire, but not worth our attention. Of greater interest were a couple of burning houses that could only have been set alight within the previous half hour, demonstrating how cocky these barbarians had been.

Elvis and the two Rangers had started to deal with the worst of five injured people, watched by Ali. A girl of about twelve or thirteen was sitting three paces in from the doorway. Supervised by a woman, who may have been her mother, she had a look of indescribable fear on her young face. Tears of pain were wetting her cheeks, not childish tears that one might normally associate with a girl of that age, but desperate tears of overwhelming pain, shock and a kind of shame. She was wearing a long skirt, but injuries to her lower legs were visible. At first she was adamant not to lift up her skirt for us to help, indicating that she would prefer to continue to suffer the pain than allow unknown soldiers to violate her privacy. However, following a period of crying while she collected her courage, helped by comfort and common sense from the woman at her side, she revealed a pair of thin white legs. There were more wounds further up, the largest penetration on the inside of her right thigh, which was bandaged ineffectively.* Elvis removed the bandage. Beneath was a bloody hole, again the size of a penny, which, looking up at me, Elvis reported had stopped bleeding at the moment when blood oozed out in profusion. His immediate reaction was to plug the bleeding with his fingers. After dressing the injury we suggested that the girl might need morphine, an offer she categorically rejected. The girl's life was not immediately in danger, but she was in pain and might become infected if not evacuated for professional treatment.

Venturing off deeper into the room, I stepped over people and apologized for treading on someone. Elvis had identified one elderly man with an injury to his pelvis area and another with a gunshot wound to his shoulder. Two other casualties had minor injuries and were dealt with by the Rangers. Needing another ambulance, I despatched Ali to tell a soldier to call for one, but the message came back that none were available. I went outside to call Lance Corporal Connor who was sensibly low in his turret. Placing my hand above my head like a dangling spider as a hand signal, I shouted "On me" at the top of my voice. He ran down the slope and received my instructions to evacuate the injured in the Warrior, which he then reversed slowly down the grassy slope.

Elvis had progressed to helping the elderly gentleman whose pelvis injury was causing him much distress. He was to be loaded into the Warrior as second priority to the girl, however, each attempt to move him brought screams of agony. Morphine was a solution, so I told Elvis to administer his morphine syrette to the old fellow. Being a personal-issue controlled drug and accountable, he refused. It was not my right to insist, so, removing mine, I passed it to Elvis to continue the good work. I was far happier for Elvis to administer the morphine, my fear being that I would probably use the auto-jet upside down and inject my own thumb with a three-inch needle.

Elvis removed the syrette from the green plastic sleeve and read the instructions. The old man may have been incoherent and dazed, but I sensed from the look on his face that his acceptance of the idea was waning; the retracted needle on this device was not even visible. Elvis took the red cap off and, without giving the man a chance to waiver any further, thrust it in the topside of his thigh with a single swift action and held it there for a few seconds. The old man released an almighty cry that overshadowed all previous complaints, but the pain

---

* It was later discovered that the injured girl's left tibia and fibula had been broken.

173

was short-lived. Within ten minutes he was ready to be moved, although I am not certain that the drug did anything more than take the edge off the pain.

Fortunately the Warrior crew had their sleeping bags on board and so we used these as stretchers to move both the old man and the girl into the compartment, normally the place for infantrymen. The elderly man suffering a shoulder injury was walking wounded and could just be squeezed on board. Elvis had done all the good work, my justification for sending him to Travnik hospital with the three casualties, which afterwards I thought was a stupid decision as it left S32 without a commander. Our own safety should have been my first priority.

Before the Warrior departed, the crew passed out two large cardboard boxes of four-man rations for the remaining people, a lifeline they were extremely grateful for. Those who were fit enough and brave enough to leave the cellar had done so to see the evacuation. An old Bosnian man, supported by a number of women, gathered around and started to badger me to evacuate them as well. They were not physically injured and so there was nothing I could do. There was no authority or provision for me to take anyone back to the protection of camp and certainly not another village. They did not care where I took them as long as it was away from Ahmici, as it was now past 1500 hours and the smoky sky was shortening the day prematurely. When we departed and later, when night fell, they would be prey to further attacks. It was a difficult call, especially when you know that you are the only hope. Nevertheless it was important not to let this highly charged atmosphere cloud my judgement any further. I was prepared to take risks, but there was simply nowhere that we could take these homeless victims. Protection of our camp was a higher military priority and, apart from anything else, the camp did not have capacity or resources for hundreds of survivors from the burnt-out villages along the valley and would have risked operational effectiveness.

The only way I could physically break away from their pleading and tugging was to say I would try my best to return. Three injured took up the room of seven infantrymen and so we could not squash the others in. It felt dreadful saying this, as I hated being deceitful and giving them false hope. Once we had left them there would be no returning. Many more people in the valley were suffering the same perilous circumstances and there was nowhere to take them either. Many would attempt the dangerous journey over the hills to Zenica. Even if they arrived safely, burdened by a family straddling all age groups, they would surely suffer the grim truth on arrival. Zenica was at capacity; there would be no shelter for them there and no food.

Once the Warrior had gone and my adrenalin had subsided a little, I realized that the two Rangers, Ali and I were isolated at this house and the vehicles were now two hundred metres away or more. For no clear reason the intensity of fire had risen and come much closer to this side of Ahmici, enough to make me feel uncomfortable. On the opposite side of the road a house was in full blaze and making a terrific noise. Having done all we could, it was time to leave. The four of us ran up the slope, one pair covering the other pair forward in a pepper-potting fashion, despite Ali not having a rifle.

Ranger Farmer and I came to a low garden wall some twenty metres from the nearest Scimitar, S32. "Blunty," I shouted at the top of my voice, but the sound of the house burning and the Scimitar engine running drowned me out. Uncertain as to whether our lives were in danger, but nevertheless feeling sufficiently vulnerable, I was keen for the Scimitar to reverse up to us. We were opposite a burnt-out coach, which provided cover from view from much of the surrounding hillside and would allow us to climb aboard with some sort of protection. Realizing that attracting Trooper Blunt's attention was hopeless, I acted swiftly, sprinting the short distance, jumping up the side of the vehicle and slithering inside the turret while keeping the smallest silhouette possible.

Despite discovering that the clutch was on the way out, Wiseman managed to reverse up the road to the wall where the other three quickly climbed in. The two-man turret had one man sitting on each seat, one man crouched above each seat, heads unavoidably protruding, and a Ranger sat cramped in the middle on the steel 'ready rounds bin'; rank has some privileges. Despite the sense of protection, we might have been safer outside as the turret was rendered virtually unfightable.

Knowing that the Scimitar would be unable to crawl home, Trooper Blunt had already called for recovery, so it was just a matter of waiting. Meanwhile Yozza radioed to tell us that he could not start his vehicle. Sitting hopeless and exposed for at least half an hour in the middle of this burning village was not ideal and not part of the plan, one that had evolved as we had gone along.

Across a field I could see a house burning and quite clearly at the foot of its front steps a dead man sprawled head first. At this stage I was not aware that the Croat tactic was to set houses alight and then shoot the men as they fled outside to save themselves. Most women and children's lives had been spared, although many paid the price of rape and some families were forced to witness the execution of their fathers and brothers.

The rumble of a Warrior could be heard nearby, but the valley seemed to be playing tricks on my ears as the engine noise was fading. Just visible through the smoke was a Warrior recovery vehicle heading east along the valley towards Busovaca, away from us and not up the hill to our rescue. The language used to describe the REME and their navigation was memorable! After calling for any "two-four" call sign looking for Sierra three-zero to turn around, we received an acknowledgement and talked the team up to our location.

On arrival, they destroyed some fencing when turning around, thankfully small beer compared to the housing problem. With encouragement, Trooper Blunt had climbed out of the Scimitar in order to prepare the vehicle for towing, leaving behind its false security. He removed the gearbox final-drive splines in record time and mostly with his head nervously facing backwards to the hillside and the intense noise of automatic fire echoing around the valley. Meanwhile Yozza had managed to bump-start his Scimitar by letting it roll down the hill, and so when we pulled level with him, I was pleased to escape the overcrowded turret of S32. Returning home in a functioning Scimitar and not being towed unceremoniously behind the REME was a must. This also afforded the group some protection with at least one vehicle having all its faculties.

Back at the Garage I received the full blow of anger from a number of the section. Feeling under-informed and vulnerable for over four hours in the village, and thus frightened, they were not afraid to vent their disapproval. There was no point preventing them for protocol's sake. If they had something to say I preferred that they got it off their chests by confronting me head on. It was important that the effectiveness of the team was restored as soon as possible; there would be more tasks soon. Furthermore, I would rather know the truth than use rank to silence soldiers and risk creating resentment and a breakdown in communications. It was difficult to judge for myself whether my actions had been right or wrong, so I had to take much of this reaction on the chin. It bothered me a great deal that they thought my leadership inadequate. Lance Corporal Connor had been put in charge of the three vehicles while I dealt with what seemed the priority. It is easy to be wise after the event.*

* A few weeks previously an officer had been criticized behind his back after a not-dissimilar scenario. He, however, had remained inside his vehicle for protection rather

There was no time to continue our conversation as the operations room had ordered us to re-deploy. S32 was already at the Garage awaiting a clutch replacement and my other two Scimitars were still 'off the road'. Consequently Corporal Ramsden from 1st Troop (S13), who had been on camp guard, had to be borrowed to make up the section.

Dooley was already on the ground waiting for us to reinforce him before carrying out his orders. He quickly briefed Corporal Ramsden and me, along with his platoon's vehicle commanders, near the Dubravica checkpoint, aided by a map laid out on the front of his Warrior. Our task was to remove dead civilians from fields near Ahmici and repatriate them less than two kilometres eastward to a roadside dropping-off point near Nadioci. The intention was that from there surviving Muslims would have access to them for subsequent removal and burial, which Muslims do after twenty-four hours. I was not particularly keen to be working under another subaltern's command, but it was Dooley's task and I was too overdosed on dramatic events to care by this time.

It was essential to create a cordon for our own protection, albeit for a few minutes. The four Warriors and two Scimitars established all-round defence in a field to the rear of a cream-coloured house that I had noticed at the village entrance that morning. This house was now burnt out, the only remnants being its ground-floor walls and two vertical charred timbers proving that it had once been higher than a bungalow.

Lying in the field were bodies of five dead middle-aged men who I had failed to notice two hours earlier during our departure; smoke had been thick and there were other distractions. A number of us debussed to assist with loading them. Still conscious of what had been said to me by members of the section, I remained consistent by helping on the ground again, rather than sitting in the vehicle. None of the lads were keen to volunteer for the task in hand anyway, and, more importantly,

---

than help soldiers on the ground administer first aid to injured Muslim civilians. His actions did not receive the approval of those present. To have sat in one's Scimitar and order young soldiers to go into Ahmici's unknown buildings and give first aid to badly injured people would have brought similar calls of cowardice. One can never win but only do what one thinks is right at the time. With no task as a distraction much of the reaction was probably fear that had been suppressed all day and later released.

the Scimitars had to have both driver and gunner mounted to watch our backs. With the vehicles in position, the armoured ambulance was reversed into the field, its rear door opened by the medic who then stood back inside to make room.

The backdrop was a hillside of burnt-out shells once called homes and a smoky atmosphere that invaded one's lungs with an unwelcome stench, created by more than just burning timbers. Distant automatic fire, the tick-over of diesel engines and the shouts of soldiers trying to overcome the noise broke any silence that these corpses might have respectfully been given. The soldiers were trying to load the dead quickly and in so doing were a little ham-fisted, the heavy corpses receiving a few knocks. The natural reaction was to say, "Be careful," regardless of the fact that they were dead. It was a sad and unusual event.

Stooping down to take hold of a dead man's ankles I noticed that he was wearing black slip-on shoes, which stopped me for a moment while I waited for some help. There is something very personal about feet and something very morbid about dead people's shoes. When the man had reached down to put on his shoes that morning I doubt he had expected to be killed in a village field that afternoon. For a fleeting second this made me consider my own mortality in this unpredictable and wretched place. A soldier helped me by lifting the corpse from under its arms and together we swung the dead weight like a heavy kit bag on top of his fellow men. Bending freely in the middle gave us some idea how recently he had been murdered.

These five dead, and I believe innocent, civilians were just a handful from the village. Many more were lying murdered and burnt alive, within what they had trusted to be the safety of their homes. The marks from this act of butchery were sufficient evidence for me to say that these men had been cut down in cold blood from a distance. Numerous bloodstained holes in jackets and trousers were the marks of scattered and inaccurate firing which had killed them, not even single aimed shots. Most striking were their tortured faces captured in their last agonizing breaths as they suffered and helplessly died. These were real faces of death that impressions cannot copy. Their wretched faces were already permanently imprinted on the minds of young soldiers, a significant education at the expense of innocent bystanders.

That said, it was their same ugly circumstances that helped distance me from the squalid reality, which had been termed 'ethnic cleansing'. The dead may have been civilians, as my own family are, but they were lying in fields. They were not sitting at home watching

178

television or standing in a supermarket car park. They were not natives of my homeland; neither were they people I had known. They did not resemble anyone I knew; a friend's father or an uncle look-alike might have struck a chord. They were all men, in their late forties and fifties, and mostly wearing rugged farming clothes, not people of my age wearing contemporary western clothes that I might associate with friends. During my patrols I had been fortunate enough to have been welcomed into a number of Bosnian homes, lovely and contented homes, but in many respects nearly a century behind what my sheltered western upbringing understood. Despite being in Europe, they were used to far greater hardships and literally lived in another world. This again helped me to dissociate from a comparison of similar imaginary events at home, a completely different emotion, I think, than finding an elderly relative collapsed on the kitchen floor.

The laden ambulance chugged away with the bodies lying head to toe. Escorted by six armoured vehicles, it was quite a cortege. At Nadioci I remained mounted and reminded the crew to concentrate their vigilance outwards instead of inwards at the bodies being placed at the side of the road. A number of their faith had already been stacked there, like a pile of logs. Two soldiers covered the bodies with blankets to afford them the most basic dignity.

The task had been extraordinary and a million miles from the early days of escorting humanitarian aid. In fact the last time we had assisted a convoy was difficult to recall, and there had been no authorized change to our mission that I knew of. Most of us had no problem with that, as these developments were making life more interesting and challenging and soldiers get on with what they are ordered to do.

The patrol returned to the area of the cemetery and postured for a while longer with the aim of disrupting the uninhibited cross-valley firing. Sitting in my turret a few hundred metres from the cemetery, I could see a grave being dug by a man with a group of soldiers surrounding him. At first I was not certain which side they were from, but then positively identified a red and white chequered board badge visible on the arm of one man. Was it a group of lazy soldiers watching a conscript dig a grave for a colleague or a captured Muslim digging a grave for himself?

Our attention was turned to the hills in the south-eastern corner of the valley. Distinctive orange tracer from automatic cannon-fire could be seen flying across the valley, its flight pronounced by the vivid contrast against the failing light. These small projectiles were too big to be mistaken for heavy machine-gun fire and the burst lengths were too long to have been from an armoured vehicle. The flat trajectory suggested the source to be from an anti-aircraft gun, probably 20 or 30mm. These weapons had regularly been seen mounted on the back of flatbed trucks, similar to the ones used against the troop in Bomb Alley. Designed for firing at aircraft, their high explosive shells self-detonate at a specific range and are capable of delivering a heavy rate of fire. This can be effective against buildings and soft-skinned and lightly armoured vehicles. The fire was being focused on Ahmici's minaret, a few hundred metres from where we had left the families in the cellar. For them it was going to be a night of hell.

# 17

## DORNE VECERISKA

Totic, the HVO commander, was still missing from the Croat camp, and the ferocity of fighting was so intense it would have required more than his recovery to secure a ceasefire. The Commanding Officer had been to and fro to countless meetings with commanders from both sides, when they bothered to turn up. A peaceful settlement was not in sight. Both factions accused the other for ethnic cleansing and displacing hundreds, even thousands, of civilians.

People frequently remind us that there are always two sides to a story. Incidents I had witnessed, however, consistently portrayed the Muslim as the underdog. Their suffering won them my heartfelt sympathy, hence my surprise to hear reports that thousands of local Croats had been made homeless, especially around predominantly Muslim Zenica. I assumed this could only be retribution. Delving too deeply in to this complex web of claims and counter-claims, accusations, ceasefire violations and so on seemed pointless as it only became more confusing. Better, I thought, to continue taking circumstances on their merits as they confronted me daily.

Having been on duty in the operations room from 0200-0600 hours, I slept in until woken at midday by Trooper Baker who informed me of a task to patrol Vitez. The town was devastated; not a soul was on the streets, except for one dead civilian lying in the gutter near the Catholic church and a scruffy dog scavenging. Debris from fighting littered the streets and the atmosphere was filled with dust from damage to buildings. The whole scene was a complete contrast to what we had known only days before.

The patrol had not progressed far before being re-tasked to a hamlet on the valley's south-facing slope. Allegedly Gola Kosa had been shelled and was now under attack from the HVO. Exiting Vitez and tracking up the Zenica hill road to Poculica, the detour was easy and quickly got us on to our new task. Corporal Bremridge led the patrol down a very narrow lane until stopped short of our target by a group of soldiers. They were occupying three or four houses on this part of the hillside, dwellings that the map did not recognize by name. Only two kilometres below us Ahmici and other villages could be seen still smouldering.

A man wearing combats and a black cop-vest jumped up on to the tracks and hung onto my periscopes for balance. By the way he was dressed I presumed him to be a Croat, but his conversation soon gave away his identity as a Muslim. He spoke very good English and professed to be the local commander, which in Bosnia can mean anything. He asked me to follow him into a house nearby where we would be able to discuss matters out of earshot of our men and in safety.

Uneasy but always refusing to be intimidated, I followed on trustfully with his cronies, leaving my lifeline about thirty metres away. The room we entered was completely bare and resembled the breezeblock interior of an army urban training building. Two soldiers stood by the closed door like menacing bouncers, but with AK-47s slung across their chests. Did they think I might run and what of it? The commander wanted to use my map to help explain his concerns. Unknowingly helpful, he pointed out Croat positions and front lines, and so, to make his job easier, I handed him a red pen and asked that he mark up all the positions he knew. His basic assessment was that Croats were advancing from Ahmici in the south and from Zenica in the north, behind them. He had only a vague idea about Busovaca and knew nothing of the situation further afield. His biggest worry was Dorne Veceriska, his own village and home to some of his unit. So this was his interest!

Before leaving the house after ten minutes of talking, a vocal man I assumed to be the second-in-command insisted on pointing out Dorne Veceriska. Fetching my binoculars, I surveyed the valley and could see prominent white smoke rising high above a village, a location that, once orientated, tallied with the name on the map. The second-in-command was becoming agitated and grabbed my binoculars to take a look. He claimed that, as we spoke, his family were there under attack from the murdering Croats and I should be there saving them – I did not doubt him. The commander, who was much calmer, then made it clear that he did not need our help, not that we could give it. Nevertheless, he said he would like us to rescue their families from imminent death, which was not quite how I understood 'no help'. The frequency of voices and hand movements was increasing, suggesting to me that emotions were beginning to run away. This, added to their repetition of the problem that I now understood and other soldiers closing in, made me feel claustrophobic and a little threatened. Keen to soften the atmosphere, I said I would see what I could do, but they wanted more and closed around me further. With few options available, I acquiesced to the commander, almost promising that I would sort the problem out, a foolhardy expedient to assist our release.

Heading back up the steep lane, I radioed the operations room to inform them of my new investigation. Not far from Dorne Veceriska Corporal Bremridge made a turning up a tarmac road, a dead end closed by the gate of an industrial estate, which was not marked on our maps. There was nobody in the gatehouse and the telephone was ringing so I dismounted to answer it, "*Dobor dan*, Monty's Pizzas" then I spoke some Serbo-Croat gibberish and put the phone down on the irate caller.

Corporal Bremridge continued on towards Dorne Veceriska and on arrival drove around the edge of the village to estimate the gravity of the situation. It was bizarre to be able to sit on a flank in relative safety with only a few shots coming close, and watch two sides engaged in close-quarter fighting. You would think identifying the divide would be difficult, but there it was, men with rifles less than two hundred metres apart slugging it out over a village. The HVO were attacking from the south-west and had made significant progress inside the village. The Muslims defending the north-east corner of the village were outnumbered and on a back foot. As a soldier, I regarded my fly-on-the-wall insight as almost a privilege.

Having stood out like a sore thumb for a few minutes and heard a couple of shots wing past us, we withdrew into the Muslim side of the village. The village was agriculturally based with every foot of land given over to food production or livestock, now conspicuously absent, and access to homes was by mud tracks. Scouting around the northern side of the village, a group of about thirty civilians or more were discovered sheltering in the lee of a house. I told Corporal Bremridge to continue, which he did for a further fifty metres until the track became so narrow as to be dangerously restrictive. Knowing that we had gone far enough, I turned the patrol about in a driveway while we had the chance.

Returning slowly along the track I stopped next to the people who cowered in unison as an explosion shook everything around us sending a shock wave that took my breath away. I ducked down in my turret and then slowly poked my head out to see a man, a madman, of fighting age running over to us. He started pleading with me to help but was speaking too quickly for me to understand him, although given their predicament, I got the flow. These were surely the families of some of the men I had seen earlier and if I had the means and the mandate, the people they would have me rescue.

The looks on these people's faces told me that they recognized the peril they were in, the HVO probably set to break through in the next hour or so. Failure to hold on to the village would see the loss of their husbands and sons, houses, means of sustenance and goodness knows what else. I radioed a sitrep to the operations room, reporting that as well as a few burning houses, so commonplace as to be barely news-worthy, the Muslim defence was slipping away and there was a group of civilians who needed to be evacuated or face possible death. The message despatched and hopefully being considered at battlegroup level, there was little that was going to be achieved by sitting in the open endangering our lives.

Having withdrawn to the Vitez Garage for a breather, we were soon ordered to return to Dorne Veceriska to monitor the fighting and establish how many civilians were in danger, although it was stressed that nothing should be read into this. Patrolling the north-eastern edge of the village once more, we pulled up next to the same people whose circumstances had not improved. Some of the crowd moved closer, including a woman who had a very new baby, no more than six or seven weeks old. To add to the confusion the sprog was wailing at full volume, affecting my concentration, and she held it high for me to see while pouring out her lamentations. It was a pretty desperate and heart-wrenching scene, but luckily being young and childless, not one that I became drawn by. I did not blame them for trying to blackmail my emotions; their lives and everything they held were about to be eradicated.

While I was focusing on their spokesman and trying to ask him to estimate the total number of civilians in the village, without giving him false hope, Corporal Bremridge came up on the radio. He warned me that a soldier holding a hand grenade had just walked past his Scimitar and was approaching us. Not concentrating properly, I flippantly replied "Seen", without fully understanding what Corporal Bremridge was implying. Seconds later my stand-in driver, Trooper Chambers, said urgently, "He's pulling the fuckin' pin out." Turning away from the blathering villagers, I faced forwards and saw this young Muslim man. He was dressed as a soldier, standing one foot in front of our vehicle with his back to us pulling the pin from the grenade. "Go, go, go," I yelled, unable to get the words out quickly enough, releasing my grip from the edge of my hatch and letting gravity return me inside the turret in what was instinctively the quickest way I knew.

184

Chambers had been ready and immediately put his foot down, half-knocking the man as he jumped out of the way. Corporal Bremridge who had also been switched on, followed so close it was as if he were attached by an elastic bungee. I grimaced, half-expecting the "dink, dink, dink" sound of a grenade falling to the turret floor, then looked back through a periscope to watch this lunatic throw it and then take cover. The grenade landed by the side of the house and, fortunately, detonated at 90 degrees to the villagers. The civilians were protected from the blast, but screams from the women could be heard as they cowered once more.

Escaping the village and at a safe distance, the patrol stopped for a breather. I thanked the lads and swore a great deal, to release something. Of all the near misses this incident spooked me the most. A mortar shell exploding nearby would have been more dangerous, but at least understandable, whereas this chilling action was by a man whose people we were trying to help. The possibilities did not bear thinking about; my sympathy was wearing thin. In direct line and two metres from my coaxial machine gun, I wished that I had been quick enough to cut the man in half. Radioing the operations room, I told them what had happened and said we would not be returning and nor should anyone else. This was acknowledged before we were tasked to re-attempt reaching Gola Kosa.

What then possessed me to return to that hillside I will never understand, but, given an instruction, I thought I could kill two birds with one stone. I would speak with the Muslim commander and, although I had nothing comforting to tell him, could at least demonstrate my integrity before proceeding to Gola Kosa as previously intended.

Two hundred metres shy of the houses a group of about fifty Muslim soldiers could be seen sitting in the sunshine on a grassy bank and milling about the buildings. Already I suspected that I was making a mistake, but, like a lemming, continued on. Close up they looked impressive, being well dressed and equipped, cleaning weapons and making preparations for operations. Some spilling onto the track, it was evident that our journey was about to be blocked.

Once more the commander approached and invited me to join him inside the house, an offer I categorically turned down, having to repeat myself again and again before he accepted this; he had succeeded in intimidating me. For the second time that morning I listened intently to their problems and explained the situation in Dorne Veceriska, news that sent him into a tirade of abuse. "Arr yoo cowad; you arr UN . . . no? You must help suffering people . . . go now back and save

185

weeman and cheeldren," he said, spitting angrily. The commander was losing his sense of rationale, supported and egged on by two colleagues. Having told Chambers to switch the engine off so that I could hear properly, I whispered down the microphone for him to start up again for a fast exit. Chambers' reply made my heart sink; the engine would not start, a problem caused by the slope; I would have to bluff the commander. I asked him to jump off the tracks for a second so that we could bump-start the engine for power to send a radio message to base. He was not happy with this request and I was forced to repeat myself strongly.

The Scimitar rolled for a few metres before being brought back to life. Chambers gave the throttle plenty of revs to clear the carburettor and, spluttering and backfiring, turned the vehicle round. Seeing that Corporal Bremridge was ready to go, we just drove up the hill as quickly as possible, keeping our heads inside the turret. A burst of automatic fire was heard behind us as we drove away, but I dared not turn to look, even through the periscope. It could have been much worse; there were a number of soldiers carrying RPG launchers; we escaped lightly. Once we had driven out of danger I radioed the operations room and informed that UN vehicles should avoid this grid square too; I had created a no-go area by trying to be helpful.

Both Scimitars needed refuelling at the Garage. There the Motor Transport sergeant told me that we would have to wait one hour because the duty fuel man had gone in to camp to refuel the generators. This was an unbelievable 'jobsworth' attitude, making me wonder whether the sergeant knew what was going on outside his comfortable garage. Still a little rattled and fired up I was not scared to be brusque and asked him whether he knew how to operate the fuel bowser. "Yes sir," he replied. "Well fill my fuckin' vehicles up then, you lazy ****."

Vitez camp was not actually in Vitez town but in a small annexed village called Bila. Having given up reaching Gola Kosa as unwise, my patrol was ready to return to camp; however, the operations room informed us that Bila was the ground of a pitched battle between HVO and BiH. We would have to wait for this to quieten down before being allowed to enter. This coincided with the untimely event of S32's turret batteries catching fire.

The fighting reported outside camp had engulfed the Officers' Mess and houses used by the Commanding Officer and UNHCR. Tudor Ellis and a few chosen men had rescued the Cheshire Regimental and Queen's Colours from the Officers' Mess in a swift operation mounted in a Warrior. Paintings and silver had also been removed and the building vacated, as it was vulnerable from the high street.

The evening briefing would have been far-fetched had it been given four months earlier, but now it was very real. The emphasis was naturally a summary of the inter-faction fighting and discussion on the anticipation of our rules of engagement being made more robust. The Quartermaster was investigating the issue of more 30mm H.E. ammunition and white phosphorous grenades for self-protection. The subaltern's house was outside the camp's perimeter wire and, vulnerable to stray fire, we had been warned off to vacate it on orders. Regardless, I slept soundly, exhausted from nervous energy and in the knowledge that members of the Royal Engineers were patrolling the area.

*Sunday 18 April: This morning I was tasked to take a pregnant woman whose waters had broken to Travnik hospital. With only a grid reference, my section and an ambulance deployed to the Croat end of Vitez, but nothing was obvious and nobody was there to meet us. I was saved from thinking what action to take next when a man started waving vigorously from a house porch. When I reached him he had gone inside the house and came out carrying a large basket of loaves. He was the baker and wanted me to deliver them to the Vitez Garage. The echelon staff had not ventured to make a collection for three days. I've heard of 'bun in the oven', but this was ridiculous! The Ops room sent a new grid, so we soon had the pregnant woman in the armoured ambulance with a scared-looking young male medic tending to her needs.*

*On the way to the hospital a group of people at the side of the road had beckoned frantically for help, but we could not afford to be diverted from our task. After dropping off the woman at hospital we returned to find nobody there, and having slowed down, got engaged by small-arms fire. Corporal Bremridge later found holes in his commander's bin and bullet slugs inside – charming!*

*My patrol was then re-tasked to collect some blankets and take them to the edge of Ahmici where the pile of bodies, still uncollected after three days, were doing undignified things in the sunshine. Unsurprisingly, the original blankets have been nicked.*

*At 1500 hrs most of the Company were 'crashed out' to deal with reports of refugees who had been ethnically cleansed by Muslims from their small Croat community near Zenica.*

187

As the recce section for the task to Zenica, I was meant to be leading the company, but Colonel Bob came along and led instead. At the top of the hill on the Zenica road the Commanding Officer announced on the air, "I am dismounting to deal with the mines". He was joined by the RSM, the two of them bravely or foolhardily kicked anti-tank mines across the tarmac road and out of the way. He then remounted and said on the radio to Martyn Thomas, "Hotel one-zero alpha, make sure the last vehicle puts the mines back," to which Martyn said, "Romeo three-zero (Dooley) you are the last vehicle, acknowledge," who then said, "Romeo two-two bravo, you are the last vehicle, ensure you put them back."

The ten armoured vehicles followed Colonel Bob to a small village where a local vicar was collected before proceeding to the village in question. Unfortunately on the approach to this ethnically cleansed village the unwieldy Warriors were too wide to continue up the narrow track. My Scimitars did neutral turns on the spot, but the Warriors had to reverse all the way, knocking down fencing and small trees. An alternative route only took us to a tipping site. Unknown locals fired a few shots at the vehicles before we withdrew to Zenica for Colonel Bob to visit the Mayor's parlour.

In the meantime we patrolled around town and stopped at the bus station to have a break. Corporal Bremridge and Kusbish gave some money to two local boys to fetch some pop and tried to explain that they would get more money on return. The kids ran off clutching a DM5 note and were not seen again.

At the end of the meeting Martyn told us that the Commanding Officer would be remaining in Zenica, leaving me to lead the company back to Vitez. On the outskirts of Zenica we passed at least two hundred assembled BiH soldiers preparing for an operation; Chambers was told not to slow down or stop. Before reaching the top of the hill it dawned on me that this time it would fall on me to kick the checkpoint mines out of the way. The mere thought of this filled me with trepidation. The way Colonel Bob had kicked the mines out of the way, with an extended leg, amused me, even more so the RSM who fully extended his leg at the same time as leaning his head back. As if doing this posed less of a risk than picking the mines up and holding them next to your chin! If one of these went off you would be picking giblets out of the trees for weeks. When we got to the check-point, however, the mines were where they had been left. R22B had ignored the Commanding Officer's instruction and who could blame him! Of course I was delighted!

As we drove past Ahmici more houses could be seen burning, further destruction that Tudor's platoon peeled off to investigate. Separating from the group to check Vitez, my section negotiated a small chicane of mines and drove up through the town centre. Ahead of us a black steel object that looked like a towed howitzer sat in the middle of the road, causing us to stop. It was in fact the engine block of a truck with front wheel still attached and the thin steel section of the chassis pointing up into the air, not a howitzer.

Ten minutes earlier these remnants of charred steel had been a petrol tanker with two Muslim men handcuffed to the steering wheel. The surrounding area was devastated. Brick debris and rubble lay everywhere, with one house completely flattened, another without walls exposing an isolated chimney and fireplace. I counted ten houses whose roof tiles had been blown clean off. Two or three men were climbing over the rubble, I imagine in the hope of digging out survivors. Unresourced to do much for them nor wanting to become a casual target, we reported this and headed back to camp the way we had come.

Covering so much mileage had weighed heavily on the Scimitars. Track pins were dangerously worn and other ailments desperately needed attention. Corporal Bremridge worked until 0200 hours getting the vehicles safe for us to use the next day. The latest information on the faction positions, gathered from a number of sources, was disclosed at the company meeting that evening. The report claimed that the Muslims had advanced to the high ground on the Zenica hill road, probably the men we had seen. The Muslim 305 Brigade had closed in on Busovaca from the west and the east and was in a position to hammer the town. The HVO had said that, if this happened, the combined strength of all their artillery would be brought to bear on Zenica town centre. The Muslims, however, were struggling for combat supplies, being land-locked from the sea. It was reassuring to be told, however, that the European Community Monitoring Mission is going to find peace by holding a meeting; a great help!

Pottering back to the house after patrol I bumped into Sergeant-Major Hughes and Sergeant Goodwin among the rows of new white portakabin accommodation. While chatting, we heard the "bang" of a firearm, a distraction I thought nothing of and dismissed as a local being stupid. Sergeant Goodwin, however, was more suspicious. Moments later an NCO ran out of the accommodation and shouted,

"Ged a fuckin' medic," immediately addressed by Sergeant-Major Hughes, who in his scouse accent said, "Eh, carm down, carm down."

Inside the portakabin a large soldier of at least sixteen stone sat puking and breathing blood from his mouth and neck. "Someone ged a stretcher," Sergeant Goodwin shouted to the assembled soldiers milling outside. Wheezing and coughing blood, the casualty was helped to the stretcher, with which four of us ran at speed with to the medical centre. This was only a short distance of some three hundred metres, but absolutely exhausting. The stretcher party had built up so much momentum that, when trying to stop, the stretcher crashed into gas bottles standing up in the theatre. Lieutenant Colonel Brookstein, the senior surgeon, very calmly thanked and released us. Medical staff, who had been sitting in the Mess, were soon seen running up the road to the emergency. The injured soldier, Lance Corporal Taff Roberts, had arrived in Bosnia two weeks previously as the replacement for Lance Corporal Wayne Edwardes, who had been tragically killed. The NCO who had shouted for the medic had been messing around with his pistol and had a Negligent Discharge. The round had entered Lance Corporal Roberts's chest at an angle, passed into his neck and exited the other side. Immediate and outstanding surgery from Lieutenant Colonel Brookstein saved the soldier's life.*

* An interview with LCpl Roberts nine years later told a different story that had nothing to do with a Negligent Discharge. There are always two sides to a story!

# 18

# THE LAST PATROL

In a matter of days whole Muslim communities had been displaced or eradicated and the goal of Croat predominance in the Lasva Valley was being achieved. The barbaric tactics used by the protagonists were nothing new; indeed Balkan history books and folklore reflect little else but inter-ethnic fighting. Deeply rooted hatred dating back to the Battle of Kosovo in 1389, concealed during the Tito years through dictatorial leadership, had resurfaced with the virulence of a malignant tumour. To Croats not actively involved in the many massacres, such as Ahmici, but living in their village, this unforgettable history justified the act. Many will have been satisfied with the outcome. Either that or their reluctance to intervene while neighbours were conveniently executed and houses set ablaze can only be explained by them turning a blind eye to save their own skins.

The massacre of Ahmici was already the subject of intense media interest and debate, a spectacle that drew international fascination. Many previously without a strong opinion on Bosnia felt compelled to comment. Judgements made on which ethnic group was the victim would be underpinned by the impact of one very striking picture of a toppled minaret. The camera does not lie!

Irrespective of numerous counter-charges by Croats accusing the Muslims of underhand activity elsewhere, this act of slaughter in Ahmici was irreversible. It would prove to be an own goal in the sympathy ratings and commit ranks of Croats to a vicarious life sentence. Regardless of equally grotesque retaliation following Ahmici, the Muslims' suffering had won the compassion of millions across the globe.

The more discerning and cynical, however, will have noticed an apparent increase in the worship of Allah. Muslims were seen in rows bent forward on their knees in the direction of Mecca, deep in prayer. Footage of such scenes supported countless journalistic storylines to emphasize the contrast of this to fighting on the front line. These people only wanted a land to call their home and the peace to make a living from it; sounds familiar? It was common knowledge that, unlike their Middle Eastern cousins, the Bosnian Muslims do not follow the strict Shariya Islamic law and pray five times a day. Maybe events had strengthened their collective faith or, never slow to capitalize on propaganda, they were deliberately manipulating the media machine.

It was essential that the clouded picture of burning central Bosnia had its definition restored. An accurate assessment was needed on the state of fighting between Croats and Muslims. Records of faction dispositions and front lines were out of date by the end of every day. For how long could fighting be sustained; who had the initiative; what would be the next target? Battle damage assessments on villages and the resulting quantity of refugees needed to be estimated. The scale of the problem required communicating with NGOs immediately so that supplies could be directed and emergency aid delivered. With many of these questions unanswered, and a stabilizing presence required, a number of patrols were mounted in the closing days of our operation in Bosnia.

Investigating the hub of the fighting in the Lasva Valley, near Gola Kosa, seemed like a good place to start. Accompanying me in the turret was Martyn Thomas. As company commander, he wanted to see and make his own assessment of the continued violence. Following us in an armoured Land Rover was Mark Laity from the BBC. The media's job was far safer, not to mention often more fruitful, when tagging onto a patrol.

The most direct route to Gola Kosa was the narrow lane from Poculica denied us more than a week previously, a path that I had attached a public health warning to. A third attempt saw progress one kilometre further along the track before coming across a group of three or four kids, one of whom aimed and tracked us with an RPG launcher. Loaded with the very familiar and deadly cone-shaped warhead, we decided not to test this boy's unpredictability or nationalistic fervour, so turned about and tried a different route.

Having considered Ahmici to be at its limit of suffering eleven days previously, our drive through it was stark and shocking. Yozza drove past the prostrate minaret and up to the bungalow from where we had evacuated the elderly woman. The bungalow was now a burnt-out shell. Just its white walls, heavily blackened by fire, and brick chimney were left standing. There was no need to waste time guessing who was responsible for these continued atrocities. Not even the Muslim propagandists would stoop to these depths. However, evidence was available to prove that, in revenge, the Muslims were guilty of employing similar bloodthirsty tactics on Croat communities. The Muslims had lost their inviolable status as a victim.

My patrol continued to the village limits where a farmer's track accessing the top fields started, one that looked negotiable in a Scimitar. Having proceeded only thirty metres Yozza stopped the Scimitar and said in a matter-of-fact Scouse accent, "There's a wire across the fuckin' tra'kk." Sure enough at four feet high a trip-wire straddled the route. Three pairs of curious eyes traced the taut wire to its source and a menacing Soviet style POM-Z grenade strapped to a tree. Such an anti-personnel mine, shaped like a cylindrical pineapple on a wooden peg, when triggered, jumps two metres into the air before exploding. Designed to decapitate victims, it was, funnily enough, the perfect height for a Scimitar turret crew. After expressing my not inconsiderable gratitude to Yozza for identifying the silk-like trip-wire, we withdrew to explore another alternative to reach Gola Kosa.

At Svrino Selo an expanse of brushwood and scrub burning fiercely at the roadside caused us to stop near a group of men who looked like dancing gypsies. Martyn and the interpreter dismounted to be told that impacting artillery rounds had started the fire. The group of men claimed to be irregular soldiers, Mujahideen recently arrived from Afghanistan. They were dressed in black polar-neck jerseys and white shemagh headdress crowned by coils of red and silver tinsel. They were holding flags and chanting, not even as provocatively as an English football crowd, and so we ignored them and continued on.

A mud track nearby had not yet been explored by us, one that Corporal Bremridge led off down. Within one hundred metres Mark Laity's Rover had bellied out on a steep muddy slope. He only managed to reverse off later and thus became separated from us. The route was tricky, bringing requests from both drivers to open their hatches; I agreed.

Corporal Bremridge spoke up on the radio and, having halted, said that a local soldier was waving vigorously at him, signals he was unable to interpret. Only one hundred metres behind them, I too could see the soldier. Nearly six months of tolerating Bosnians and their habit of exaggerating everything, however, told me to ignore this typically obstructive behaviour and advise that we continue down the track where, if we wanted, we would go. "*Kaboom*," a deafening explosion literally stopped Corporal Bremridge in his tracks, and a grey cloud engulfed his Scimitar.

Before the cloud had dissipated I was relieved to hear Corporal Bremridge speak coherently on the radio, if a touch rattled. More pleasing was seeing his head appear from the turret. Once the dust had settled he stepped out cautiously on to the vehicle's engine decks to investigate the damage. I did not need to tell him of the potential danger that dismounting and walking around the vehicle posed. His prognosis, gained from leaning over the side, was not serious, although Sparky, who was driving, could not get the Scimitar to reverse. The detonated mine had somehow dislodged a five-ton shackle and wedged it between the drive sprocket and track, the sort of bizarre occurrence that a thousand re-attempts could not repeat. Helped by adrenalin and limited options, Corporal Bremridge found the necessary strength to free the shackle and our patrol withdrew to safety.

Mark Laity's crew were on hand to survey the vehicle's damage and record it on film. The driver's front bin had been split open like a banana-skin and its tools vaporized into thin air, completely vanished. Some of the track was bent, in truth all cosmetic, but not a bad effort for an anti-personnel mine. The mine was most likely an M-RUD, a Yugoslavian version of the claymore mine. Had it been an anti-tank mine the whole crew would have almost certainly been killed. Corporal Bremridge answered questions in front of the camera in a nonchalant, if not perplexed, manner. Trooper Sparkes, who had had his head out of the driver's seat, showed the television camera the deep scratches on his helmet where, miraculously, shrapnel had skimmed over his head; he was visibly shaken by the event.

As the interview was being conducted, a burning house was noticed a few hundred metres away. Despite having been started recently, the fire was out of control. No arsonist would be stupid enough to remain at the scene, but could not have been far away either. Nevertheless, we made our way over to the blaze, the cameras following us, and, cocking my rifle, I stalked around the back of the building ready to meet a challenge. I was right; nobody was there, but another home had been lost. Being exactly ten days from the Croat assault on Ahmici, it might easily have been a Croat home, a Muslim reprisal. The situation was out of control.

In camp Martyn debriefed me on the morning's events. While talking, a runner arrived with a task from the operations room. A number of army Bedford trucks needed escorting to Miletici where they were to drop off coffins and collect twenty-three women and children who had become stranded there. A suitable refuge had been identified in Nove Bila where they would be taken to safety. I re-directed the task to Corporal Payne who commanded the section with Elvis as the other vehicle commander.

In camp the Officers' Mess was once more in use, although the Battalion's Colours, pictures and silver had not been replaced because of the continued high threat. Later on Abes found me at the bar and commended me for the way the troop had been surviving recent events. He was obviously unaware that I had done a good job trying to get most of them killed at some point or other. The mine incident that morning was mentioned in particular. He was glad that the Scimitar drivers had sensibly been closed down and thus protected from the blast. My integrity wavered with an agreement, seeing no point in telling him that this was not in fact the case.

There was a number of officers in the Mess newly arrived in theatre. They belonged to the Prince of Wales's Own Regiment of Yorkshire and The Light Dragoons, members of the incoming battlegroup. The Light Dragoons were a reconnaissance regiment based in Germany, just like ours, and their B Squadron was to relieve us in the first week of May. The Squadron's advance party comprised its headquarters and from every troop the troop leader and corporal. The next few days were spent showing my replacement, Captain Charlie Renwick, some of the sights of the Kozica and Lasva Valleys prior to the rest of his soldiers arriving.

Hours later, on my way back to the house, I bumped into Corporal Payne and Elvis walking to their accommodation. Their trip to Mileteci had been successful, but fairly harrowing. While conducting this task, they had discovered three men dead in the Muslim village. The men were found with hands tied behind backs kneeling with their heads in buckets of water. They had been drowned.

On the 30 April Charlie Renwick joined me in my Scimitar for another handover patrol. After a delayed departure due to a red alert warning of Serb artillery, we were released from the shelters and mounted up. Our first stop was Dorne Veceriska, the previous visit to which had been unnerving, leaving us unsurprised to return and discover how much more the Croats had managed to achieve. There were very few homes that were not burnt down and consequently the village was deserted. It smelt of burnt flesh, which hung in the air and could not be avoided. Unable to do anything useful, we headed through Vitez and back up the Zenica hill road to look at the BiH's T-55 tank and then back down to Poculica.

How pleased I was to bump into the Muslim commander who I had upset near Gola Kosa two weeks previously. Extraordinarily, he greeted us like friends and asked whether we would like to go to his base for a coffee. It was always wise to have an excuse up one's sleeve and so, not trusting him, I looked him in the eye and, politely declining, told him of our busy patrol schedule.

Jelinak village is beyond Putis at the top of what looks like a small hanging valley. I had never ventured there before and, in the closing days, wanted to hand over as much of the patch as possible to my successor. At the crest of the track into Jelinak we were warmly greeted by a house on fire. The flames were so fierce that it must have been ignited that hour. Other houses smouldered and the occasional sound of gunfire echoed off the buildings and valley slopes. Colonel Bob had helped negotiate another ceasefire in the past few days by banging a few local commanders' heads together, but this had little effect in Bosnia. The warring factions had very weak chains of command and even less discipline. The soldiers were all too drunk and primitive to care and the leaders too hamstrung on old scores to arbitrate through diplomatic means.

In Jelinak my patrol pulled up next to two huge pigs lying dead on the ground. The undersides of their carcasses were black and smouldering, which emitted an indescribably pungent stench. At this stage it was unclear which ethnicity the village was, but, becoming prejudiced, I instinctively assumed it to be Muslim. Livestock had been seen needlessly slaughtered in the fields near Ahmici, but these were pigs; Muslims do not keep pigs? Was I wrong; was Jelinak Croat? Perhaps there were some Croats living in Jelinak and Muslims had returned and killed the only thing they found, by chance a pro-Muslim statement? But then the Croats might have taken them there to dese- crate the Muslim soil. Both sides were now as bad as each other; I was confused.

My understanding was made no clearer when two local soldiers approached us from the cover of a building. One jumped up on to my Scimitar's tracks. His shirt was Bundeswehr issue (German Army), the German Federal flag still sewn onto the shoulder. The Croats have long been allies of the Germans and were often seen wearing these shirts, so I presumed he was Croat, but it may have been a coincidence. He indicated for me to follow him; he had something to show me. Corporal Bremridge advised caution, but there was no reason why they should be truculent with me.

Having dismounted from my armoured comfort-zone I realized that Corporal Bremridge had had a point. But I now chose to take a risk rather than admit error and dismissed his caution with youthful bravado – after all, I was bullet proof and an expert on Bosnia! With my rifle held firmly in two hands, I followed the soldier around the back of a nearby house. In front of us the ground was blackened where a fire had been. Walking closer, I could see that the subject of the fire was human.

The body had not burnt very well and was now just a dark brown-black torso. The face was a man's. His contorted look of horror, paralysed at the moment of death, reflected the kind of traumatic finish he had suffered. Had I previously known this man I would certainly have been able to recognize him. The detail on his face was such that he just looked like he had been spray-painted in a matt-black finish. His clothes had gone and his hair was frazzled, but every other feature was perfect, down to the pores of his leathery skin.

Below his waist was a different story. His legs were missing, but nearby were two leather knee-length boots. One had fallen over, the other stood on end. Protruding from both were the white knuckles of knee-bone joints covered in blood, indicating to me that this victim's legs were still inside the boots. Worse still, the boots and legs were not burnt, posing the question: when had the legs been hacked off at the knee and what of the thigh-bones? Next to the torso were remnants of two other beings. One was just an upper torso and head, the third just an unidentifiable blackened head. They had been so effectively destroyed by fire that they barely resembled humans and therefore did not create the same impact. The soldier showed me where they had been shot. On the wall of the house were three dark red bloody marks at head height. It did not need detective work to unravel the order of events.

A fortnight witnessing the aftermath of the Bosnian people doing their worst to each other had made me think differently. The sight of three burnt and dead bodies lying there was not what made this awful. Firemen see burnt dead bodies frequently, something that is tragic, but the circumstances can be comprehended – a fatal domestic accident. What was disturbing in Jelinak, like many other villages, was the manner in which these people had died, many at the hands of their former neighbours. Attempting to imagine the sequence of events was hard to ignore, if their terror was in fact within the capacity of one's simple imagination. To fully appreciate the fear they had undergone, hearing a friend being executed and knowing you are seconds away from the same fate, could surely only be achieved by actually experiencing the same.

The terrifying thought of this execution was reinforced by the smell of burnt human flesh that made me gag when I crouched too close to

197

inspect the bodies. Maintaining a phlegmatic attitude, one that probably appeared disrespectful, had been a mechanism protecting me over the previous two weeks. There was no room to be emotional. It was easier to block it out; instead I gawped at the spectacle with fascination, not believing it to be real. Only later was I to appreciate that some senses are unable to block out unwanted signals and become indelibly recorded. The burning flesh smell had penetrated my subconscious and achieved life-long memory.*

Fifteen minutes in the village listening to this soldier told me that he was a Muslim. He gave me a spool of Fuji film that he had found near the bodies. Had the murderers taken photographs of their victims' final moments as they helplessly suffered this atrocity and then left the spool for a Muslim to discover? Regardless, there was no doubt in my mind what had happened in this village. Every one of my senses was working overtime taking in the experience. This was not a battleground but a medieval ransacking. Had it been a fiction book based in the late 1980s it would have been considered unrealistic. I knew that once this atrocity was reported we would soon be returning to Jelinak.

Q. Major Woolley, do you know the date in which this destruction occurred and killing?

A. Well, it can only really — the last time I was anywhere near there was the 15th of April, on the night when I was in Putis, and I was there then on the 30th of April, so it was anywhere between those two dates.

Q. So you've got no specific knowledge?

A. No, although most of the activity I understand went on between the 16th and the 25th of April I understand just from my knowledge.

Q. This village was predominantly Muslim; is that correct?

A. That's right.

Q. And the Serb front lines in relation to Jelinak, can you explain to the Court where they would be? Would they be nearby?

---

* Some years later I was in the kitchen at home when my mother burnt pork chops under the grill. I was very nearly sick.

A. Well, from Jelinak, the Serb front line is not even significant, there's no weapon capable of being launched from a Serb position, certainly not to the east, but the nearest Serb frontline to the west and north-west was Turbe which was about 20 miles away, in range of artillery.

Q. Bearing that in mind, what was your presumption as to which military force generally inflicted the damage on that village?

A. It was the HVO that had attacked Jelinak.

Q. But you didn't see the particular attack?

A. No, no.

Q. This is a conclusion?

A. This is a Muslim village. Serbs are miles away. Conclusion: Croats attacked this village. There was also some — there was also two pigs in the village that were still smouldering when we arrived there, and I don't think pigs smoulder for 15 days when lit. I assume they were brought along and destroyed there to desecrate or soil the village, make a point about Muslim faith, if you like, and they were still smouldering when I arrived there, suggesting they had been lit or shot or something like that only a few days before.

The patrol continued through Jelinak and a kilometre on into Loncari. As well as houses decimated by fire, telegraph wires and fences were down. A burnt cow lay dead in a field. It was stiff with rigor mortis. Its legs were not flopped on the ground, but sticking straight out as if it was a plastic toy knocked over on to its side. The cow's body was half its normal size again, bloated with gases. Several sheep lay dead and covered in blood in a wooden pen nearby. Clearly they had been shot dead with sporadic automatic fire. There was no sign of any activity in the village; the place seemed deserted.

Back in the valley floor I directed the patrol towards Busovaca and the Kozica Valley where the ceasefire was far from being upheld. The most intense fighting locally was reported to be near a village called Kula on the valley's watershed. The trenches on the hill there were wide and shallow, affording limited protection. The stand-off between the two sides reminded me of scenes from the American Civil War.

My patrol stopped by a house near a small orchard. Seven or eight

HVO soldiers were gathered behind the protection of the house's white walls. With occasional shots ringing out, it was obvious that these men were having a break from fighting in the trenches. When they turned to look at us they were all smiling. The spring sunshine was glorious; it was a very pleasant scene, the reality only exposed by their uniforms and assault rifles. One of them called out something, followed by the unison of friendly laughter from his mates, but I did not understand the joke. Gesturing if I might take a photograph, they approved. Their trench was dug straight across the track and so, wanting to continue, we drove over the top of the orange sandy soil, flattening the berm in front which was unlikely to please them.

Not two hundred metres separated the warring opponents. Too unique an opportunity to miss, we halted to spectate from the side-lines. Again it was most surreal, like standing on the centre line of a football pitch, just a little more serious and not as noisy. There was no movement of men, just the occasional single shot from the trenches, each side ensuring their opponents kept their heads down.

At the far end we crossed through the Muslim lines and looked along their trench system. About ten or so soldiers were lying in cover. One man nearby, who had adopted a good firing position, let off a few aimed shots – I had not seen many of those in Bosnia! It never entered my mind how much trouble we could get into by telling the BiH to follow us back to the HVO lines in support of a full-blown assault. But then one shouldn't take sides; the Croat soldiers in the orchard had seemed such pleasant chaps, just like a friendly neighbour from next door!

Not wanting to overstay our welcome we pushed on further and did our best to conceal the vehicles in a wood. Hidden from the threat of stray bullets, we broke from our patrol for a cup of tea and a break for the drivers. After some consideration the consensus was that we had seen enough and should return to camp in time for lunch. As the Scimitar straddled the HVO trench on our way back across their lines, I looked at the group of soldiers to wave cheerio. There was only four or five of them and none were smiling. A soldier lay on a canvas stretcher splattered in bright blood. He was not screaming, but gasping and overwrought with shock. One soldier had taken the lead and was in the process of dressing the soldier's injured stomach.

What the procedure was for such a casualty did not bear thinking about. No doubt he would be driven in a car to a makeshift dressing station, probably equipped with illicit medical supplies poached from a humanitarian convoy. Whether the HVO casualty evacuation system was capable of reaching a hospital in time, and if it did would there be the necessary help, I did not know. Would hospitals in predominantly Muslim areas, such as Zenica, be sympathetic to a Croat? Did the Geneva convention mean anything to these civilians dressed in camouflage?

Twenty minutes later we were back in camp for lunch. I selected pork casserole.

*Saturday 1 May: Today an American TV station filmed a day in the life of Colonel Bob. He was wired up to a microphone so that everything he said could be recorded. Sadly, in order to give the cameras the drama they were after the day was all a bit too staged for me. We were given orders outside the hairdressers, a first! My section was tasked to lead the Posse – the tail really was wagging the dog today! After visiting the HVO HQ in Travnik we patrolled to Poculica. Colonel Bob sent me down a steep slope towards Jelinak with the task of checking whether it was suitable for Warrior. I radioed back that it was barely fit for mountain bikes. The Colonel, his two other Warriors and a convoy of media and groupees had to go the long way via Putis. We waited for ages in Jelinak and bumped into the man who had shown me the bodies. He wanted to know about the film – as if it might be back from the developers! The stench in the village was still incredible. When the CO arrived the TV cameras were all over him; he seems to have been transformed from Commanding Officer to celebrity. We sat mounted providing all-round defence to the assembled crowd who, waiting for General Morillion (Commander of UNPROFOR) to arrive, had gone to witness the horror of the three burnt bodies.*

*Back in camp the troop has completed work on the other two Scimitars for hand over. Security on the ground is reported to have improved in some locations, making routes safe enough for food convoys to be delivered. 'A' Company made farewell presentations; everyone in the troop has been given a Cheshire pennant and I presented Martyn with a 9<sup>th</sup>/12<sup>th</sup> Lancers shield. Because the troop has been attached to 'A' Company for four months we have become as close to many of them as some of our own squadron. Our experiences with 'A' Company are in many cases quite different from those of B Squadron who we rejoin tomorrow. Although the official flag change is some days off, in the morning The Light Dragoons will conduct patrols without our guidance. It is going to seem strange being in camp for five more days preparing to leave while our replacements learn the ropes for themselves. They'll soon get the hang of it. After*

201

*the presentation I asked David Sherlock for his thoughts on the tour. His reply, "You cannot live on the edge, but you must pay it a visit now and again."*

The Cheshire Battlegroup went to Bosnia with the mission of escorting convoys of humanitarian aid to pockets of beleaguered Croats and Muslims cut off by the successful strategy of Radovan Karadzic. At the time of the battlegroup's arrival, the HVO and BiH had been in loose co-operation against their common enemy, Karadzic's ruthless Bosnian Serb Army. Consequently the battlegroup's mission had been reasonably straightforward in terms of intent and execution; there was a clear and achievable aim and troops were able to operate in relative safety.

Nevertheless, for those suffering persecution at the hands of the Bosnian Serb Army, the situation was acute. On the ever-encroaching front line, BSA offensives rampaged through towns and villages with a scorched-earth policy. Innocent civilians were killed or displaced, and women were raped, but essentially it was the work of an advancing army tasked by its command with land reclamation at any cost. The Cheshire Battlegroup was, on the whole, not in a position to witness these actions.

The situation across Bosnia, however, was very much more complex, a tinderbox which soon ignited into a full three-sided civil war, further complicated by groups within groups. Inter-ethnic rivalry was fierce and fighting exceeded conventional rules, although in many ways nothing was much different if compared to the numerous unsolved confrontations around the world. One fact, however, did make this tribal war unpalatable to democratic governments; it was in Europe. If hostility was going to be prevented from spilling wider, something had to be done about it.

One had only to read a history book to understand that the unruly nature of Balkan politics, blended with ethnic prejudice, a culture of fighting and a combustible temperament had been the ingredients of regular bloody wars. Having lost Tito's unifying leadership, it should not have been a surprise to see these people revert to barbarism once more.

As United Nations soldiers without the appropriate mandate, equipment or numbers to enforce peace, options were limited in attempting to minimize or contain this hostility. Senior officers could have advised politicians that the safest course of action was to batten down inside camp with heads in the sand, or troops could have just gone home. In hindsight, the international community might have acted more quickly and robustly and nipped the problem in the bud; if there is one thing the Balkan people respect it is strength and power. The rhetoric of the UN and Western governments could have been replaced by forcible proactive intervention and, arguably, the situation would not have escalated as it did. But if nothing else, there was a political and ethical imperative to do something, even if only to monitor the problem and escort the convoys of humanitarian aid.

Supported by the United Kingdom's political and national will to assist, the battlegroup made its resources work to best effect. The tempo and unpredictability of political and military action in Bosnia, however, was such that there was no choice but to react to events. The leaders of this three-sided Bosnian war were playing a cunning game off each other and off UNPROFOR and calling the tune. Consequently operating parameters became blurred within the weak and in-appropriate rules of engagement, which thankfully were not often tested. There came a requirement for flexibility, the emphasis shifting – mission creep – from the initial basic task of humanitarian aid escorting to a more proactive role of policing; call it what you will.

Meanwhile, in order to attempt solving a complicated problem in Bosnia, the international community intervened with a simple plan, "Not in our backyard, thank you". Although the best plan available was adopted, unfortunately its strategy failed fully to take account of an alien culture, which despite its geographic proximity to European cities such as Milan, Vienna and Zurich, was a world apart and in a previous Age. Its aim was to solve the territorial quarrel by simply dividing the land into ten discrete parts. Far from harmonizing Bosnia's people, however, this plan, which rode roughshod over centuries of ethnic identification and boundaries, completely polarized the populace. Instead of compliance and a lasting peace, this plan was the catalyst that triggered the inter-faction fighting and, worst of all, ethnic slaughter that occurred in the spring of 1993. This inhuman behaviour between Croats and Muslims was the most pure form of civil war, one where neighbours and communities tore each other apart like savage dogs.

Not only had the international community intervened in something it could not completely understand or control, helping create this unnecessary bloodshed, but intervened again in 1995 to stop hostili-ties, freezing time at a point where hatred between ethnic groups was at its most intense. Serving as part of SFOR in a peacekeeping role in 1998, I witnessed these polarized ethnic groups being coerced to tolerate this contrived post-conflict peace. The end-state had left nobody the winner and everyone the loser; consequently all sides were dissatisfied. Some opinion maintains that international intervention occurred at a time when the loose Croat-Muslim alliance was on the brink of turning the situation around against the Bosnian Serbs, which, after three years of being the underdog, was poor timing and unfair. A natural and decisive conclusion was never reached.

Half a decade after the worst of the fighting, this artificial peace was fascinating to monitor. Guilty of contributing to the instability, the international community started the process of attempting to return refugees to their original homes. These were the burnt-out ones they had been expelled from by the people who hated them. This plan included sending Muslims back into Ahmici, and many villages like it, to rebuild their homes on the assumption that old scores would be forgotten, given the appropriate incentives. European governments were keen to fund this in-country solution as it was preferable and cheaper than accepting the displaced people as immigrants.

If a neighbour kills your father, rapes your mother, kills your family's livestock and burns down your house and barn, then spends five years living contentedly next door, what a concept to send the remnants of that family back to their burnt-out home to rebuild a life. The events of 1389 had been passed from generation to generation, so how were the actions of 1993 going to dissolve conveniently from memory?

Following the Dayton Peace Accord in 1995, when peace in Bosnia was agreed by all sides, the next obvious step was to re-equip the Bosnian (ARBiH and HVO) Federation's army using international money! The Train & Equip programme was designed to give the Muslims and Croats sufficient military training and hardware for regional force ratios to be balanced more evenly. At the same time, the international community publicly backed one of Karadzic's former aides to form a new Bosnian Government in Pale. Madame Plavsic subsequently handed herself in as a war criminal and was sentenced at The Hague in 2003. It is not the first time that Western governments have supported the underdog, in this case helping Muslims and Croats protect themselves against the Republic of Serbska's Army (VRS, formerly BSA). As seen elsewhere in the world, Western intervention can completely reverse a nation's fortunes, and in some cases ensure that the people of a region are divided forever.

My simplistic view leads me to conclude that the problem presented to the international community in the early 1990s might have been approached instead in one of two different ways. As in centuries before, in the long term it could be considered as kinder to let the warring sides fight it out to the bitter end and to its natural conclusion. This would have allowed supremacy to be established on their terms; survival of the fittest. Although painfully afflictive, the likelihood of Bosnia emerging with real winners and losers would have been greater and the result quicker. The people might then have been more willing to accept their fate, rather than resenting a ceasefire imposed on them in perpetuity. Fighting, however, might have spread across Yugoslavia and beyond, north into a recently liberated eastern Europe. International leaders only needed to consult their history books to remember the potential that the Balkans has for sparking a bit of trouble, so they might have done more sooner.

An alternative would have been for NATO to intervene early with force by air and on land. For the people who respect power, a lesson and demonstration in the capability of large-scale force-projection might have prevented or curbed the spillage: the fighting between Serbs and Croats in Croatia's Krajina, into Bosnia and later Kosovo, and the tremors in Macedonia. The weapons that were used by all factions through the 1990s could have been confiscated from the start and the whole bloody mess averted. This lesson was learnt by the West and applied in 1999 for the war in Kosovo.

The middle way had its difficulties, which is easy to see now with hindsight. The middle way was the international community's concept to solve Bosnia's territorial problem by dividing it into ten seemingly arbitrary cantons, the plan that helped precipitate the bloody atrocities of spring 1993. Furthermore, it was then the Dayton Peace Accord in 1995 that was to force a peace and place all hatred in suspended animation until a time, to be determined, when it will be released again. Much of the carnage might never have happened, neither too the deaths of British and European soldiers who lost their lives in the Service of Peace, a peace which, for all their sacrifices, is still only held together by an international band-aid. Interference with or ignorance of centuries-old culture and customs can bring expensive lessons; the British Raj during the Indian Mutiny of 1857.

Without fully understanding the Balkan people, and by attempting to treat them in the same way that politically correct Western governments do their own citizens, the international community interferes and returns all the components of potential war back to the start, to 1992, to 1389! A bastard is born, a 'unified' Bosnia, forced upon the people by foreign governments' policy and bereft of the natural and strong leadership required to bond such disparate ethnic

205

groups. Instead a multi-national force is deployed to keep the peace, on an open-ended commitment that is expensive and difficult to withdraw from. Meanwhile the people are asked to forgive and move on, an insensitive request that demonstrates the international community's arrogance and lack of proper understanding and ensures there is enough bottled-up hatred to fuel a Balkan war for the rest of time.

Perhaps this view is melodramatic; this could not happen now, not after half a decade of bloodshed in the 1990s; it is the twenty-first century and Bosnia is progressing. Foreign aid injected into the Balkans has transformed life; modern factories are being built. Factories create jobs and jobs give economic prosperity, which aids stability. Prosperity and stability encourage further investment and give people and government hope for higher goals – European Union Membership. But who is prospering? Many of the entrepreneurs of early post-war Bosnia, who saw an opportunity and struck, are the men of influence today; they are driven in black limousines with darkened windows; there is no more fighting because they are too busy making money, for the moment! Yes, there is a mood of progress in Bosnia today, but much of the progress is superficial: corruption, distortion, forgery and the black market are rife and lie beneath the façade of new Bosnia. And for the majority, not much has changed.

Leave a Bosnian main road and travel a short distance along a track and you will journey back in time to a medieval land, where memories have not been blurred by a decade of enticements; here you will find that the people are just the same. The Balkans is not cured, it is in remission; the story is not over, another chapter has merely finished. How many years will elapse before this dormant volcano erupts again, before the inherent culture of this people is sparked to fight and settle old scores once and for all? The sentiments of Chancellor Otto von Bismarck were probably right!

Q. Major Woolley, you said in the beginning of your testimony that you received training and education in the law of armed conflict, the rules that apply to war. In relation to the principles of protection of civilians and protection of civilian property, can you give the Court an opinion on the nature of the attack, whether you, as an educated, experienced military soldier, believe it was an unlawful operation or the damage and the injuries that you saw was legitimate?

206

JUDGE CASSESSE: Sorry to interrupt you. Could you maybe rephrase this question because actually it's not important — it is for the Court to decide whether it was lawful or unlawful. The question is whether it was a military operation or — let me see, the words used by the witness. He said there was, in a way, a choice between military action or civilian slaughter. So without classifying the action as lawful or unlawful, whether it was, rather, a military action or a civilian slaughter, to use his own words.

MR. SMITH: I'm happy with that question, Your Honour.

A. Again, from what I saw, from what I was told by the woman, from the smoking houses, from the smoking civilian houses, the dead — couple of dead men of what I would describe as non-combatant age, from a man who was in civilian clothing in a jumper who had got a shot in the back, suggesting he was withdrawing or running away or something, from a woman who saw — with a very nasty face, who was probably about 50 or 60 years old, a woman with a gunshot wound to the head, a single shot to her head, and from a whole cellar of anything from old men to children, a small girl of 12 years old, from seeing that and seeing no defences, only a few men earlier on in the day of combat age with rifles, my impression was that, whether there had been any soldiers in this village at all, of which there was only a very, very small example, these few men I've talked about, at the end of the day, these houses, these civilian houses, had been burnt down, were on fire – these were not houses that had any signs of being defended by soldiers or had any fortifications – and I think when you see 12-year-old girl with bullet wounds and men who, even if they could fight, with gunshot wounds in their backs, or women with gunshot wounds in their heads, it tells me that this is a slaughter of civilians.

MR. SMITH: I have no further questions, Your Honour.

# Epilogue

# THE HAGUE

Five men indicted on 10 November 1995 for war crimes perpetrated during the massacre of Ahmici voluntarily surrendered themselves on 6 October 1997. Quite by coincidence this was one month before the 9th/12th Royal Lancers deployed to Bosnia for a six-month tour of duty as part of the British contribution to SFOR. Holding the rank of captain and appointed Operations Officer, I was later to come into contact with aspects of the International Criminal Tribunal for Yugoslavia's (ICTY) internationally collaborative procedure. Executed by special SFOR units, People Indicted For War Crimes (PIFWC) would be seized and immediately extracted to The Hague. It was in the spring of 1998, following these five surrenders, that, from our base in Mrkonjic Grad, I was contacted by the ICTY. They requested me to *rendezvous* with them in Zenica prior to going to Ahmici to retell the story in a series of official statements as I had witnessed it. Having met with Al Moskowitz, we surveyed the shattered landscape of Ahmici and retraced the steps of my patrol of exactly five years before, an event that is described at the beginning of this book.

The visit was an important exercise for the ICTY, a visit where the credibility and detail of my evidence was realized. A subsequent visit to Ahmici months later was eventually to lead to me giving evidence in person at The Hague. The case of the five men who surrendered and a sixth man who was seized twelve days later was known as the Kupreskic case. The original indictment included two additional accused men. On 19 December 1997 Trial Chamber II granted the Prosecution's request for leave to withdraw the indictment against Marinko Katava on the grounds that there was insufficient evidence. On 23 December 1997 the Prosecution was granted leave to withdraw the indictment against Stipo Alilovic following his death. The amended indictment alleged that during the armed conflict between the forces of the Croatian Community of Herceg-Bosna, the Croatian Defence Council (HVO) and those of the government of Bosnia and Herzegovina, from January to May 1993, the HVO systematically attacked villages chiefly inhabited by Bosnian Muslims in the Lasva River Valley region of central Bosnia. The accused were charged for their alleged involvement as HVO soldiers in the persecution of Bosnian Muslims in the village of Ahmici-Santici and its environs from October 1992 to April 1993 and in participation in an attack on Ahmici on 16 April 1993. The report states that during the attack the village was shelled from a distance and then groups of HVO soldiers went from house to house attacking Bosnian Muslim civilians and burning their houses, barns and livestock. The trial started on Monday 17 August 1998.

JUDGE CASSESSE: I trust everyone had a good lunch — Counsel Radovic.

Counsel Radovic: Thank you Your Honour.

Q. Tell me, Major Woolley, as far as I was able to understand, you are an infantryman, or armoured units, or what is your category?

A. I'm from an armoured reconnaissance unit, cavalry.

Q. Does artillery come under your specialist training?

A. Not under my specialist training, no.

Q. And what about anti-aircraft guns, is that part of your training too?

A. . . . No but I have a good all-round knowledge of the all-arms battle, and that includes air defence and artillery, and infantry work and armoured work.

Q. Did you see anti-aircraft guns, the ones that the HVO had at their disposal in the surroundings of Vitez, did you personally see them?

A. I didn't see the guns, but I saw fire from a gun, from an HVO area, which with its rate of fire, the size of the tracer, the trajectory of the gun, made me understand that they were clearly anti-aircraft guns.

Q. How did you know that it was a 30mm anti-aircraft gun?

A. I didn't know it was a 30mm gun, I said it was between 20 and 30mm, because anti-aircraft guns are normally anything between 23mm, 20mm, sometimes as little as 12.7mm and sometimes as much as 40. That's why I said between 20 and 30, roughly.

Q. Very well. Do you know, in concrete terms, what anti-aircraft guns were at the disposal of the HVO and the Muslim side?

A. I think most of the units had former JNA weapons, and most of these weapons are based on Russian or Soviet type patterns, the ZPU or ZSU type anti-aircraft guns. Mainly ZPUs, ZPU-4 12.7mm, 20mm, some 23mm and even 57mm in some cases.

Q. Very well. I'm now interested in knowing how you decided upon this category between 20 and 30mm.

A. The rounds that were fired over the hillside had firing intervals in that, I'm saying the rate of fire showed me that they were, first of all, not machine gun, which puts them in a larger bracket — Okay? They were also not of a rate of — do you want me to continue, or are you going to talk?

Q. Yes, you can carry on. I can ask you the next question in that regard. Do you know that anti-aircraft guns are conceived in such a way as to have limited possibility for reducing the barrel downwards, just like with tanks, you can't raise the barrel upwards, which is the case with Russian tanks, for example. And this one can't go downwards. Do you know of that fact?

A. That's not correct. You can depress an anti-aircraft gun to fire in a direct role, and in fact, I was fired on by Serb guns in January over near Kladanj, where anti-aircraft guns were fired at me in a direct role from the other side of a valley.

Q. But do you know whether it was the same type of weapon, because I imagine that not all types have the same combat possibilities?

A. Anti-aircraft guns can fire in the direct role and they can be depressed. They can be elevated up to the vertical and, in fact, beyond it, all around 360 degrees. Soviet anti-aircraft guns fire in all directions, including on a flat trajectory on the horizontal. The flat trajectory of the ammunition going across the valley shows that the rounds were of a high velocity. They were being fired at a rate of fire where there were about up to, say, ten tracer element or rounds in the air at any one time, and this is consistent with an anti-aircraft gun. Tanks fire rounds one at a time. Machine-guns fire with a rapid rate of fire where you have a lot of rounds in the air of a much smaller nature.

Q. Tell me what the time was when you filmed the men carrying the weapons.

A. Which men carrying which weapons?

Q. On the photograph that was shown to you. One photograph shows people not wearing uniforms with automatic rifles, and I'm interested in knowing when that picture was taken.

A. That picture, if you're referring to the picture that has two men in brown jackets carrying AK-47s, that was taken at about 11.00, 11.30 in the morning.

Q. On their civilian clothing did they have any signs showing that they belonged to any army?

A. No, they didn't.

Q. What, according to the rules of the British army, would you do with individuals carrying firearms, without having any insignia as belonging to an army? Which category would you place those individuals in?

A. Depends how they are dressed.

Q. Like the people dressed that you took the photo of. If the British Army were to meet men dressed like that in the operation zone, what would you think — who did you think these men belonged to, what category?

A. If that's a general question, if I came across, in any war, men dressed in civilian clothing, with a rifle —

Q. In any war, yes.

A. Yes. It depends which side they were on. If I could speak to them and establish they were on my side, I would take no action. If they were firing at me and they were wearing civilian clothing, I would shoot them. I don't really understand what you're trying to get at.

Q. I am trying to get at whether you would consider them to be soldiers.

A. In this specific case I would regard them as soldiers because –

Q. No, I'm asking you in general terms. Generally speaking, if the British army were to encounter an adversary firing at them without military uniforms or military emblems, who would you consider them to be?

A. Well, I wouldn't know because they would have no emblems on them. The point is here, and what I think you're trying to say is, are these soldiers or not. Because these men are in Bosnia, and because Bosnia doesn't have a professional army with professionally trained soldiers, my experience is that you have any man with any weapon dressed in any clothing can be a soldier. So I don't see what you're trying to say.

Q. Very well. I would like an answer. I'm not trying to say anything. I just would like to have an answer to the question, are they soldiers without uniforms with weapons, and without having any signs on their civilian clothes as showing that they belonged to an army of any kind? Would you not agree with me if I say that if they are civilians they would have to have emblems showing that they belonged to some army, or a five-pointed star or something else? This is just an ad hoc, random example. Anywhere on their clothing.

A. If a man is wearing civilian clothing, he could be anything from a civilian to a soldier. This situation, whether it was the same for another British Army situation somewhere else in the world, at the end of the day if you have somebody with a rifle, whatever they're wearing, then I would regard them by looking at the weapon and not looking at what they were wearing, and especially in Bosnia. What they were wearing was irrelevant, because I would say these two are soldiers is the point. I never doubted that they were soldiers. But what sort of soldiers they were, whether they were professional front-line soldiers or whether they were local defenders, I don't know. I don't know whether they were there in the morning or whether they'd come as a result of the engagement in the morning. The fact that they were standing there and they had no — I was not

212

aware of them having taken part in any fighting, suggests to me that they probably came afterwards, unless they hid while their friends, and families, and old people and children were slaughtered.

Q. Well, I'm not asking you for your conclusions, I'm just asking you what you saw with your very eyes and heard with your very ears. What you conclude is your own conclusion, but in court it is customary for witnesses to set out the facts and then the Court decides on those facts. That is to say, whether it was so or not so. So let us keep to what you saw and heard.

A. Before you asked me my opinion of what they were — looked on as by the British Army, Okay? So that's an opinion, isn't it? So if you want the facts, these two men were two men of combat age, they were wearing civilian clothing but were carrying rifles —

JUDGE CASSESSE: Mr. Smith.

MR. SMITH: Your Honour.

MR. RADOVIC: That's right. And the part of my question — I asked that part of my question because it belongs to your professional expertise.

JUDGE CASSESSE: Let Mr. Smith speak.

MR. SMITH: I want to raise one point. I think there is a difficulty arising in this cross-examination, and the difficulty is I think there is confusion. The witness may well be confused from general questions to specific fact questions, and in the beginning my friend was asking questions of a general nature and only wanted to ask from a general point of view. This witness was trying to keep it in relation to what he saw and what he did, but my friend wants it had in a general way. Now the witness, when answering a question in a general way, that general question is being criticised by my friend for not relating it to the specific facts. So it's a mixture of concept and what he saw and what he heard.

JUDGE CASSESSE: Let me try and rephrase the question put by Counsel Radovic, with Counsel Radovic's permission. I think you — probably the gist of your question was that you were keen to know from the witness whether under, you said,

British military law, British rules, a civilian in civilian clothes, with no distinctive emblem but carrying weapons, would be regarded as a lawful combatant or as an unlawful combatant. I think this was probably the sense of this question.

A. Okay. Generally speaking, he is an unlawful combatant if he's got no uniform or insignia, or is quite clearly not a soldier. But the point is, going back to specifics, is that —

JUDGE CASSESSE: So far this is the general question. I wonder whether —

A. Can I continue?

MR. RADOVIC: That is precisely what I wanted to hear.

JUDGE CASSESSE: I wonder if you are interested now to take up the point taken by Mr. Smith, in classifying the actual behaviour of those two people.

MR. RADOVIC: Let me put it this way: First of all, I wanted to hear that these were unlawful combatants because they did not have any insignia on their clothes showing that they belonged to an organised unit. And we stopped at that point, as far as I'm concerned.

A. Can I continue with that? I'd like to be more specific.

JUDGE CASSESSE: Why not?

A. Yeah, I think we all know from the theatre of operations in Bosnia, whether the side is Serb — or Bosnian, Serb, Croat or Muslim, the nature of how the war came about, you do have situations where men of combat age, and any age, in fact, can pick up weapons and become part of forces. Some are police forces, some are the army, but generally, if they have a weapon they are, in many cases that I was aware of, part of armies. They might not be on the front line with a formed unit, but they might be part of a local defence, defending their families and children from being slaughtered by opposition. That's how I see it, and that's my experience of my time out there. Just because somebody didn't have a uniform on didn't mean he wasn't a soldier defending something like a village, for example, Ahmici.

214

MR. RADOVIC: Q. Tell me, witness, are you an interested party in any way in this case?

A. I am not an interested party in any way. Why do you ask that question?

Q. I'm asking you this question because you go far beyond what you are asked.

MR. SMITH: I object, Your Honour.

JUDGE MAY: I object to this line of questioning. Just a moment. This line of questioning is wholly unjustified, in my view. The witness was, first of all, asked his opinions by the Prosecution about military matters and he gave them. You, Mr. Radovic asked him his opinion and he gave it. Now you choose to allege that he's somehow an interested party. It may well be he's interested in the sense that he has reported what he saw that day, but apart from that, I do not see that he's an interested party and I regard it as an objectionable question.

JUDGE CASSESSE: Counsel Radovic, could you move on to another question, please?

MR. RADOVIC:

Q. Now, I would kindly ask you to look at this map and tell me — you can look at the photograph behind you, the big one. So this is the main road that leads from Vitez up to Zenica, right? I'm interested in the following: To the best of your knowledge, do part of the houses of the village of Ahmici go across this road?

A. I understand that — I'm not sure whether the houses go to the south side of the road. I generally — yeah, I think they do. The name of Ahmici is actually on the north side of the road on the map, and all my references have been really to a map – my experience is from the map, and the problem with the houses in Bosnia is that you can have small groups of houses that don't even have a village name. So it would be speculation for me just to say now that the houses south of the road were Ahmici or that they weren't Ahmici.

Q. All right. In your opinion as an officer who is a Major now, was this road of strategic importance for the HVO in case of an armed conflict with the Muslims, of strategic importance?

A. This road runs basically east/west. And let me first say that any road is of importance for lines of communication and supply, but generally a road running east/west, from what I understood the situation to be, was not quite as relevant as a road running north/south, because generally your operations, the HVO operations, were south/north leading out of the Busovaca area and that linear sort of front line running from Busovaca across to the west, south of this sort of area. So if I was a Croat wanting to advance, depending on what my objective was, I'd be going north, and, therefore, to have this road would be nice, but I wouldn't have thought necessarily essential, other than distributing logistics across my frontage to the east and to the west.

Q. And tell me, this road, doesn't it link Vitez and Busovaca?

A. Correct. Yes. So there you go. You've answered the question. It is of some importance, because it's nice for the HVO headquarters in Vitez to have a little bit of a link with that of the bases in Busovaca. Very good.

Q. Tell me, if there were a group of HVO in Vitez and a group of HVO in Busovaca, is cutting off a line of communication between these two groups part of warfare strategy in any battle?

A. It could be, yes.

Q. I mean, to separate these units and then to destroy each group separately; isn't that correct?

A. That is a very typical way of conducting operations. Yes, that could be done.

Q. You said that you did not notice in Ahmici any significant presence of the BiH army. What did you mean by that when you said that? That is to say, this should be elaborated in two directions. First of all, did you notice any presence of the BiH army? And, if so, because you said you did not notice a significant presence, how was this presence that was there manifested?

A. What I saw, as I said earlier, was no evidence of any formed Bosnian or Muslim army. There were no defences that I saw. There was no barbed wire, there were no trenches, there were no sangars, there were no houses which were fortified. The only thing I saw that I knew was Muslim and that resembled anything to do with fighting were a few gentlemen carrying Kalashnikov weapons.

Q. If I understood you correctly, you base your conclusion on what you saw precisely that day, on the 16th of April?

A. That's correct, yes.

Q. That is to say that before that you did not come to the village of Ahmici?

A. No. I drove past the village of Ahmici, but I saw from the main road, if you use that as a confrontation line, no defences at any point. Had I seen any defences or build-up of forces, I'm sure, anywhere along that front line I would have noticed them.

Q. Tell me, when with your armoured vehicles you got into Ahmici, did you move exclusively along the road or did you go apart from the road? Did you go into the fields?

A. No, I didn't, but what we did do when we advanced was stop occasionally, and using our high magnification sights, look around, into woodland in order to see any activity, because it's very important to look after ourselves. We didn't go off the road because you don't know whether there are any mines off the road.

Q. Tell me, on the basis of which facts did you conclude that there was danger of minefields?

A. I didn't conclude that there was any danger, I was just being prudent because if you stick to tarmac you have less chance of being blown up. I was not in any way trying to risk my life or that of my soldiers or my government's property, in fact; and therefore, we stuck to the tracks, as we do today and as I did when I was recently in Bosnia.

Q. In the part of Ahmici that is just by the road and part of Ahmici is on the other side of the road, after all, could you exactly identify every house that would be Muslim as opposed to houses that would be, for example, Croat?

A. All I had was an understanding that, generally speaking, houses with four-sided roofs, pyramidal shaped, were generally Muslim and that houses with Swiss-style two-sided roofs were generally Croat, and that was a good rule to go by.

Q. But you do allow that there were exceptions?

A. Absolutely. But generally speaking, houses all around a minaret tend to be Muslim.

Q. One thing that I'm not quite clear on in your conduct, when you went with your armoured vehicles and before you picked up the dead bodies, did you check previously whether there were any other wounded, or did you start picking up the dead bodies once you had asserted that there were no other casualties, wounded?

A. Referring to the specific task in the evening, at about 6.00, I was tasked just to assist Lieutenant Dooley and therefore we just conducted the removal of those five bodies and then finished with that task and went back to our base in Vitez. So to answer the question, we didn't make a point of going into any more buildings to try and find people that were injured because that was not our task.

Q. The dead bodies that you found, did you inspect each of them individually, or what did you do? Because you spoke of the possibility of wounding from one position or another, back wounds, and so on. For example, the body where you found that the wound came from, the entrance wound was from the back. Did it have an exit wound?

A. Because we were vulnerable, I did not have the time to inspect bodies. What I do remember of the bodies was that they were lying in the way I believe they fell, on their front or on their back or whatever. They were not there as a result of being piled up, they were there having been running away. There were several patches of blood on those bodies in most cases, which suggested to me that they had been engaged maybe with automatic fire.

Q. Very well. I've understood that. But I'm not quite clear whether you looked for an exit wound or, if not — let me ask this more exactly: How do you know that the back wound was an entrance wound?

A. I don't remember talking about any back wound in this particular case. I talked about a back wound of a man alive, although very annoyed. The men that were lying dead — the five men in the field, they had all sorts of injuries, and I didn't have the time to particularly inspect them because the entry wound seemed to have done significant damage and a back wound — an exit wound seemed irrelevant, really, because they were not moving.

Q. Very well. Then we agree, with regard to the dead bodies, that you cannot say whether they were shot from the back or from the front.

A. No, but they were — from what I could see, they lay where they had been shot or within yards of where they had been shot because they were lying in a way that was random; in other words, they might have been fleeing.

Q. Tell me, please, the opinion you have just given us belongs to the area of forensics, the mechanisms of the wound, but what I'm interested in is in what you saw with your own eyes, that is to say, whether they were entry/exit wounds and whether all the wounds were in the back. You said just now that you did not inspect the bodies and that quite possibly they could have been entry wounds, that is to say, from the front; is that correct?

A. They could have been any wounds. As I just said, I didn't have the time to inspect them. There were five civilians lying in the field, and they were lying where they had been shot, and the fact is that there were dead men, some elderly, who were very dead. As a result of entry or exit wounds, it seemed irrelevant.

Q. That's right, yes. Okay. That's all right. Tell me, do you know whether, on that day, there were dead Croats as well?

A. I didn't see any dead Croats, so I had no need — I have no understanding or belief that there were any.

Q. Very well. Believe it or not, it doesn't matter; the facts are what interest us. On the basis of what indices were you able to differentiate between dead Muslims and dead Croats?

A. The houses. The dead people that we picked up were sitting next to houses that had been burnt out. You can make an assumption that maybe the houses were set fire to and they exited and were shot, but that aside, I didn't see that, so we can't presume that. But there were dead people next to houses in a Muslim village, the houses having been destroyed, the houses all very near a minaret, and these are the facts that led me to believe this. And also evidence from earlier in the morning where the woman had told me, you know, that she had witnessed an attack by Croats early that morning and that — she was obviously Muslim, with her house, which is about 15 yards from a minaret, et cetera, et cetera.

Q. Very well. But the people you found in the field that you mentioned, they were neither at home — and the woman that you talked to couldn't have told you anything about them.

A. No. I agree, yeah.

Q. That means that, in fact, you are giving a conclusion whereas you have not got a concrete incident, and the conclusions are on the basis of what you heard from the Muslim woman and from the other stories, but no measures were taken for the identification of those individuals. Have I understood you correctly?

A. That's right, no specific identification of them, but as I say, the series of facts which I've described led me to believe that these were Muslim –

Q. That's all right. You've already told us that, yes. And now my final question — perhaps I've already asked it, perhaps not — but it has to do with the five men that were mentioned, at the beginning, that you met with Kalashnikovs at around 11.00 a.m. Did you in any way inform yourself of whether they were from Ahmici or whether they had come from outside Ahmici?

A. No. And as I said earlier, I wasn't sure where they had come from, I didn't speak to them, specifically those men, and if you remember, I did say I was surprised that they were still in one piece, having had no combat, because they were there in the village, and had they been there when the attack went in, they would have probably got involved in it so . . .

MR. RADOVIC: Thank you. I have no further questions.

JUDGE CASSESSE: Thank you, Counsel Radovic. Mr. Smith, any re-examination?

MR. SMITH: Just a few questions, Your Honour. Re-examined by Mr. Smith:

Q. Major Woolley, I just have a few questions to clear up in relation to the questions that Mr. Radovic just asked you regarding the dead bodies that you picked up from the side of the road. You don't know the addresses — you didn't know the addresses of where they, in fact, lived, did you?

A. No, I didn't.

Q. So it's quite possible they could have lived in the area just next to where they were found?

A. Correct, yeah.

Q. And my friend also asked you some questions in relation to the legitimacy of an operation such as Ahmici, and he mentioned the importance of routes as far as being legitimate military objectives in terms of securing them, and you agreed with that, that some routes can be legitimate military objectives and thus can be secured or can be secured within the meaning of the laws of war?

A. Yes.

Q. The villages of Loncari and Jelinak, how far off the main road are they, off the main route between Vitez and Busovaca?

A. They're quite a way off the Busovaca-Vitez route, but the route then bends round towards Zenica, obviously a Muslim area, and therefore I would say they're of less relevance to the Croats, to the HVO.

Q. If I can produce to you this map, it's a 1:50.000 map of the general area of Vitez and Busovaca, and you'll see the villages of Jelinak and Loncari, and can you relate that map to that main route and point out the villages of Loncari and Jelinak?

221

A. There is Loncari and here is Jelinak(indicating), and I understand — let's have a look — Busovaca I think is down this route, down here, this is the road that links Vitez and Busovaca down here, and, of course, here we have Ahmici. So this is the road that we've been looking at all day, and yet here is Loncari and here is Jelinak which, with regard this line of communication, are pretty irrelevant with regard picketing or securing of this route here. Is that the question you wanted answering?

Q. If the HVO wanted to secure the route between Vitez and Busovaca, is it militarily necessary to cause the destruction, and in the particular case of Jelinak, the killing to secure that route?

A. No. Jelinak is a long way away from that route. Jelinak is here (indicating), and this is the main route linking Vitez and Busovaca, and all that you would require to do to ensure the security of that route is push out up to the highest ground in order that you have a good field of view and fire, in order to picket that route as we've described, and therefore, Jelinak, I think, is far too far to the north, with several hills between it and the road, to be of any relevance, certainly with regard burnt bodies with limbs chopped off, dead livestock and burnt-out civilian houses.

Q. I would like to ask that same question of you in relation to the village of Ahmici. Was it, in your opinion, militarily necessary to cause the damage and the killing that you saw right into the village of Ahmici and right up the road, in fact where you went, in order — if that was an objective, in order to secure that route? Was that damage and that killing and that injury militarily necessary? Is there another way of doing it?

A. It is absolutely unnecessary to destroy civilian houses, especially undefended ones that have no signs of fortification, should I say. Certainly not necessary to maim or injure or attempt to kill or kill children or old people, or livestock, for that matter. The way to do it is to destroy any armed units that are in that village, take any prisoners of war. Any civilians or refugees who are causing a disturbance, to use a provost unit to deal with them so that they don't interfere with the security of your operation and the lines of communication.

222

I don't see any point in destroying a village and its people to conduct that intent.

Q. Apart from those four men that you saw with rifles at the beginning of the village, were there any other obvious legitimate military targets within the village, like military installations, communications centre, anything that would tend to suggest that it was an obvious military target?

A. In the village on the day of the 16th, I saw — and subsequently anyway, I saw no dug-in positions, sangars, communication centres, any weapons. All I saw which gave me a feeling of anything military was four or five men at about 11.00 who were not in uniform and were carrying AK-47s.

MR. SMITH: No further questions, Your Honour.

JUDGE CASSESSE: Thank you. I assume there is no objection to the witness being released. Major Woolley, thank you so much for coming here to court to give evidence. You may now be released.

The case finished on the 10 November 1999 after 111 trial days. Sixty witnesses were called by the Prosecution and ninety-nine witnesses were called by the Defence. The Trial Chamber pronounced its judgement on 14 January 2000.

**Dragan Papic** was acquitted and released from the Detention Unit immediately.

**Zoran Kupreskic** was found guilty on the basis of individual criminal responsibility for:
Crimes against humanity (Article 5 – persecutions on political, racial or religious grounds).
*Sentence:* 10 years' imprisonment. Found NOT GUILTY on the basis of individual criminal responsibility for: Crimes against humanity (Article 5 – murder; inhumane acts) and Violations of the laws or customs of war (Article 3 – murder; cruel treatment).

**Mirjan Kupreskic** was found guilty on the basis of individual criminal responsibility for:
Crimes against humanity (Article 5 – persecutions on political, racial or religious grounds).

223

*Sentence:* 8 years' imprisonment. Found NOT GUILTY on the basis of individual criminal responsibility for: Crimes against humanity (Article 5 – murder; inhumane acts) and Violations of the laws or customs of war (Article 3 – murder; cruel treatment).

**Vlatko Kupreskic** was found guilty on the basis of individual criminal responsibility for:
> Crimes against humanity (Article 5 – persecutions on political, racial or religious grounds).

*Sentence:* 6 years' imprisonment. Found NOT GUILTY on the basis of individual criminal responsibility for: Crimes against humanity (Article 5 – murder; inhumane acts) and Violations of the laws or customs of war (Article 3 – murder; cruel treatment).

**Drago Josipovic** was found guilty on the basis of individual criminal responsibility for:
> Crimes against humanity (Article 5 – persecutions on political, racial or religious grounds).

*Sentence:* 15 years' imprisonment. Found NOT GUILTY on the basis of individual criminal responsibility for: Violations of the laws or customs of war (Article 3 – murder; cruel treatment).

**Vladimir Santic** was found guilty on the basis of individual criminal responsibility for:
> Crimes against humanity (Article 5 – persecutions on political, racial or religious grounds).

*Sentence:* 25 years' imprisonment. Found NOT GUILTY on the basis of individual criminal responsibility for: Violations of the laws or customs of war (Article 3 – murder; cruel treatment).

Following the determination by the Trial Chamber that the sentences were to be served concurrently, the above sentences indicate the highest penalty imposed on each of the convicted.

## The Appeal

The Prosecution filed its notice of appeal against the Trial Chamber's findings regarding Josipovic and Santic on 31 January 2000. The appeal hearing took place from 23-25 July 2001. The Appeals Chamber rendered its Judgement on 23 October 2001:

**Zoran Kupreskic:** The Appeals Chamber found him not guilty, reversed his conviction and ordered his immediate release.

**Mirjan Kupreskic:** The Appeals Chamber found him not guilty, reversed his conviction and ordered his immediate release.

**Vlatko Kupreskic:** The Appeals Chamber found him not guilty, reversed his conviction and ordered his immediate release.

**Drago Josipovic:** The Appeals Chamber allowed his appeal in part and reduced his sentence from 15 to 12 years' imprisonment.

**Vladimir Santic:** The Appeals Chamber allowed his appeal in part and reduced his sentence from 25 to 18 years' imprisonment.

# APPENDIX

# B SQUADRON
# 9TH/12TH ROYAL LANCERS
# (PRINCE OF WALES'S)
# – OPERATION GRAPPLE 1

| | | | |
|---|---|---|---|
| Maj | A M Abraham | Capt | D M Bennett |
| Capt | T R Hercock | Capt | S J I Ward |
| Lt | B V Beddard | Lt | W J O Fooks |
| Lt | J P B Freeeland | Lt | M Jones |
| Lt | M R Woolley | WO2 (SSM) | A F Sterenberg |
| SSgt (SQMS) | J Pearce | SSgt | P D G Saunders REME |
| Sgt | S M Bowmar | Sgt | J R Clarke |
| Sgt | K Costello REME | Sgt | A D Finlay |
| Sgt | P Gaylor | Sgt | D R Holroyd REME |
| Sgt | S Lindasy | Sgt | A Mason |
| Sgt | L M Pilcher | Sgt | D R Richardson |
| Cpl | A Bithell | Cpl | G Bremridge |
| Cpl | S Carter | Cpl | D A Clarke |
| Cpl | E P Dent | Cpl | C H Ducker |
| Cpl | R L N Duncan ACC | Cpl | T C Gelsthorpe |
| Cpl | D A Henderson | Cpl | K W H Holley |
| Cpl | N P Kenton-Barnes REME | Cpl | M McGrath |
| Cpl | C M Mitchell | Cpl | C A Mitchell REME |
| Cpl | C M Payne 935 | Cpl | A G Price |
| Cpl | R Ramsden | Cpl | J Richmond |
| Cpl | S Smethhurst REME | Cpl | S W Ward |
| Cpl | G P Webb | LCpl | M P Burn |
| LCpl | J Coogans | LCpl | D Hallewell |
| LCpl | C R Hillman | LCpl | A J McDonald REME |
| LCpl | A P Melbourne | LCpl | C S 'Elvis' Priestley |
| LCpl | A Pumford | LCpl | D D Rickford |
| LCpl | M N Simpson | LCpl | K L Swift |
| LCpl | J W Visser | LCpl | S Vyse |
| LCpl | C L White | LCpl | P M Wick |

| | | | | |
|---|---|---|---|---|
| Tpr | L I Baker | | Tpr | M Blunt |
| Cfn | S Brennan REME | | Tpr | S R Chambers |
| Tpr | C P Doherty | | Tpr | D Dolbear |
| Pte | M N Durston ACC | | Tpr | R A Fleetwood |
| Tpr | M P Franks | | Tpr | T J Godfrey |
| Tpr | N D Green | | Tpr | J D Harrison |
| Tpr | T J Heeley | | Cfn | I M Hoffman REME |
| Tpr | J P 'Yozza' Hughes | | Tpr | L R James |
| Tpr | S N Kusbish | | Tpr | M E Large |
| Tpr | D G Ledgard | | Tpr | L Machen |
| Tpr | G J Manger | | Tpr | S M Mansfield |
| Tpr | P J Marson | | Tpr | D J Martin |
| Tpr | S B Meadows | | Tpr | P Millband |
| Tpr | P D L Mills | | Tpr | D R Nardone |
| Tpr | S C Orr-Munro | | Tpr | M C Payne 333 |
| Tpr | R O Pritchard | | Tpr | N P Ransome |
| Tpr | M W Roberts | | Tpr | Robins |
| Tpr | O R Robinson | | Tpr | S Russell |
| Tpr | M J Skates | | Tpr | J South |
| Tpr | C W Sparkes | | Cfn | A P Watmuff REME |
| Tpr | B R Whittaker | | Tpr | J P E Wilkinson |
| Tpr | T J Wilson | | Tpr | R B Wiseman |
| Tpr | A C Wright | | | |

# INDEX